Why Did I Marry You Anyway?

Why Did I MARRY YOU Anyway?

OVERCOMING THE MYTHS THAT HINDER A HAPPY MARRIAGE

REVISED AND EXPANDED

Barbara Bartlein, R.N., M.S.W.

CUMBERLAND HOUSE
NASHVILLE, TENNESSEE

WHY DID I MARRY YOU ANYWAY?
PUBLISHED BY CUMBERLAND HOUSE PUBLISHING
431 Harding Industrial Drive
Nashville, Tennessee 37211

Cover design: Gore Studio, Inc. | www.gorestudio.com
Book design: Mary Sanford

Library of Congress Cataloging-in-Publication Data
Bartlein, Barbara, 1951–
Why did I marry you anyway? : overcoming the myths that hinder a happy marriage / Barbara Bartlein. — Rev. and expanded.
p. cm.
Includes bibliographical references.
ISBN-13: 978-1-58182-632-6 (pbk. : alk. paper)
ISBN-10: 1-58182-632-X (pbk. : alk. paper)
1. Marriage. 2. Man-woman relationships. I. Title.

HQ734.B275 2007
646.7'8—dc22

2007040405

Printed in Canada
1 2 3 4 5 6 7—13 12 11 10 09 08 07

CONTENTS

A PERSONAL NOTE FROM THE AUTHOR

I remember the scene like yesterday, though I was only thirteen at the time. Standing in the driveway of our suburban bungalow, I had my face buried in my father's shoulder in an awkward show of affection. His clothes, shaving gear, a few pictures, and his *World Book* encyclopedias were carefully piled in the backseat of his gold Chevy Impala. With tears in his eyes, he said, "I guess you knew what was happening all along." He then turned, got into his car, and drove away.

I rarely saw him after that.

Yes, I guess I did know what was going on, but I never completely understood it. And I sure didn't know how I felt about it.

In some ways, I was relieved. There had been so much yelling and fighting the last year or so of my parents' marriage. And Dad seemed angry so much of the time, especially when he was drinking. I never really knew what all his anger was about—and don't even to this day.

All I know is that my life was never the same. I thought it would just continue and maybe improve—that is, no yelling. I didn't comprehend, at the time, the huge implications of divorce. I didn't know that I would essentially lose my mom at the same time because of the hard work it took to support four children. I didn't understand the financial hardship of a single-parent household. I didn't realize that this meant the family I had known was gone. And I didn't recognize that we would lose all the fun along with the yelling.

It was just a lot lonelier after that day, though we never talked about it. The hours after school with no one home, summer vacations with no family outings, and Saturday mornings with Mom at work.

I think we all pretended. Pretended that nothing of significance had happened. Pretended that it certainly didn't bother us. We were tough. We all struggled in our own way, but we never talked about it—as if talking would make the pain come alive and consume us.

But one thing is very clear. The distress of our broken family haunted us all for many years. And I'm sure if one looked hard enough, remnants of sadness can still be found today . . . after forty years.

These days I try not to judge my parents (after the guillotine-type of evaluation I put them through during my teen years). I did not walk in their shoes, and I can't really imagine what their lives were like. I long ago accepted that they did the best they could, which is surely the first step toward true forgiveness. But at times, I wonder what my life would have been like if they would have stayed together.

Did they try hard enough? I don't know. I do know that my mother has stated many times, with a sigh, that she wishes she had tried harder. I know she had regrets, as the lasting effects of the divorce became clear. And I know that my dad loved her until the day he died. So why couldn't they make it work? I don't know.

But I do know that their experience led me to try very, very hard in my own marriage. It also convinced me to help couples work relentlessly on theirs. I warn couples of the lasting repercussions of not trying hard enough and believing the myth that it is easier just to walk away.

I know that a happy, successful marriage is not an accident. It is not a fluke. It is the result of hard work, dedication, and a commitment that is carved in stone.

This book is a result of twenty-three years of marriage and twenty-two years of experience as a professional marriage counselor and psychotherapist.

If it helps even one couple stay together and find the happiness that I have found with my husband, Charlie, it is worth it.

ACKNOWLEDGMENTS

I wish to sincerely thank all the wonderful people who have encouraged and supported me through the writing of this book. This includes my agent, Doris Michaels, for her enthusiasm and energy. Ron Pitkin, Stacie Bauerle, and the team at Cumberland House, whose expertise guided the book through the stages of editing and production. My fellow speaker, Byrd Baggett, who believed in the book and recommended my work to Ron. And my copy editors, Barbara McNichols and Eleanor Hanold, and Mary Sanford for their language expertise.

Grateful acknowledgements to Dr. Carole Schoffstall and all the instructors from Beth-El School of Nursing for their commitment to nursing and the guidance of my career. Dr. James Blackburn, Dean of the Helen Bader School of Social Welfare at the University of Wisconsin–Milwaukee, for encouragement, recommendations, and suggestions. And Dr. Harry Prosen, Chairman of the Department of Psychiatry and Behavioral Medicine at the Medical College of Wisconsin for his support over the years.

A special thank you to Jeffrey Gitomer, who first encouraged me to write and published my very first article; Sam Horn, who gave me the title for this book and consulted with me on a regular basis to make it better; and C. Leslie Charles, whose wonderful book, *Why Is Everyone So Cranky?* and ongoing support inspired and motivated my efforts. I can't thank you all enough. You have changed my life and I will be forever grateful.

A special thank you to all my fellow authors and friends from the Maui Writers Conference. The motivation and guidance were invaluable. I wish to thank LeAnn Thieman for allowing me to participate in *Chicken Soup for the Nurse's Soul,* my entrance into the publishing world. Thank you to all my friends in the National Speakers Association, especially the Writers Professional Emphasis Group. And heartfelt appreciation to my dear friends and fellow writers Michael and Cathleen Biehl for years of support and encouragement.

I am forever grateful to the Birthday Club, not only for their companionship but for their assistance with the manuscript. Cheryl Rugg, Cindy Stigler, and Carol Maier were especially helpful with their ongoing critique, encouragement, and rare insights on men and marriage, much of which is included in the text.

I wish to acknowledge the special friendships and years of ski trips and beach vacations with Ellen Croke, Gerry Harmon, Deb and Michael Dwyer, Julie and Mike Toepfer, and Maggie and Mark Fischer. These were some of the activities that helped keep our marriage and family strong. I also wish to thank the members of Professional Dimensions, who have provided friendship and professional networking.

Love and appreciation to my family of support, which includes Debra, Larry, and Dave Schmidt; Rea Katz; Richard, Ben, Becky, Andrew, and Michael Bartlein;

Robert, Judy, and Jake Bartlein; and Penny Brosky. Thank you so very much for helping in many ways.

I wish to thank my son and fellow writer, Ken Brosky, for his encouragement, coaching, and inspiration. He understands better than most just how truly difficult writing can be. My daughter, Stephanie, who refused to listen to my whining and complaining and told me, "just write." And my niece, Jocelyn Brosky, who made me laugh when I should have been writing.

A special thank you to my mom, Wilma Gunther, for her prayers, donated resources, and always believing in me no matter what. Words can never express how much I appreciate you and your love.

And a kiss, hug, and lifelong devotion to my beloved Charlie. You are my best friend, lover, companion, and business partner. You are simply the very best thing that ever happened for me. I cannot imagine my life without you.

INTRODUCTION

Disposable Marriages in a Throwaway Culture

Most married couples expect their relationship to last. In fact, more than 70 percent of adult Americans believe that "marriage is a lifelong commitment that should not be ended except under extreme circumstances." Even among divorced and separated Americans, 81 percent still believe marriage should be for life.[1]

Yet, first marriages have a 45 percent chance of breaking up and second marriages have a 60 percent chance of ending in divorce. Twenty-five percent of people between the ages of eighteen and forty-four have divorced parents.[2] "Divorced person" is currently the fastest growing marital status category, with the number of divorced adults quadrupling from 4.3 million in 1970 to 17.4 million in 1994.[3]

Collectively, we have created a culture of divorce: disposable marriages in a throwaway culture.

Divorce has been normalized through acceptance of failure, "no-fault" divorce laws, and popular media portrayals. It has become de-stigmatized, as obtaining a divorce has become easier. With divorce becoming a more acceptable solution to marital unhappiness, partners quit trying. A recent study found that adopting favorable ideas regarding divorce actually tends to lower the quality of a person's marriage. As divorce has become an easy option, marriages have become more unhappy.[4] Partners simply do not try very hard to stay together when they believe divorce to be a valid solution to their problems—despite what they say in public.

Even those seeking help for a troubled marriage may discover competent assistance difficult to find. Many therapists are not trained in marital therapy and too often view divorce as a positive option and a path to fulfillment and personal growth. They may urge clients to "follow your feelings" and "do what is best for you." Though well meaning, they play cheerleader for the divorce culture and promote "therapist-assisted marriage suicide."

Yet, divorce does not seem to make adults happy. According to new research on happiness and divorce, two-thirds of unhappy spouses who stayed with their marriage instead of divorcing were happy five years later. Of those unhappy spouses who did leave the marriage, only half were happy after five years.[5] While the assumption has always been that getting out of an unhappy marriage will make you happier, it appears not to be true.

According to research, married people are the happiest. They report less depression, less anxiety, and lower levels of other types of psychological distress than do those who are single, divorced, or widowed. In fact, marital status is one of the most important predictors of happiness, with 40 percent of married folks saying they are very happy with their life in general, as compared to just under a quarter of those who are single or who are cohabiting.

Marrieds are also healthier and live longer than their single counterparts. Non-marrieds have significantly higher rates of mortality: 50 percent higher among women and

250 percent higher among men. The unmarried are far more likely to die from all causes, including coronary heart disease, stroke, pneumonia, cancer, cirrhosis, automobile accidents, murder, and suicide. Researchers have found that there are even positive effects from the "nag factor"—the routine nagging that spouses engage in actually encourages a positive lifestyle and decreases destructive habits such as smoking or drinking to excess.

A healthy marriage may also be the starting point for a growing net worth. Not only is divorce very costly in the short run, but the long-term effects of not being married dramatically affect how financially secure you become.

The longer people stay married, the greater their wealth accumulations. At retirement, a typical married couple has accumulated about $410,000, compared to about $167,000 for the never married, about $145,000 for the divorced and just under $96,000 for the separated. This could be due in part to the fact that married people behave more responsibly when it comes to money because they have more responsibilities. By pooling money, labor, and time, married people create far more opportunities for building wealth.

Spouses also have better access to health and life insurance coverage, pensions, and social security. Being married provides "insurance," as spouses almost always leave their worldly goods and benefits to their partners.

There is even a value to in-laws. They tend to help a family when needed. In-laws also provide potential access to inheritance. In the past five years about 29 percent of married couples received financial help from in-laws, and about a quarter of families with children received financial transfers.[6]

There are also dramatic effects on children when parents divorce. A 1997 study of children's use of time found that children in one-parent families got about nine hours less from their mothers and about thirteen hours less from either parent per week than did children in two-parent families. Children raised in single-parent households are more likely to be poor and to have health problems and psychological disorders. They are also more likely to commit crimes and have poorer relationships.[7]

With all the evidence of the benefits of staying married, why don't people work harder on their marriages? At least, in part, because they don't know how.

This book provides concrete answers to the common problems in building, maintaining, and renewing a long-term marriage. It is designed for couples just beginning their lives together, partners who recognize some areas that need improvement, and couples who want to increase their intimacy. It can be used with or without counseling, but it is specifically designed for couples who want to work on their marriages.

Each chapter outlines a frequent complaint of marriage with the common myths that block solution to those problems. This "MythInformation" is the information from media, literature, other couples, and even misguided therapists that confuses relationship building.

The quizzes and tools at the end of each chapter give you an opportunity to practice new skills and behaviors. Take the quizzes to get a snapshot of where you are today, and implement the tools to make changes for the future.

Investing your time and energy in your marriage will be some of the most rewarding work you will ever do.

HOW IS THE HEALTH OF YOUR RELATIONSHIP?

We all want a "healthy" relationship. But what exactly is this? How do you attain it? As you will find out in this book, a healthy relationship does not just magically happen when you meet the "right" person. A healthy relationship is based on friendship and understanding. And like any friendship, it requires effort, communication, and flexibility.

I often hear from couples that they want their partner to be their "soul mate" and their best friend. But how do you create this kind of bond? The best place to start is to evaluate the health of your relationship. How well do you know your partner and their view of the world? Take a few moments to answer the following questions to find out.

1. I understand my partner's philosophies about life.

   Yes No

2. I consider my partner to be my very best friend.

   Yes No

3. We often touch and kiss for no particular reason.

   Yes No

4. I call my partner several times a day.

   Yes No

5. I understand my partner's dreams for the future.

   Yes No

6. We find our sex life is fun and satisfying.

   Yes No

7. We touch base everyday about how our day is going.

   Yes No

8. If I have a problem, I talk with my partner.

   Yes No

9. We have scheduled activities that we look forward to.

   Yes No

10. We have similar values and goals.

Yes No

11. I think that my partner has high integrity.

Yes No

12. I can't wait to get home at the end of the day.

Yes No

13. We have favorite traditions for many of the holidays.

Yes No

14. I feel that my partner respects me.

Yes No

15. We enjoy many of the same activities.

Yes No

16. My partner understands my family.

Yes No

17. My partner makes me laugh.

Yes No

How many "Yes" answers did you have?

15 or more: You have a strong relationship built on friendship.

9–14: You have a good base but additional work will enhance your relationship. This is a good time to utilize additional tools.

8 or fewer: Get busy or you and your partner risk drifting apart.

How did your relationship stack up? Talk with your partner about any "no's" on your list. What could you both do to create "yes" answers to the questions? Use this quiz as a starting point for discussion and change. You will find in the following chapters ideas, quizzes, and tools to help you become closer. After finishing the book, retake this quiz and see how you are doing.

Why Did I Marry You Anyway?

1 Why Did I Marry You Anyway?

STRATEGY 1: BUILD COMMITMENT TO STRENGTHEN YOUR MARRIAGE

I guess you could say I was an old maid. Well, maybe not by today's standards, but this was the '70s. I was almost thirty years old and still single. Not just single, completely single. No boyfriend, no prospects, and shocked with the realization that the best relationship I had had so far was with my cat, Whiskers. I could picture myself twenty years from now feeding a dozen cats and dressed in a baggy muumuu with my hair in brush rollers.

Most of my high school classmates were already married (some also divorced). My older brother, cousins, and neighborhood friends were married. I had even heard that the thin, homely girl with protruding teeth who sat next to me in high school chemistry was married, following expert orthodontics after graduation.

Now I was sitting at my younger sister's wedding in a

long, formal "maid"-of-honor dress, between Aunt Bertha and Uncle Stuart. I knew what was coming.

"And where is *your* special young man?" started Aunt Bertha.

Smiling weakly, I replied, "Just haven't found the right one yet."

"'Atta girl," interrupted Uncle Stuart. "Don't just settle for anyone. Only the best for my favorite niece."

"Well, I can't believe a gal as pretty as you can't find a husband," said Aunt Bertha.

"Maybe she doesn't want a husband," Uncle Stuart responded.

"Of course she wants a husband. Everyone wants to be married."

"Not everyone," Uncle Stuart started laughing.

"And just what do you mean by that?"

"Nothing, dear." Uncle Stuart gave me a wink.

"Sometimes I wonder," Aunt Bertha sighed, "why did I marry you anyway?"

At that point, I quickly made my getaway. Carefully avoiding the "singles" (losers) table, I leaned against the wall by the dance floor to survey for opportunities. Glancing down at my yellow, crêpe dress, I noticed a pronounced swirl of dried green frosting streaking the front. *No wonder I'm standing here alone,* I thought. *I look like a frosted donut.*

Aunt Bertha was right. It would be nice to find someone. She should know. Married for over forty years, she and Uncle Stuart were devoted to each other and had always seemed happy. It would be nice to find a relationship like that.

It wasn't that I hadn't been looking. I looked at college, at work, on the street, in bars, cafés, and restaurants. I explored opportunities on mass transit, including buses, trains, shuttles, and airplanes. I went on arranged dates, blind dates, and disaster dates. I even allowed my mother to set me up with a friend's son who they assured me was "perfect." Yes, perfectly *awful*—thank you very much. After listening to him discuss Guernsey cows for three hours, I had him take me home.

Myth: There have to be sparks or it's not love.

I was nauseous and tingly all over. I was either in love or I had smallpox.[1]

WOODY ALLEN

Now there is nothing wrong with Guernsey cows, but I've lived my whole life in the city. I barely know the difference between a Guernsey and a Great Dane.

I was looking for love. The kind of love that I saw in movies and read and dreamed about. I was totally convinced that if I met the "right" person, the sparks would fly and my life would be perfect. We would get married and live happily ever after. I didn't know then what I know now, after twenty-some years of marriage and a career counseling hundreds of couples.

I, like many, had limited knowledge of love, often confusing infatuation for the deeper bond of love. I wanted that invigorating charge of a new relationship and convinced myself that this was "true" love. I embarked on a series of liaisons that could best be described as "Loser Alley," seeking security and stability with the men least likely to provide it. I used to say that if there were a loser in a room, he would eventually Velcro himself to me. Looking back, I probably met some nice guys from time to time, but I was certain to fly by them as quickly as possible. After all, they were boring. There wasn't any excitement. No high. No instant attraction.

I often have couples come in for therapy concerned because they have lost the passionate "high" of when they first got together. They wonder if they have "fallen out of love." Or even worse, were never in love. I explain to them that the feelings they had when they first met were due, at least in part, to chemicals. Current research into the "chemistry of love" shows we actually get "high" when we are first attracted to someone because of the release of serotonin, dopamine, and norepinephrine in the brain.[2] These neurotransmitters contribute to a rosy outlook on life, increased energy, and excitement. As couples immerse themselves in a relationship and focus on each other, these "love feelings" emerge. They become convinced they have found the perfect person to meet all their needs. The chemical rush of early love is exhilarating and exciting, leading them to believe that "nothing" could change their feelings or burst their bubble of romantic bliss.

I carefully explain that these feelings are probably infatuation and not the kind of love that grows in marriage. They look at me with disbelief and confusion as I start discussing the difference between infatuation and love. Before they can ask for their money back, I hand them a copy of the following comparison. I have had it for many years, (it was actually taped to my refrigerator during my years on "Loser Alley"). I find that it is still valid.

Love vs. Infatuation

Infatuation is instant desire; it's one set of glands calling to another.

Love is friendship that catches fire; it takes root and grows one day at a time.

Infatuation is marked by a feeling of insecurity; you are excited and eager, but not genuinely happy; there are nagging doubts, unanswered questions; little bits and pieces about your beloved that you would just as soon not examine too closely. It might spoil your dreams.

Love is the quiet understanding and mature acceptance of imperfections; it is REAL. It gives you strength and grows beyond you to bolster your beloved; you are warmed by your partner's presence even when away; miles do not separate you. You want to be near, but near or far, you know the love is yours and you can wait.

Infatuation says we must get married right away. I can't risk losing the relationship.

Love says be patient, don't panic, the relationship is secure; you plan your future with confidence.

Infatuation has an element of sexual excitement; if you are honest, you will admit it is difficult to be in one another's company unless you are sure it will end in intimacy.

Love is the maturation of friendship; you must be friends before you can be lovers.

Infatuation lacks confidence; when away from each other, you wonder about cheating; sometimes you even check.

Love means trust; you are calm, secure, and not threatened. Your beloved feels that trust and becomes even more trustworthy.

Infatuation might lead you to do things you may regret later, but love never will.

Love lifts you up. It makes you look up; it makes you think up; it makes you a better person than you were before.

AUTHOR UNKNOWN

After most couples read this comparison, I can see the disappointment on their faces. They display, perhaps, a hint of longing to sign up for a marriage retreat on an Andes hilltop where they can walk with monks and meditate at some ancient burial site instead of coming to see me. They came to couples counseling to "get back" the magic and excitement, only to hear that this isn't the stuff of marriages. They want the perfect romance with music and fireworks, but learn that marriage is more like a quiet evening spent listening to crickets.

I tell them clearly, so they understand, *infatuation does not last*. It can be the start of something real, a love that grows, but this growth takes effort. It does not magically happen. To build the structure for something more concrete than a flirtation or a fling means focusing on the foundation of the relationship. This is usually not what they came to hear.

Myth: Marriage is based on love.

If there is such a thing as a good marriage, it is because it resembles friendship rather than love.

MICHEL EYQUEM DE MONTAIGNE

I try to cheer them up by explaining that in some respects it really doesn't matter anyway, because marriage is not based on love. This is the stuff of fairy tales, romance novels, and popular media. Most couples who get divorced still love each other, or at least have strong feelings about the marriage dissolving. Otherwise, divorce would be simple. The separating parties would enter a room, sign papers, and perhaps kick the tires on the way out like they were selling a car. No emotion, no problem.

But it *is* a problem. The couples I have seen with shattered marriages have shattered hearts and shattered spirits. They are often completely befuddled as to what went wrong. They had mistakenly believed that love was enough—only to find that it barely counted at all.

They usually begin to argue with me at this point, telling me how much they love each other and that after all, "All You Need Is Love"—the Beatles should know. And, if love isn't the foundation to a marriage, what is? Just what the heck am I talking about?

I explain to them that marriage is built on commitment. This foundation piece creates the climate for trust and love to grow. It is not automatic in a relationship; it grows over time. And it requires work, not magic, not fairy tales. Like the beautiful ash trees in my yard, commitment grows over time with careful attention and nurturing. I stress to them that the more they cement this foundation into place, the happier their marriage will be. And yes, the love will grow. Not the roller-coaster love of early infatuation, but a mature love of respect, understanding, and mutual admiration.

Building commitment needs to be the number one priority in a happy marriage. Chasing love does not grow a marriage. It is commitment that grows the love. For there will be days that you won't experience overwhelming feelings of love for your spouse. You may not be consumed with wild passion so strong that you want to rip off your clothes in a frenzy and make love on the linoleum. There are days you may not feel love at all. In fact, there are moments you barely like them.

This is where commitment comes in. Because, guess what? He or she may not like you so much, either. Not that there is anything wrong with you, mind you, but that is just the nature of living with other people. People can be annoying and frustrating. They squeeze the toothpaste in the middle, they leave towels on the bathroom floor, and they drink directly out of the milk carton. I mean, are they even *thinking* about germs or do they just have full faith in pasteurization? It's enough to make a sane person crazy.

Now, I know that *you* don't have any of these awful habits, but some people do, and if you look really, really close, you might notice a very small problem in yourself here or there, too. Like cramming everything you possibly can into a closet, so that when your spouse opens the door, all the stuff falls on their head. Or backing your brand new van into a pole. (This happens to be one of mine. My husband asked me if I had seen the pole. *Hello!* If I had seen it, do you think I would've hit it?)

The point is that marriage isn't always smooth sailing, and you have to be committed to make it work. Comedian Rich Hall does a hilarious bit where his girlfriend presses him on his level of commitment by asking, "Would you still love me if I were hit by a bus?" His answer? "Stay out of the bus lane." Yes, stay out of the bus lane. But just in case you do get mowed down with bad luck, it's nice to know that your spouse won't be on the next bus out of town.

"But *why* do we have to focus on commitment?" my clients ask, usually with a look of disbelief and despair. "If we love each other enough, it will work . . . the commitment will grow." And I say softly, "You have it backwards. Love is not enough. Life and marriage is so much more complicated than this. This is not a fairy tale or a movie. You need protection that can stand up to the storms that come your way, and the shield for marriage is commitment."

Myth: All we need is love.

The men in my life went to bed with Gilda . . . and they woke up with me.

RITA HAYWORTH

I let them know they are not alone. We are taught to believe in wild, romantic love and its ability to leap buildings in a single bound and perhaps take a bullet without any bodily harm. I had believed it myself.

I still remember the idealistic experience of my first love—the guy I was sure was "the right one." I was on a ski trip with other students from the University of Wisconsin. It was spring skiing in Aspen, Colorado, and the snow was powdery and soft, not at all like the ice chunks and dirt mounds that we navigate in the Midwest. The weather was crystal clear, with brilliant sunshine that warmed your face and lifted your spirits.

As the week of skiing came to a close, there was a "wrap-up" party in one of the rooms. After talking and laughing until 1:00 A.M., I said my goodnights and started for the door. A young, handsome man named John offered to walk me to my condo. I had seen him on the hill several times during the week but had not really talked with him before.

As we strolled down the quiet Aspen street, moonlight lit the snow and illuminated the mountains. The cold, dry mountain air was mysterious with tiny ice crystals sparkling in the moonlight and haloing the streetlights. We laughed at the stories we had heard and told a few more of our own. Funny and charming, John said, "I've watched you all week. I would really like to see you when we get back to school."

When we arrived at the door to my room, he leaned over and kissed me. Not a long kiss. Just the short kind that can't get a person into too much trouble if it's not welcome. It was magical. I felt like time was standing still. My mind was spinning. What does it mean when you are kissed in the moonlight at the base of a mountain? As I watched him walk away, I thought, *This must be the one. This is so romantic.* A kiss in the Rockies is surely more significant than a kiss at sea level. A moonlight walk with sparkling ice crystals counts for something. This was meant to be. This was serious.

We did date when we returned to school, but other than skiing, we actually had little in common. I believed in marriage, he didn't. I wanted kids, he didn't. I was ambitious, he wasn't. The amazing thing was I kept trying to make it work in spite of the overwhelming evidence that it wasn't working at all. I thought, *If I just try harder. . . .* I thought that since the magical moonlight had started it, the least I could do was finish it. This was my fairy tale and I wanted the happy ending.

It didn't work that way. He became involved with one of my close friends and dumped me. I couldn't believe it. I loved him. I thought he loved me. But there was no real commitment. And other than meeting at the base of a mountain, there was little base to the relationship.

Myth: If I just try harder, it will work.

It takes two to make a marriage a success and only one to make it a failure.

HERBERT SAMUEL

We are taught to believe in high-altitude romance and the myth: "If we love each other, it will work." We watch movies like *Sleepless in Seattle* and *You've Got Mail* that convince us that finding the right one is all there is to it. After all, Tom Hanks and Meg Ryan presumably lived happily ever after. While I am a big fan of Tom Hanks and I love romantic comedies, they are not real life. It is no more realistic than the carriage-out-of-a-pumpkin maneuver by Cinderella's fairy godmother. The problem is, most people don't believe the pumpkin trick, but lots of folks believe that a rooftop kiss or a cyber moment can determine their lives—and that leaves *me* sleepless.

These movies give the impression that the main concern is finding "Mr. or Ms. Right," and the rest will work out. And many of us believe that. We *want* to believe that. We buy into the magical belief that "Love Is All You Need." So we keep looking on rooftops and—in today's world—on the Internet.

Couples often come to see me when the infatuation begins to fade and their idealistic beliefs about marriage start to crumble. At first, they are hopeful, then discouraged, and then downright angry. They feel like they have been given a bill of goods. The lament is always the same: "I just wish it was like when we first met. It was wild and passionate then." Well, no kidding! Something new usually *is* exciting, whether it is a relationship, a car, or a pair of shoes. But everything gets dented and worn after a while.

Couples want their marriage to work. According to the Coalition for Marriage, Family and Couples Education, Americans say that a happy marriage is their number one goal, and 85 to 90 percent will get married at least once. But too often, they think that a great marriage will just happen. In fact, when it doesn't work, they mistakenly assume they have simply married the "wrong person." They terminate the relationship and resume the quest to fulfill fairy-tale expectations. Usually by their second or third serious relationship, they see similar issues and (hopefully) begin to question their basic assumptions.

Myth: If I find the "right" person, we will live happily ever after.

Many a man has fallen in love with a girl in light so dim he would not have chosen a suit by it.

MAURICE CHEVALIER

By believing this myth, they do not really have to take responsibility—for themselves, for their actions, or for the success or failure of their marriage. This attitude is often reflected in how people talk about marriage. They say, "Well, it just didn't work out. It was one of those things." This implies the success of the marriage lies outside of themselves and their actions. But the truth is that the success of any relationship lies *with you*. A distinguishing feature of happily married couples is that, after years of trial and error, they have finally acquired the judgment to choose a mate carefully and wisely.[3]

But couples aren't excited when I tell them to focus on commitment; they want the high of infatuation.

CASE STUDY: John and Wendy

John, age twenty-six, and Wendy, thirty-five, sought marital counseling after eighteen months of marriage. While it was John's first marriage, Wendy was divorced, with two young children, Ryan, age six, and Brittany, age three.

Dressed in old blue jeans and a flannel shirt, John saunters slowly into my office and falls into the overstuffed chair, making it clear he does not want to be there. He avoids eye contact with Wendy and frequently stares out the window. Working as a carpenter for his father's construction company, he describes his schedule as "flexible" with frequent "downtime" when business is slow. He reports he is presently "laid off," and spends his days "lounging" at home.

Wendy is dressed in a navy suit with a matching blouse. Crisp and businesslike, she states that she works as a secretary for a small legal firm. She gets up at 5:00 a.m. to get the kids to school and arrive at work on time. She often works ten-hour days when the firm is in the middle of a trial. Both came to the initial session feeling discouraged and disappointed.

The night before, they had a lengthy and loud argument when John came home after midnight from an evening at the bars with his friends. John has a very active social life, plays on several softball teams, and belongs to a pool league. While Wendy occasionally meets him for a drink when her children are visiting their father, she has not done so lately because of responsibilities at work and home.

Both parties report that they "feel cheated" since getting married. It is not what they expected. Wendy tearfully describes their home life as being like roommates. She had hoped that John would take more of an interest in the children and that they would "partner" with duties around the house. Instead, she feels like a waitress, with all the household chores on her shoulders.

John states that Wendy is trying to "cramp his style" and dictate to him what he can do. He thought marriage would be more fun, like when they were dating, but the magic seems to be gone. "She used to like partying with me," John states. "We would go dancing and to football games, and we'd party with my friends."

I explain to them that marriage is not like dating. Dating does not include the realities of everyday life: mortgages, bills, taxes, laundry, etc. I explain that "early in the relationship, these tiresome details are often put aside to have fun, to connect. Yet they will be there eventually, no matter whom you marry."

"I just didn't think marriage would be this much work," says John. "I'm beginning to wonder whether I married the right person."

I ask John what the "right person" means to him.

"You know, someone where you just 'click.' We shouldn't have to work so hard at it," John replies.

I explain to them that all long-term marriages require work. They don't just happen. It's not magic. It requires commitment so that the trust can grow, and trust is critical. It is hard to be yourself and develop a relationship if you worry that at the first sign of problems your spouse is going to leave.

Over the next few sessions, it became clear that John wanted out. He wasn't ready to deal with a new wife and two children. He had married Wendy because he was attracted to her, but he had not really considered the issue of commitment. He didn't seem to understand that this was the major issue. No matter who he married, the relationship would require more effort than he was willing to give at this point. He believed in the myth of finding the right person and living happily ever after.

Wendy had once again married someone with whom there was physical attraction but who could not give her the stability and predictability she desperately needed. She had not looked deeper for his ability to make commitments. In subsequent sessions, she came to the realization that John wasn't really committed to anything, much less the marriage itself. He wasn't pursuing a career, further education, or even a full-time job. He continued to work for his father because it was comfortable and he had no accountability. He had a pattern of taking the easy route and looking for easy answers. No wonder his approach to marriage was so nonchalant.

I explained to Wendy that the best relationships are based less on chemistry and more on intellect and logic. I told her about the kiss in the mountains and how I was such an expert in finding my "type"—only to discover it was exactly the type that was no good for me. I cautioned her to run the other direction if she felt an immediate attraction, an instantaneous connection, upon first meeting a man. Chances are, it will be simply more of the same, like a vanilla ice cream cone at Baskin-Robbins. And I made Wendy repeat after me, "The familiar is not what I need."

■ ■ ■ ■ ■

I talk with clients about the myth of finding the "right person," explaining that few people really understand what "right" means and what is "right" for them. People who desperately need stability, like Wendy, hook up with unstable folks. People who fear abandonment choose those who can't make commitments. Many fail to learn from their mistakes. They get involved with the same type of person over and over again—looking for stability with partners afraid of commitment, looking for a soul mate with someone they can't trust, chasing a fairytale.

My clients are often emphatic about what they want in a spouse, but it may not match at all with what they really need. I understand the "looking for what I want instead of what I need" dilemma because of the strange way I met my husband. To this day, I say, "He's not my type," meaning he is not the type I thought I wanted. I was still looking for love in the mountains and on the rooftops. My husband was not what I wanted, but I assure you, he is exactly what I need.

I had just returned to Milwaukee after nine years in Colorado. Discouraged and broken-hearted after the breakup with mountain man, I took a nursing position at a local hospice and enrolled in graduate school. I think that's how I got so many college degrees: whenever my life wasn't working, I went back to school.

About the third month on the job, a young man named Michael was admitted to the unit. Only thirty-three years old, he was dying of a brain tumor discovered eighteen months previously. An engineer and accomplished sky diver, Michael owned a business designing skydiving equipment. I was assigned to be his primary nurse.

Myth: I know what I want.

It doesn't much signify whom one marries, for one is sure to find out the next morning that it was someone else.

WILL ROGERS

I walked down the hall and entered Michael's room to get a psychosocial history before planning his care. He was reclining in a leather Barcalounger watching TV, his half-eaten tray of lunch food pushed to the side. He was paralyzed on the right side from the tumor, and his cane leaned against his chair along with the nurse's call button.

After I introduced myself, Michael made it clear that he preferred to be called by his nickname, Shoobie. He explained that all of his skydiving friends have nicknames: Wishbone, Charlie Oatmeal, Freakbrother, Wildman, and others. Pulling out a picture calendar showing sky divers linked in a star free-fall pattern, Shoobie described how they would go to jump meets across the country, often living out of the back of a van.

"See, that's a twelve-man," he explained. "It's great! I've done it all. And I'm not done yet. You see, when I die, I'm going to roller-skate straight down Pikes Peak."

We both laughed at the thought.

Suddenly, there was a knock on the door and eighteen people walked into the room, several carrying six-packs of beer. With every person in the room looking at me, Shoobie asked if they could have a party. Never one to worry about rules, I assured them it was fine and closed the door on my way out.

Shoobie—always the host, always in a good mood, joking with his friends—shared many evenings like that with the sky divers. I was amazed at how many nice people he knew and how much they thought of him. One evening after his friends had left, he asked, "Why do you look so sad tonight?" And I soon found myself telling him about my failed engagement, the kiss in the mountains, and my Loser Alley of love.

> Myth: I know my type.
>
> **Your partner doesn't have to fulfill all your needs . . . just the most important ones.**
>
> AUTHOR

He told me that I needed to find a "nice guy." As if I didn't already know that. I wasn't sure I would know one if I fell right over him.

"Well, what about someone like Charlie Oatmeal?" he asked.

Laughing out loud, I responded, "Charlie Oatmeal! He's not my type. He's too quiet, too soft-spoken. Don't be silly!"

Talking softly, Shoobie said, "Maybe the type you want isn't the type you need." And he got into bed.

As we entered the dog days of summer, Shoobie's health clearly deteriorated. Not as many friends came to see him anymore, and Shoobie had limited energy when they did. He began to sleep most of the day or was barely conscious. At times, the nursing staff thought he would die in his sleep—only to find him sitting up and lucid a few hours later.

After one particularly difficult day, I noticed the elevator doors open. I intercepted Charlie Oatmeal as he started down the hall.

"Charlie! He really isn't doing very well. You may not want to stay," I reported.

He paused for a minute, and then looked me in the eye. "Will he know that I'm here?"

"Uh, well yes, I suppose. They say even people in a coma can hear. He'll probably know you're here."

"Well, that's good enough for me." He turned and started down the hall to Shoobie's room.

Charlie spent the next six hours at Shoobie's bedside. Holding his hand, he related one skydiving story after another. When I was free of my duties, I went and sat on the other side of the bed to listen. Occasionally, Shoobie would smile as Charlie talked of jumping nude into the Running Bear Nudist Colony or of being stranded in a cornfield miles from the drop zone.

"Shoobie sewed the best jumpsuits ever made, you know," Charlie said to me as Shoobie smiled.

"No, I didn't know that," I whispered, watching carefully. Shoobie was right. There was something very wonderful about Charlie. A special kind of person sits at the bedside of his dying friend telling stories and making sure he is not alone. I have never claimed to be a rocket scientist, but at that moment, I got it. The type I had been looking for was not what I needed. I needed someone who knew how to commit to relationships, even in the worst of times. I found myself staring at Charlie as he comforted his friend.

Shoobie died two days later. He was given a sky diver's burial—his body cremated and his ashes taken up to ten thousand feet. Charlie participated in the burial jump and described to me later how the contents of the urn slowly rose in a spiral as a stream of light came down through the clouds.

The next week, Charlie called and asked me out. We were married the following spring. When we honeymooned in Colorado, I could have sworn I heard Shoobie roller-skating straight down Pikes Peak.

That was twenty-four years ago. Shoobie was right.

It was clear to me then—and it's clear to me now—if I

had met Charlie any sooner or perhaps under different circumstances, I would have walked right by. After all, *he's not my type.* It certainly was not the romantic, kiss-in-the-mountains meeting I had expected. After all, we met over a deathbed. Not very romantic. However, meeting and marrying him was the best thing that ever happened to me. He is able to make commitments, which makes me feel secure, loved, and cherished. This is my most important need.

Charlie certainly does not fill all my needs—just the most important ones. For example, I am a voracious reader. I like fiction, non-fiction, biographies, history, business books, and any other books I can get my hands on. Charlie reads periodicals, usually of the length that can be read in the bathroom. I would love to have someone who would sit and discuss books, share philosophies, and analyze great writing. I can picture myself having afternoon tea discussing great literature with my partner on the balcony overlooking the lake. But that's not Charlie, and that's okay. I can join a book club to fill those needs.

Now I wish I could tell you that I never had another problem in my life since I married Charlie, but I know you would begin laughing hysterically and maybe injure yourself falling off your chair. I would love to tell you that we are perfectly compatible and have never had to work on even one little issue in our marriage, but my children would call a hotline or tell the tabloids what life is really like at our house. One day, Charlie asked me where I got the material for this book. As my teenagers say, "Duh!" Like all marriages, we have had to work at it, but more on that later. The commitment has given us the foundation on which to do the work.

Commitment does not end the day you say "I do." Your public declaration of commitment on your wedding day in front of family, friends, and clergy is important, but it's only the beginning. To have a healthy marriage, you have to focus on commitment and make it a priority. Commitment is more than a promise; it is more than a one-time decision. It is an ongoing focus on your marriage. It increases the value of the relationship "precisely because reasons will always exist not to honor it."[5]

There are a million and one reasons to walk away from a marriage. And you will find a great deal of support and understanding from other people if you want to do so. After all, many of *them* have also walked away. You will have no difficulty finding therapists, attorneys, and friends who will urge you to "take care of yourself" if you are unhappy, as if marriage is always supposed to be happy. Divorce appears easy. Many states have "no-fault" legislation that makes it quick and acceptable. We have normalized divorce to the extent that it is viewed as an easy option when things aren't working.

I'm often asked, "Just how committed do I need to be? How much more do I need to do? After all, I said 'I do.' Isn't that enough?" And I answer, "No. You must be willing to do anything." "Anything?" *Yes, anything.* The couples I see that create long-term marriages are so committed that if I tell them to stand on their heads every day, they do it. If I ask them to study Yoga together, they go sign up. If I suggest gourmet cooking, they search for innovative cookbooks and exotic spices and, perhaps, buy a new stove. Sometimes, when they try my suggestions, things get dramatically better and they want to nominate me for Therapist of the Year. They become convinced I know the magical answer just for them, when the real secret is their commitment. When couples are willing to take sugges-

Myth: Saying "I do" is enough.

The secret to staying married for thirty-six years? Just keep coming home.[4]

BILL COSBY

tions, to try new strategies, it demonstrates and builds their commitment to each other. It is the attitude that they will make it work, dammit, no matter what it takes from them—and that is precisely the attitude that makes it work. Committed couples have an attitude of winning, of success.

They verbalize and demonstrate their commitment to their partners through compliments and words of encouragement and reassurance. They plan for the future together. There is never a question of whether the marriage will work because they are both committed to "making it work." As one partner increases his or her sense of commitment, the other feels more at ease verbalizing his or her own commitment, and a cycle of commitment and building takes place.

Myth: I can make my partner more committed.

The difference between involvement and commitment is like ham and eggs. The chicken is involved; the pig is committed.

MARTINA NAVRATILOVA

Commitment provides the base, the foundation on which the partnership will be built. If this building block is shaky, the rest is at risk of tumbling down.

So you are committed and your partner isn't? Well, join the club. This is actually fairly common. Maybe because of magical thinking or enticing infatuation, too many people walk down the aisle and say "I do" while looking for the door, ladder, or fire escape just in case things don't work out. They don't realize that the growth of the marriage is directly related to facing problems and working together. The investment is exactly what gives it the value.

I frequently ask couples at the first session to rate their commitment on a scale of one to ten with ten being the absolute most. It is usually very enlightening. Perhaps one partner will be at a ten and the other at a two. Well, you don't have to be Freud to figure out that there is a problem. One partner is trying to make the commitment for both of them. The problem is . . . you can't do that. You can't convince someone to become committed; you can't force him or her. No amount of talking, nagging, cajoling, urging, threatening, or demanding is going to make it happen. It has to come from within, something with which each partner feels comfortable. And some people just don't commit to anyone or anything.

Sometimes, when I ask the one-to-ten question, they both quickly say "ten" without a moment's hesitation. They are sure. They are convinced. They *are* committed. Then they display the "yeah . . . but" disease. They "yeah . . . but" everything I say or suggest. "Yeah . . . but, we already tried that." "Yeah . . . but, I don't have time for that." "Yeah . . . but, that will never work for us." I then have to point out that they are right. Nothing will work. They have the "yeah . . . but" disease and it's eroding their commitment. I explain that they really aren't at a ten. They are more like a two or a three and that is what we have to talk about.

CASE STUDY: Susan and Dwayne

Consider Susan and Dwayne, married for six years. They postponed having children due to busy careers and financial concerns. Now they constantly argue over whether it is "time" to have children and make a "commitment" to being a family. Both have had decreasing fulfillment in the marriage, as they have spent little time nurturing and building the basics.

Dwayne: We can't wait forever, Susan. And anyways, you hate your job! Why don't you stay home for a while and be a housewife?

Susan: Is that what this is about? You are looking for a solution to my career problems?

Dwayne: No, I want children. I thought you did, too.

Susan: Well, I do. But not now. I just don't think we are getting along well enough now to consider it. I wouldn't want to have children and get divorced in a few years.

Dwayne: *Divorced?* (Getting upset) What do you mean divorced? Aren't you happy with me?

Susan: Well . . . yes. But, it just seems that we fight a lot lately. All you ever want to talk about is having kids. I'm just not sure.

Dwayne: Not sure about kids? Or me?

Susan: Well . . . both. I'm just not sure the family thing, you know, the white picket fence and all that, is what I'm looking for.

Dwayne: Well, when are you going to know? I thought that was what marriage was all about.

Susan: I'm just not sure what I want.

■ ■ ■ ■ ■

Dwayne and Susan are going to have a difficult time dealing with their problems and issues because their commitment is not clear. This couple has not made the marriage a priority in their lives; their primary focus has been their careers. They clearly will not find the love, security, or fulfillment in their marriage with just their "leftover" time and energy. A "leftover marriage" is about as exciting as any other leftover.

HOW COMMITTED ARE YOU?

Reality forms around a commitment.

AUTHOR

Commitment provides the base, the foundation on which the partnership will be built. If this building block is shaky, the rest is at risk of tumbling down. How would your commitment rate on a scale of one to ten? How much effort do you put into your own commitment?

1. When I argue with my spouse, I threaten divorce or separation.

   Always Sometimes Never

2. I have stormed out of the house during an argument without letting my spouse know when I will return.

   Always Sometimes Never

3. I make it clear to my spouse that I have doubts about the future of the marriage and am not sure it "will work."

   Always Sometimes Never

4. I refrain from telling my spouse that I love him/her, because I shouldn't have to say it.

   Always Sometimes Never

5. I am reluctant to plan for the future and fully commit my money because I don't know whether the marriage will work.

   Always Sometimes Never

6. I question whether I married the "right" person.

   Always Sometimes Never

7. I often wonder whether marriage would be easier with someone else.

   Always Sometimes Never

8. I think if you love each other enough marriage should just work out.

   Always Sometimes Never

9. There are days where I question whether I still love my spouse.

    Always   Sometimes   Never

Scoring: How many "never" responses did you have?

7–9: Excellent. You are clear about your commitment and are communicating this to your spouse.

4–6: Good. Keep working. You will reap results by changing your behavior.

Fewer than 4: Actively work on increasing your commitment. Utilize the following tools to build this quality in yourself.

BUILD YOUR COMMITMENT

A winner makes commitments. A loser makes promises.

AUTHOR

TOOL #1 Ban the "D" word from your vocabulary. Under no circumstances is divorce ever mentioned unless papers have been filed. Mentioning or threatening divorce basically means, "I am not fully committed." This erodes the trust. Ban all talk about divorce, even in jest. It is no joking matter.

TOOL #2 Do not discuss previous relationships with each other. These discussions do not serve any purpose and tend to make people feel insecure and unsure. Remember, whenever there are comparisons, someone comes up short. Your spouse is who you are married to. Keep your focus on the present.

TOOL #3 Agree that you will not storm out during an argument. These dramatic exits tend to deliver the message, "I may leave and not come back." If you do need time to cool down, go to another room or let your spouse know you are taking a break but will be back at a certain time—then come back when you said you would, or before.

TOOL #4 Agree to do something you do not want to do because it is important to your spouse. This may be a movie, a new sport, or simply going for a walk. Your participation demonstrates your commitment to bend, to make it work. It shows your willingness to respond to your spouse's needs and wishes.

Building commitment is the most important task for you and your partner. By actively using the tools and working on these building blocks, you establish the groundwork for further growth in your marriage. With a firm foundation, trust and love will grow.

Losing love is like a window in your heart,
everybody sees you're blown apart,
everybody sees the wind blow.

"GRACELAND" BY PAUL SIMON

2 I Can Never Count on You

STRATEGY 2:
CREATE A CLIMATE OF TRUST TO GROW YOUR LOVE

It took me about three years to start trusting Charlie. Not because he wasn't trustworthy, he was. In fact, he would constantly surprise and amaze me. He showed up for dates and called when he said he would. At times, I would confront him. Why are you calling? And he'd calmly remind me, "Because I said I would." Oh, that's right. You said you would. This behavior was new and seemed very foreign. It was what some call "normal." I didn't know what normal was.

It was clear to me that I was "recovering" from years of distrust from investing in untrustworthy people. I had little experience with men who did what they said they were going to do. After all, Dad had left. And my relationships had all been disasters.

I already told you about mountain man, but I didn't

really tell you the whole story. I didn't tell you that all my future dreams were linked to him. I left out that we bought a house together, with all the appliances, including a washer and dryer (my first washer/dryer, by the way). I omitted the fact that I had already picked out a pattern for my wedding dress and planned to embroider roses and flowers around the hem with silk thread. I had my heart in this relationship and perhaps just a bit of my soul.

It's not that I didn't suspect something was wrong. I did. I could feel it. It seemed that he had gotten very close with one of my friends, but after all, she was happily married. I tried to talk with him about it, hesitantly asking, "Are you involved with her?" He rolled his eyes and said, "How could you even suggest such a thing?" But then why did I feel so funny when they were both in the room?

I asked her, "Are you involved with him?" Looking surprised and shocked (which immediately made me feel guilty), she assured me, "I'm only his friend. Actually, I'm trying to help you. I'm trying to give him another person to talk to, which will take some pressure off your relationship. You are imagining things." I smiled sheepishly and noticed that I couldn't eat lunch because my stomach hurt.

I tried to talk with her, only to hear her expound on the value of open marriage—a concept popularized at that time through a book written by a husband-wife team. The basic premise of *Open Marriage* was that it was fine to be married, but there was no reason to have it be exclusive. It was perfectly okay to see other people. In fact, it would enhance your marriage if you did so. (The authors have since gotten divorced, by the way.) You'd think I could have figured things out at this point, but after all, she was one of my best friends. Best friends don't sleep with your fiancé—no matter what book is popular at the time.

At this point, it was clear to me that I was simply crazy. How could I ever suspect such a thing from two of the people in my life that I cared so much about? I was simply hallucinating, not seeing reality, letting my imagination get the best of me—*almost paranoid,* for heaven's sake.

Myth: It's me. I must be crazy.

It is an equal failing to trust everybody, and to trust nobody.

ENGLISH PROVERB

I had obviously moved into another dimension: the *Twilight Zone* of relationships. I could imagine Rod Serling with a cigarette in his hand standing off to the side of my living room. "Barbara thinks she understands what is happening and what is her reality, but she has traveled to another dimension; there's a signpost up ahead . . . *The Twilight Zone.*"

It's like the episode in which a couple finds themselves in a small, rural town with identical houses and perfect landscaping. It looks like paradise, except there are no other people, and sometimes they hear the laughter of a child in the distance. The man leans too hard against a tree and it tumbles over. In panic, the couple realizes that the trees are artificial, built on wooden stands. They begin to examine the houses and find they aren't real either. They have fake finishes and non-working appliances.

Suddenly, a large hand comes out of the sky and picks up the couple. The twist? They have become "toys" in a dollhouse village for a giant child on another planet. What appeared to them as reality was not real at all.

This is the way it is when there is no trust in a relationship. You begin to question your reality: what you are seeing, what you are hearing, and what it means. Your esteem crumbles as you second-guess your intuition and yourself. If it's not them, it must be you. You feel powerless—like a play toy in a fake set—to understand the truth and what is happening. You start to feel insane, but it really isn't you. It's living without trust. The lies put you in another dimension that makes you crazy.

Of course, it soon became all too clear that my fiancé and best friend were involved. They had been sleeping together for some time. She was planning to leave her husband and move in with my fiancé. So much for our house. Sell the washer/dryer. Forget the embroidery. My world collapsed. I had given him my heart, thinking of a future, and now I couldn't see a future at all.

It reminds me of my first car—a Volkswagen Bug that I bought when I was twenty-five years old. I had saved for months to buy the car with $500. The first thing I did to it was add an elaborate car stereo (with a cassette deck and four speakers). That car with its sound system was my pride and joy. It wasn't much, but it was mine, and I had waited for it a long time.

One day, my sister borrowed the car to go to the store. Upon her return, I proudly asked, "What did you think of the sound system?"

"What sound system?" she replied.

"What do you mean, 'what sound system?' The radio in the dash with a cassette deck and four speakers."

"There's no radio in the dash. Just a hole with wires hanging out."

Panicked, I ran to the car and confirmed what I already feared. Indeed, someone had hastily stolen the car stereo and ripped out the speakers, leaving large, gaping holes with frayed edges and hanging wires. I realize a VW Bug isn't very much. I know it's not a Lexus or a Mercedes. But it was all I had. It was everything to *me.*

It is like that with the heart. Maybe the relationship didn't mean as much to him. I guess it's obvious it didn't. But it meant a lot to me. I had given it all that I had. I had given him my heart and let him peer into my soul. And after the lies, after the deceit, all that was left was a large wound with frayed edges. These types of wounds take a long time to heal.

You don't need infidelity to feel crazy. There are many other ways that trust gets trampled in a relationship. Addictions are notorious trust destroyers. Whether alcoholism, drug addiction, or gambling, addiction always includes an element of lying that erodes the relationship as surely as infidelity. Welcome to *The Twilight Zone*!

It may begin with little lies. "I only had one drink." "I didn't go to the casino tonight." "I had to work late." The addicted person may begin to believe that "little white lies" don't really matter. In fact, they may believe they are just protecting their spouse from getting upset. But, after years of deceit, reality becomes very murky. The couple gets so used to living with lies that they wouldn't know the truth if it walked up the front walk and rang the doorbell.

Myth: Little white lies don't matter.

Don't trust the person who has broken faith once.

William Shakespeare

I let couples know that the white lies do matter. Without trust, their love will never grow. They both have to work on it, be committed to it, and study hard. I tell them, "The world is crazy enough. You do not need it at home. There are plenty of people who will misrepresent the truth to sell you a used car or a Ginsu knife. You do not need one in your bed. At home, you need someone to count on.

Couples are quick to tell me they "completely" trust each other. No problem there—thanks for asking. But they are often just thinking of situations like the one that happened to me: cheating or extramarital affairs. While, obviously, this is a big issue (there is a reason adultery is included in the big ten rules), trust involves so much

Myth: But, of course we completely trust each other.

I have seldom known a person who deserted the truth in trifles and then could be trusted in matters of importance.

BABE PALEY

more than this. Trust is the sum of hundreds of everyday experiences that affect our ability to connect with another. Little things. Almost insignificant things. Things like keeping promises, showing up on time, not criticizing when angry and refraining from comical mother-in-law imitations at the neighborhood cocktail party. But they are not insignificant, because they affect the ability of you and your spouse to become intimate and operate as soul mates. The first step to building trust is looking at yourself.

You must *be* trustworthy. Consider the following dialogue:

Julie: Where were you last night until two o'clock in the morning?

Sean: There you go again. You don't trust me. You are so jealous. I told you, I was just out with the guys.

Julie: But you said you would be home at midnight!

Sean: Well, is that a crime? Are you the police? I don't have to report to you. You act like my mother.

Julie: I am not your mother. I just think you should do what you say you are going to do.

Sean: Well, you said you wouldn't buy more clothes, but you went shopping last week again.

Julie: Is that what this is? Are you retaliating because I went shopping? You are such a child.

Sean: I'm a child? You are the one making such a big deal out of this.

Julie: Well it is a big deal. I worry about you when you aren't home. I worry that something happened to you.

Sean: You don't need to worry. I know how to take care of myself. I was just having fun and lost track of time.

Julie: But you always lose track of time. You said you would be home at midnight.

Sean: So shoot me. It's obvious I can't do anything right.

This dialogue can continue for hours because both Sean and Julie are missing the key point. Building trust requires doing what you say you are going to do—walking the walk, not just talking the talk, being predictable and accountable. Your spouse must know he or she can count on what you do and say because you follow through. People are not likely to be trusting about large things, the big issues, if they can't trust you to do the small things.

I remember a guy I dated in college. He was supposed to pick me up one evening for a dinner at a gourmet French restaurant, after visiting his parents. I spent most of the afternoon getting ready, including purchasing a new outfit, cutting and styling my hair, and undertaking major defoliating efforts. He never showed. I sat there waiting for two hours past the time, silently giving him every excuse I could think of for why he might be late: the roads are slippery, he had a heart attack, he was arrested due to mistaken identity. I finally had to accept that he was not coming. I had defoliated for nothing!

The next day he begged me to give him another chance. I am very embarrassed to report that I did—only to have him do this again a few months later. (By the way, this is one reason I'm never too hard on clients who make the same mistakes over and over again. I needed an intensive training program myself.) One day, the lightbulb went on. Why on earth would this guy be a good partner when he can't even show up for a date? This isn't exactly the tough stuff here. I shuddered to think of the dinners that would sit on the table getting cold waiting for him. Or the family outings he would forget. I could picture myself giving birth in a taxi because he failed to show up for labor and delivery.

It wasn't that he didn't always have good excuses; he did. In fact, some were extremely creative: "The dog fell into the neighbor's swimming pool and if I wouldn't have jumped in, she would have drowned. Of course, I couldn't leave her all upset." (Never mind that I was upset.) But excuses get old, and intentions don't count.

Myth: My good intentions count.

Trust everybody, but cut the cards.

FINLEY PETER DUNNE

I caution people not to get suckered with "good" intentions. My date may have *planned* to pick me up at 8 o'clock, but he still never showed. So he *meant* to call—he still didn't. He can't get credit for just an intention . . . that is not how the world works.

You don't get a degree because you intended to go to school. Or a paycheck because you thought about showing up for work. You have to follow through. Intentions don't count. I get so tired of hearing "I should've," "I would've," and "I could've." Enough already! The should'ves, would'ves, and could'ves of broken promises and commitments are not impressive to me, and they shouldn't be to you. When evaluating human behavior, I always look at what people actually do, not what they say.

When I tell this to my clients, particularly those who are not in the habit of following through, they look at me like I am an alien. They often begin to argue with me, insisting that "meaning" to do something should "count" for something on the relationship scorecard. I can only imagine that they were given a lot of credit as a child for *tasting* the beans on their plate, even though they did not actually chew or swallow them.

Positive intentions that do not lead to positive actions slowly erode trust. Your partner cannot rely on you to follow through. Consistency is the key, whether in marriage, parenting, or stirring a Hollandaise sauce. Consistent behavior creates a marriage of confidence and security.

Outcome and results are what count—not what you meant to do or what you thought you would do. It reminds me of when I took my first nursing job in Denver, Colorado. Fresh out of school, I worked on a large medical/surgical unit of a teaching hospital. Each morning, a team of physicians would make Grand Rounds, visiting the sickest of patients to discuss their care and make recommendations.

They stopped one morning to see one of my patients who was postsurgical and had experienced multiple complications, including a postoperative infection and a bleeding disorder. They stood at the door reviewing the latest lab reports with enthusiasm and excitement.

"Look at this," exclaimed the attending physician. "His white count is decreasing. I think the infection is finally under control."

"Yes," said another. "His platelets have also improved. Things are definitely looking better."

"Well, there is *one* problem," I interrupted. They all turned to stare at me, wondering who would be so impertinent to disrupt their academic discussion.

"Yes, and exactly what is that?" demanded the attending physician.

"The patient's dead," I replied.

In unison, they slowly stepped forward and stared at the patient, quickly realizing that I was right. They had been so busy looking at the detail that they had missed the big picture. White counts and platelets were not really the issue.

It is the same with relationships. The details of who did what, what was said, and what was promised aren't the real issues . . . trust is. If you are struggling in a relationship because of a discrepancy between what your partner says and does, ignore the words and focus on the action. Remember, intentions don't count; action does. Look at the big picture—not just the words.

When you are trustworthy, trust builds in your marriage. And trust grows the love, and love builds the happiness. Trusting people are confident and happy. They are viewed by others as happier and friendlier than distrusting people.[1] Trust builds over time and provides a foundation for your marriage.

It takes hundreds of everyday experiences to build trust in a relationship, and sometimes only one to tear it down. The rebuilding only starts when there is honesty and a renewed commitment to work on the relationship.

Myth: It was just one time.

The toughest thing about the power of trust is that it's very difficult to build and very easy to destroy.

THOMAS J. WATSON

CASE STUDY: Jack and Helen

Jack and Helen came to see me after twenty-one years of marriage. Jack works as a tool and die maker at a local factory. Helen is a housewife, taking care of their four children, ages ten to nineteen. Both enter very hesitantly and move to opposite sides of the couch in my office. There is noticeable tension in the room as Jack begins to describe the financial problems that brought them to counseling.

As Helen nervously fidgeted on the couch, Jack reported that they have close to fifty-six thousand dollars' worth of debt that began with the overuse of credit cards, which has resulted in a series of equity loans on their house. Jack raised his voice and glared at Helen while describing his embarrassment at the local bank when he was turned down for a loan. "They informed me we already had a loan for close to forty-five thousand dollars, which I knew nothing about," he stated loudly. "She forged my name to the papers to get the money."

As I gathered further information from both of them, it was clear that the financial problems had developed over a period of years. They had both used the credit cards to make purchases they couldn't afford, but Helen had apparently tried to "fix it" by taking equity loans. She used the money to pay down the high credit card balances, only to repeat the cycle.

"I thought I could solve the problems," she reported. "But we just kept getting deeper and deeper into debt. I began to fall behind in the bills and soon, I was borrowing money on the line of credit to pay everyday expenses. Then I received an offer in the mail to borrow 110 percent of the value in the house. That was the beginning of the end. I couldn't make the payments, and now they want to foreclose."

Feeling deceived and lied to, Jack acknowledged that he should have paid more attention to the financial situation but that he "trusted Helen to handle it." He couldn't believe that they had gotten into so much financial trouble without her saying anything to him. Helen recognized that she should have talked with Jack about what was happening but stressed that she never lied to him. She just did not tell him everything.

"Lies of omission are not full honesty," I explain. "And though your intent was not to worry Jack, perhaps it was also a way to avoid the conflict. There were probably questions you did not want to answer and discussions you did not want to have." I explained to both of them that part of marriage is partnering on everyday living, the joys *and* the challenges. Money and finances need to be discussed and worked on together.

In the following months, Jack and Helen were slowly able to rebuild their marriage and their lives, but the trust between them was severely damaged. While the issue may have initially appeared to be money (and money is a big issue in marriage), the core issue for this couple was trust. The years they had spent building their marriage were ripped and torn apart by the events of just a few months. While rebuilding is possible, it will be hard. There are severe, deep wounds that can easily be reopened at the slightest provocation. Years of building a marriage and strong partnership became tarnished because of poor decisions and poor communication. Clearly, the keeping of secrets and lack of honesty made their problems much worse than they needed to be.

■ ■ ■ ■ ■

For a happy marriage, building the trust is essential. As the trust grows, you truly have the opportunity to become best friends and soul mates. Focus on this foundation piece in your relationship.

HOW TRUSTWORTHY ARE YOU?

Self-trust is the first secret to success.

RALPH WALDO EMERSON

To build the trust in your relationship, start with you. Are you doing your share to build the trust and increase your partner's confidence in you?

1. When I say I am going to do something, I do it.

   Always Sometimes Never

2. If I will be late in making a commitment or coming home, I call.

   Always Sometimes Never

3. I keep my spouse's confidences and do not share them with other people.

   Always Sometimes Never

4. I am careful not to discuss information about my spouse with other people.

   Always Sometimes Never

5. My spouse can count on me to listen to concerns without judgment or ridicule.

   Always Sometimes Never

6. When we are with other people, it is clear my spouse is the most important person in the room to me.

   Always Sometimes Never

7. When I am angry with my spouse, I am careful not to use information that he or she has confided in me in an attempt to win the argument.

   Always Sometimes Never

8. I refrain from name-calling or sarcasm when I am upset with my spouse.

   Always Sometimes Never

Scoring: How many "always" responses did you have?
7–8: Excellent. You are a trustworthy person, focused on building trust in your marriage.
5–7: Good. Keep working. You will reap results by changing your behavior.
Less than 5: Get busy. Use the following tools to improve your trustworthiness and the trust in your marriage.

BUILD THE TRUST IN YOUR RELATIONSHIP

Love all, but trust a few.

William Shakespeare

Focus on the small things you can do to enhance the trust. Try the following tools:

TOOL #1 Make an agreement that if you will be late, you will call after ______ minutes. Set the number of minutes that works for you and your partner. This is a simple tool that makes your behavior more predictable. It lets your partner know he or she can count on you. As this tool gets implemented and followed repeatedly, trust builds.

TOOL #2 Agree that you will not discuss your private conversations with others. Verbalize this agreement with your spouse. If you are not sure where the discussion will go, it is difficult to feel open and willing to disclose. There sometimes is a tendency to talk "outside of the marriage," especially if you are upset. Unless the listener is a trained counselor, usually the feedback you receive is what you want to hear and not objective. It won't be a useful mirror for your behavior or approach. Rather than talk to others, talk to your spouse.

TOOL #3 Agree as a couple that you will not use information to hurt each other, no matter how angry or hurt you may feel. You will not be eager to open up if you fear that the information will be used in the future to win an argument. These "cheap shots" are designed to purposely wound the other person. If used consistently, there is a wounding of the spirit, which erodes the foundation of a marriage.

TOOL #4 Make a rule that each of you has to say what you mean and mean what you say. Actively work on eliminating game playing. This means being honest and forthcoming. When asked what you are thinking or feeling, be honest with your partner and try to express it as clearly as possible. So when asked, "What's wrong?" rather than saying, "NOTHING!" in an angry tone, say, "I feel angry because _____." Each partner can TRUST that the other will tell the truth.

3 You're Absolutely Perfect . . . Now Change

STRATEGY 3: FOCUS ON BEING THE RIGHT PERSON

As a young girl, one of my favorite activities was playing board games with the kids in the neighborhood. We loved all the popular ones—Monopoly, Parcheesi, and Risk—and we played for hours in my neighbor's basement. Then, as we entered pre-adolescence, our favorite game was Barbie. Feeling a special kinship with this character, because of my name, I imagined my future self as Barbie. I would have long, flowing hair, a pencil-thin waist, an exaggerated chest and, of course, the *perfect* man in my arms.

In the Barbie game, we played to win a date with the man of our dreams. We would fight over who would get Ken, who was always our first choice, or Skip, a close second. None of us wanted Poindexter. He sounded and looked like a nerd, and no girl wanted to be married to a nerd, although now of course nerds like Bill Gates control the world. What did we know?

While it was a ridiculous game from my past, looking for Barbie or looking for Ken is not as uncommon as it may sound. Most people form a mental image of what they want in a spouse from an early age. Is that true for you?

I had always envisioned myself with a tall, handsome, Harvard-educated businessman, complete with an outgoing personality and lots of charm. If I closed my eyes, I could picture exactly how he would look and act in imaginary love scenes staged on a large, open staircase in a beautiful mansion. I think my romantic setting was from *Gone with the Wind*.

But the man I met was more like Poindexter. Charlie worked as a computer operator, not a CEO. He had a high school education, not a Ph.D. He was very shy, not a Rhett Butler. While I knew that he was the right one for me, he did not fit the image I had constructed over so many years. Of course, I didn't exactly have the pencil-thin waist and large chest that fit the Barbie image either. Fantasy and reality can often be very far apart. This became obvious when we traveled across the United States shortly after getting married.

We decided to take a van road trip for six weeks and see the West. Traveling a total of 6,324 miles, we journeyed through the Dakotas, Wyoming, Utah, California, Arizona, Colorado, and Nebraska. As this was a trip of a lifetime, we agreed to keep a daily journal of our travels and the sights we saw. Each night, we both wrote a paragraph or two on the day's events and any noteworthy details, with Charlie also writing down the mileage—*definitely a guy thing.*

The entries began innocently enough, with glowing descriptions of the Mississippi River and the beauty of the Badlands. We no sooner got to the Black Hills, however, and the record began to offer a glimpse into what was really happening:

"We ran out of film at Mount Rushmore and Charlie lost the extra roll."

"We bought insect repellent and a thermos but Barb left them at the wayside."

"Charlie keeps taking pictures when I move. They will all be blurry."

"Barb is getting testy from sleeping in the van."

"Charlie is always hungry."

"Barb never wants to stop."

You get the picture. We quickly discovered that the journaling reflected our irritation with our traveling companion. Two weeks into the trip, I screamed at Charlie: "You are absolutely perfect, now change." He just stared at me and then quickly ran to write a journal entry.

I know, I know, trips are like that. My mother and her husband once went on a trip with their very best friends of over twenty-five years only to return in stony silence. They never spent time with those friends again.

This is exactly the point. Marriage is a trip, a journey. And it is highly unlikely that your spouse will pass the microscopic scrutiny that can occur after six weeks in a Chevy van or five years in a one-bedroom apartment. He or she certainly will not fit the vision of your perfect mate. *No one* is that perfect.

By the way, I recently found our trip journal in the back of a bookshelf. Everything that we wrote about each other is still true.

Myth: Marriage should be like the honeymoon.

Whatever you may look like, marry a man your own age—as your beauty fades, so will his eyesight.

PHYLLIS DILLER

The clash between dreams and reality is a major factor in the "Honeymoon Is Over" syndrome that I frequently see in counseling. Within a year or two of marriage, couples find that the day-to-day management of a house, career, and family differs tremendously from the excitement and energy of a relationship in its early phases. The illusion of the perfect spouse first fractures and then crumbles to a heap on the floor next to the dirty clothes. One's partner does not look so great in the morning and seems to have acquired thousands of annoying little habits that are certain to test anyone's sanity.

Spouses complain that their counterparts do not do things the *right* way (i.e. their way). Some express befuddlement as to what they saw in this person in the first place. As one young wife put it: "I had no idea that passing gas was so important to men!"

Myth: If only you would change, everything would be perfect.

The crisis of yesterday is the joke of tomorrow.

H. G. WELLS

As the relationship settles into a routine, it is both what one wants in marriage—stability—and what one does not want—boredom. When days are very bad, clients may wonder whether life would be easier or more exciting with someone else.

Couples are hesitant to discuss these feelings, worried that their spouses will feel angry or hurt. What they do not realize is that their partner probably feels the same way. Ironically, talking about feelings would help them reconnect and rekindle intimacy, but such discussions are difficult. The couple does not understand yet that mature love not only means accepting one's partner's imperfections, but also actually embracing and enjoying each other's differences—as the French say, *vive la difference!*

Too often, rather than accepting the differences, one

or both partners embark on a mission to change the other person. The spouse's many "flaws" are absolutely obvious, certainly correctable, and it is clear that a comprehensive remedial program is in order. A spouse begins coaching, cajoling, lecturing, explaining, and nagging his or her partner to change and do things differently. *Just be more like my vision, would you? Just try!*

The spouse continues to believe that "if only" their partner would make these few adjustments, he or she could still be the ideal mate, the one dreamed about. Focusing on a spouse's "faults" rather than on oneself entails that more and more energy is put into "fixing" the problem. Consider the following couple.

CASE STUDY: Sam and Marsha

Sam and Marsha sought counseling after eighteen months of marriage because they were "disagreeing about everything." Sam, a computer programmer for a local Internet company, works long hours and frequently brings home a bulging briefcase to attend to in his home office. Marsha works as an underwriter for an insurance company. Both work extra hours so they can save for a down-payment on a first home.

"I feel like I am doing *everything* around this place," complains Marsha. "He just goes to work, comes home, and retreats to his office."

"It's part of my job," Sam responds. "I have to get some of these big projects off my plate and into the next stage. Anyway, you spend too much time on this place anyway. It doesn't have to be cleaned every day."

"Yes, I know all about your big projects," says Marsha. "You have papers all over the dining room table, strewn throughout your office, and stacked up on the counter in the kitchen. Can't you organize and clear away the clutter?"

"I have to spread things out when I am working on a major project," explains Sam. "It takes too much time to put everything away and then bring it out each time I want to work on it."

"Well, the house always looks messy," says Marsha angrily. "*The trouble with you is* . . . you think your stuff always takes center stage, that it is the first priority. Well, I wish I could leave my stuff out all of the time, too."

"But I have to get this work done," Sam responds. "It's the only way I know how to do it. I have to see it and organize it."

"Why don't you do it the way I do?" Marsha says. "Use an accordion file or something so the house doesn't look so messy. Messiness drives me crazy."

"I've never worked that way. I need to spread things out so I can see them," Sam repeats.

"But, it's not just the work. It's everything. You leave clothes laying around, you don't throw dirty towels down the chute, you just don't want to be neat," accuses Marsha. "I didn't realize what a slob you were until we got married."

"I didn't realize you were such a neat freak," he retorts. "*The trouble with you is* . . . you never just sit down and relax. You are always running around picking up and fussing. The house doesn't have to be *that* clean. Sometimes I don't feel like I can relax in my own home."

I interject, "It's very common for couples to have different thresholds for cleanliness in a house. This is an issue on which the two of you need to find compromise and agreement. Perhaps, Marsha, you could create additional space close to Sam's office that he could use for his work, and this would prevent Sam from having his papers all over. Possibly, Sam, you could make more of an effort to pick up and participate in regular cleaning."

"Yes, I could use the back closet for organizing the work," suggests Sam, eager for a solution. "I'll try harder to throw dirty clothes down the chute and pick up around the house."

I add to the suggestions, "The two of you could set aside a few hours each week when you both clean. The work likely would go quicker and it might ease the tension around Marsha 'always' cleaning."

"Well, we could try it," agrees Marsha.

■ ■ ■ ■ ■

This couple was able to arrive at consensus and a tentative solution to the tensions and irritations they had been experiencing in their daily lives. And, as they focused on solutions, they stopped viewing their partner as the problem that needed to be "fixed." They each began to look at their respective contributions to the tense climate in the house.

Myth: The Blame Game is to help you.

Marriage is more about being the right person than finding the right person.

AUTHOR

Specifically, Marsha began to recognize that Sam's approach to his work was not going to change a great deal and her attempts at making him "neater" were likely to continue to lead to friction in the household. Sam came to understand that Marsha "needed" a different level of cleanliness and order than he did, without which she felt anxious and unable to relax. With their new levels of awareness, they were able to work together to find solutions and compromises.

When we look at our partners instead of ourselves, we play the Blame Game (i.e., viewing what happens as being outside of ourselves). The Blame Game blinds us to our own role in the problems we may be experiencing. It stops honest self-evaluation, which can lead to personal and relationship growth. Whenever people blame, they avoid taking responsibility for their own actions.

The Blame Game keeps the focus on your spouse instead of on you. You may look at your spouse as a "fix-up" project, feeling it your duty to point out his or her flaws and shortcomings. You may even believe you are doing your spouse a favor when you outline such defects in detail with recommendations for correction. While your intention is certainly to be helpful, he or she likely may not hear it that way. Quite the contrary, let me assure you, only criticism is heard.

I joke in my seminars about my *Husband Training Program.* This fictitious program includes a tape on the twenty-five best responses to the questions, "Is my butt too big?" and "Did you use the guest towels?" These questions must hit home, for I routinely have people ask to buy the tapes after public presentations.

I let people know, however, that in spite of the concentrated focus and intense effort of the training program, my husband has changed very little. One day it hit me like a lightning bolt: If he hasn't changed in more than a decade, I might as well accept things as they are!" I am embarrassed such a shift took so long, but I am pleased to say that I stopped nagging about the little annoyances and instead looked at the things *I* did that were annoying. I stopped correcting him and focused on what I could do better. I replaced the criticism with encouragement, the irritation with laughter, and the blame with responsibility. Maybe not so amazingly, a lot of our problems disappeared.

Myth: You are nagging me to death.

When you do what you have always done, you get what you always got.

UNKNOWN

Do I do these things perfectly? Hardly. But as I tried harder, I noticed that Charlie tried harder too. And when two people focus on self-improvement and work hard to each be a better person, magical things happen in a marriage.

Does this mean you ought *never* to point out problems or issues with your partner? Of course not. Some issues need to be addressed, negotiated, and compromised. Still, too often the fix-up work we attempt deals more with basic personality than minor behaviors. After counseling hundreds of people for over twenty years, I believe it is very difficult to change basic personality.

In reality, how one views issues with one's spouse will have a great deal to do with the happiness in a marriage. A recent study showed that spouses in a happy marriage tend to view negative events involving their spouses occurring because of extenuating, outside events rather than due to personality. A spouse might say, "She must not be feeling well" or "He had a hard day at work today." Spouses in unhappy marriages, on the other hand, view their mate's negativity as a character flaw, saying things like, "She is always like that." In addition, they view positive remarks and actions from their spouse as a result of outside influences rather than part of his or her personality, saying such things as, "He must just be in a good mood today."

The researchers concluded that the happier a person feels in a marriage, the more he or she will give a partner the benefit of the doubt. The less happy one is in one's marriage, the more negatively one perceives one's partner.[1]

I would take this a step further. I think the more you give your partner the benefit of the doubt, the happier your marriage will be. And if you focus on negative thoughts about your spouse, your marriage will be less happy.

My husband has in the past jokingly asked our kids to put "NAGGED TO DEATH" on his tombstone. He was referring, of course, to my focused, ten-year improvement effort to make him a better person. The last ten years, however, have taught me that rather than trying to get my husband to do something to please me, I would be wiser to focus on pleasing him and doing what is good for our relationship. Take a positive approach—that's the secret.

Some nagging can actually be helpful, however. Considerable research shows that the "nagging," or encouragement, partners give each other in the areas of health and wellness pays off. According to some studies, people adopt a healthier way of living when they marry.[2] Their partners actually "nag" them into a healthier lifestyle by urging them to quit smoking, limit drinking, and eat healthier.

Myth: You're the only one with #!@* for brains.

All men make mistakes, but married men find out about them sooner.

RED SKELTON

In addition, both men and women live longer if they are married than if single. For men, staying married boosts the chance of surviving to age sixty-five from about two out of three to almost nine out of ten. For women, marriage increases the likelihood of surviving to old age from 80 to 90 percent.[3]

Moral? Focus your energy on what is in your spouse's best interest. He or she will know you are asking to make changes because you care, not just so you can get your own way. Forget the socks left on the floor; go for a walk together instead.

I warn my clients that they have to be very careful about criticizing their spouses. Most of us, at times, have "shit for brains"—you know, those occasions when we hit our forehead with the heel of our hand and mutter to ourselves: "You idiot!"

I'm not sure who initially identified this brain disorder, but my first encounter with it was with one of my close friends, Cheryl. She and her husband had spent the last year remodeling their kitchen, while working full-time and going to school. Trying to do much of the work themselves, they spent months with the kitchen ripped down to the studs—no plumbing, no cooking appliances, and a refrigerator on the back porch. After a year of washing dishes in the bathtub, eating on an end table in the living room, showering in the root cellar, and making coffee in the bathroom, they completed the kitchen just in time for the arrival of their new baby.

Driving through the neighborhood several weeks later, Cheryl's husband noticed a house for sale that was a "fixer upper." He turned to her and said, "Wouldn't it be fun to buy a big house like that and remodel it?" Not believing her ears, she said, "What? Are you kidding? We barely lived through the last remodeling without killing each other. Do you have shit for brains?"

Many of us have stories such as these. Trips, projects, and undertakings that look great on the front end but leave you wondering, "Whatever was I thinking? Where was my brain?" Similar to the man who crashed his Winnebago after putting it on cruise control to go back and make a sandwich, we can have a brain drain that leaves us bewildered.

Like the day my hairdryer quit. I was in the middle of a major styling effort and the thing just stopped. I flicked the switch a few times and threw it in the wastebasket. Charlie quickly came running, excitedly announcing those familiar words: "I can fix it."

He spent the next three hours in the basement, armed with his tool belt, happily whistling as he worked on the hair dryer. Smiling and triumphant, he emerged from the depths waving the appliance with a new, fifteen-foot yellow cord.

To demonstrate my appreciation, I plugged the dryer in and hit the switch. It immediately began to smoke, and then stopped in a shower of sparks, which left the side of my face blackened and the power extinguished in the house. Shocked and speechless, I slowly began to laugh as I looked in the mirror and saw my reflection. Charlie was crestfallen. He couldn't believe that his "fix-it" project wasn't a success. But he began to giggle, too, when he viewed my Al Jolson face and realized I wasn't hurt.

Our mirth was somewhat tempered, however, when we went in the basement to restore the power. The force of the power surge had blown all the circuits in the house and shorted the system. Replacing the electric box and circuitry cost over $1,500 before the electrician was finished. All to keep from spending $20 on a new hairdryer.

Myth: We should save the best for the guests.

Respect for ourselves guides our morals, respect for others guides our manners.

LAURENCE STERNE

"Shit for brains" happens in marriages. Sometimes you do it together and sometimes you manage it all by yourself. But it happens. Whether it is forgetting to enter a check in the checkbook, letting the bathtub overflow, hanging a door upside down, or forgetting to pick up a kid at school, we all make mistakes. How you handle this garbage in your marriage will have a profound impact on your happiness.

When we accept shortcomings in others, we also accept them more readily in ourselves. We acknowledge our humanity. Most of us try our best. And people respond to life better when they receive encouragement instead of criticism.

The best responses to shit for brains are humor and learning—laugh at the funny parts and learn from the mistakes. It is said that you cannot grow wiser unless you grow older. But many people get older without growing wiser. Wise people learn from mistakes—both their own and those of others.

Accepting a spouse for who he or she is involves letting the spouse know you feel he or she is special and not taking him or her for granted.

When I was a kid, I remember the "guest towels." Made of a deep, soft pile with gold and blue embroidery on the seams, these beautiful towels were untouchable and we knew it; they only found a place on the towel rack when guests were coming. Even then, we were not allowed to use them. We would use paper towels in the kitchen to make sure those guest towels stayed clean and in good shape.

One evening, some friends of my father's from the Lion's Club stopped by to discuss business. One of them went into the bathroom and wiped ink all over one of those beautiful towels. I could hear my mother sigh when she saw what he had done.

After the company left, I asked my mother, "Why do we save the best towels for people we really don't care about and who don't appreciate them? I think we should put our torn towels out for them and use the nicest ones for the people we really love, like our family."

She thought quietly for a minute and said, "I think you're right. The nicest things should be saved for the people we love."

Looking back on that incident, I believe we often "give our best" to people we barely care about, and offer leftovers to those we profess to love the most. We may be pleasant all day at work and come home in a foul mood to our spouse and children. Or we dress up for a special occasion, but never dress up "just for our spouses." I remember my daughter asking me when she was eight years old, "It's Saturday. Why are you putting on make-up? Just for Dad?" *Yes, just for Dad.*

To create a pleasant home life, consider the following rule: *Treat your spouse at least as kindly as you would treat a total stranger.* How do you talk with people in supermarket lines, at the bank, or a restaurant? That level of courtesy should be the bare minimum at home. We owe each other at least that much, and we can always do more.

How do we dress and act in public? Do we look as pleasant at home? We say we love our families more than anyone else, yet often the people closest to us see us at our worst. They get what is "left over" after we give everywhere else first. When we give our best to our families, we create households of honor and respect.

By the way, we can also do "extras." We can surprise a spouse with a favorite food, movie, or favor. But it is not a game to see "who gives the most." We ought not give with the notion of winning poker chips so that our loved ones "owe" us. We give because we are committed to a person. An attitude of "you owe me" becomes a predictor of problems. In a 1988 study, spouses who showed kindness to one another, but only with an "I'll be nice if you are nice" attitude, broke up within five years.[4]

Sometimes when couples practice the "treat each other as you would a stranger" test, it feels awkward. They report feeling nervous as they go out of their way to be polite or considerate. As one woman put it, "It just doesn't feel natural; it feels like we are play-acting." I responded by saying, "That's good! We can *act* differently, and pretty soon it is no longer acting. It becomes who we are and what we feel."

When your behavior feels awkward, then you know it is new. And when you do new things in a marriage, new things happen. It is always crazy thinking to believe you can get different results when you follow the same old behaviors.

Focus on being a hero to your spouse. Put your loved one on a pedestal and say how much he or she means to you. Honor your spouse every day with kind words and actions. Show the respect usually reserved for royalty and you will receive great riches in return. Since you are the only one "living" your story, make sure you are living it the best you can.

HOW ACCEPTING ARE YOU?

American women expect to find in their husbands a perfection that English women only hope to find in their butlers.

W. SOMERSET MAUGHAM

Evaluate how accepting you are of your partner and eliminate the Blame Game.

1. I do not make verbal attacks on my spouse or lecture him/her on what "should" be done.

   True False

2. I express appreciation for the nice things my spouse does for me.

   True False

3. I give my spouse more positive messages than negative messages.

   True False

4. I admit when I do something wrong and apologize.

   True False

5. I treat my spouse as well as or better than I treat co-workers and neighbors.

   True False

6. I maintain a pleasant personal appearance even when I am "just home."

   True False

7. I can identify three things I can improve to enhance my marriage.

   True False

8. I look for humor in everyday events and share them with my spouse.

True False

Scoring: How many "true" responses did you have?
7–8: Excellent. You are building honor and respect in your household.
5–6: Good. Look for opportunities to improve your response to your spouse.
1–4: Get moving. You need to take a careful look at yourself and what changes you need to make. Utilize the following honor tools to build honor and respect.

HONOR TOOLS

We ought not to treat living creatures like shoes or household belongings, which when worn with use we throw away.

PLUTARCH

Establish basic ground rules with your spouse as to how you will interact with each other to build honor and respect. Create a list together and write it out. Make sure both of you agree with each item. Sign the list and put it on your refrigerator. Whenever you disagree, refer to this list to remind yourselves of the ground rules and the commitments you made to each other.

The following items can be useful. Focus on the "honor tools" specific to your relationship.

- ✔ We both agree not to raise our voices when we are upset with each other.
- ✔ We will not swear or call each other names.
- ✔ We will make an effort to say one positive comment to each other every day.
- ✔ We will not go to bed angry.

- ✔ We will treat each other at least as well as we treat total strangers.
- ✔ We will make efforts to connect each day.
- ✔ Neither of us will storm out in the middle of an argument.
- ✔ We will not make disparaging comments about each other's friends or family.
- ✔ We will believe each other and give each other the benefit of the doubt.
- ✔ We agree to keep our marriage the number one priority in our lives.
- ✔ We agree it is okay to remind each other of the priority of our marriage when other things get in the way.
- ✔ We will apologize to each other, even if we think we did nothing wrong.

Add some rules you think are important just for the two of you. While it may be hard to adhere to these rules, especially when you are angry, you will find they can make a tremendous difference in the growth of your marriage. Adhering to these rules helps you to build honor and respect so both of you feel secure in your relationship and ensures that you grow into the best people you can be.

We are family,
I got all my sisters with me.

"We Are Family" by Sister Sledge

4 You Are Just Like Your Mother/Father

STRATEGY 4:
SET HEALTHY BOUNDARIES WITH FAMILY

When Charlie and I got married, the phone rang all the time. Not with well-wishers or friends, rather with calls from my father. Depending on the day, he would call two, four, eight times or more. He never had much to say. In fact, I think at times he forgot he had just called. I am sure he was lonely, and I felt sad *for* him. It was heartbreaking that he was not happy with his life. I knew I could not fix that for him, but I felt I *had* to let him call—even though it interfered with my married life.

Charlie was patient, but many times Dad's calls would interrupt our conversations or our activities. While I wanted to put Charlie first, I felt guilty and responsible for Dad and believed I owed him my time and attention. One day, after ten or more phone calls, Charlie blew up.

"You have to put a limit on his phone calling. I can't

stand it," he shouted. "Once, twice a day would be fine, but it is eight, nine, ten times a day. You have to stand up to him and make him stop calling."

"And just how am I going to do that?" I implored. "I can't control what he does. I've told him not to call so much, and he just does it anyway. If I confront him about it, he gets really sad, and then I feel bad."

Charlie responded: "Well, how about if I tell him?"

"I don't know if I can trust you to do it nicely," I confessed.

Charlie persisted, "We *have* to do something . . . it is interfering with our marriage and our lives. I didn't marry your father."

So I promised Charlie that I would talk with my dad and set limits on how many times he would be allowed to call.

I sat down with Dad and firmly explained our concerns about the calls, the effects on our marriage, and the necessity for change. I then outlined in great detail clear limits to the times and frequency for phone calling.

Nothing changed.

Dad acted like we had never talked about the calls and I acted like the problem was fixed. Meanwhile, the tension at home just continued to build. Then one day Charlie said to me, "You are just like your father. You think if you ignore a problem, it will just magically go away."

Becoming immediately defensive, hurt, and angry, I blurted out, "Well, you are just like your mother, thinking you can bully people into what you want them to do."

We did not talk the rest of the day; or maybe it was a week.

This type of situation is not unusual. Couples frequently come to counseling because of problems with extended family—too much contact, too much interference, too many problems. They find they are fighting about issues that are not really theirs, yet they do not know how to stop. They do not know how to set appropriate boundaries with the rest of the family, and when they try to say "No," they feel guilty.

Myth: I always feel guilty.

Absence is one of the most useful ingredients of family life, and to dose it rightly is an art like any other.

FREYA STARK

I explain to clients that guilt is not a true emotion or feeling. It is really a mixture of several feelings that can be very confusing. Guilt is like a Catch-22, where your best is never good enough. If you are not careful, you will get lost in a haze of good intentions and missed opportunities.

That certainly was the case for me. If I kept the peace with Dad, then Charlie was mad. If I tried to set limits, then Dad was angry. It surely was a no-win situation. I found myself increasingly frustrated as I tried to deal with a wave of feelings, including anger, depression, and guilt. When I began to analyze the situation, I found the Guilt Wheel, pictured on the next page, to be useful.

I noticed a pattern in my interactions with my father. I would set a limit, suggesting perhaps that one or two phone calls a day would have to be sufficient. Then I would proceed to give in when he failed to comply. I would say "Yes" when I wanted to say "No" and then feel angry—angry with him for pushing me in a corner and angry with myself for giving in and not standing firm. In this cycle, discouragement and depression would follow, and I saw no way out of the predicament. It seemed no way existed to resolve the situation so that Charlie was happy, Dad was happy, and I was happy.

The guilt would begin to creep in and grow. Messages would replay in my head about what a "good" daughter would do. *Why wasn't I more patient? Were his*

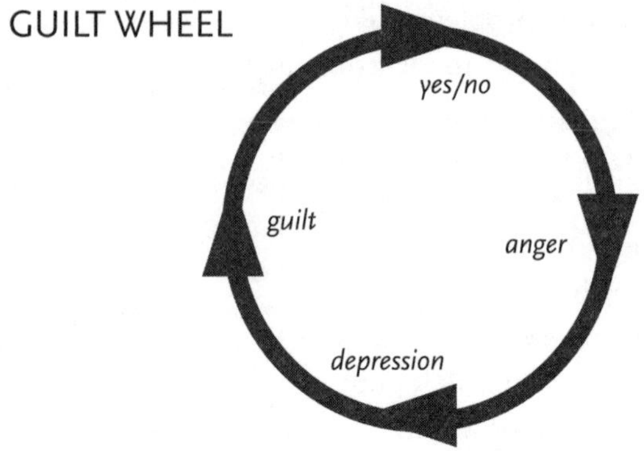

demands really too much to ask? If I allowed it, guilt would consume me to the point that I felt I did *nothing* right. It took me a long time to realize that the real issue, the real problem, was saying "Yes" when I wanted to say "No."

When I realized my desire to say "No" was being suppressed and contributing to my depression, Charlie and I had a long talk and agreed we would be firm with Dad without being angry or harsh. We would set a definite limit on the phone calls of once per day, explaining to Dad that we also wanted a chance to call him. Dad was angry and hurt in the beginning, yet he gradually grew not only to comply but also to accept the limit we had set. By not being able to rely on us to fulfill his every need, he found himself reaching out and networking with other people.

Dad began volunteering at a local hospital. He started going to senior citizen dances, where he became popular with the ladies. With the ratio at these dances of a hundred women to one man, he found that he was especially attractive to the opposite sex. He appeared happier and much more content. Years later he told me those were some of the happiest years of his life. Did all of this happen as a result of limiting his phone calls? Of course not—little in life is so simple. It was, however, one important step in Dad's taking charge of his life instead of expecting his children to fulfill his needs.

We had many wonderful years after that with my dad. He often visited for Sunday dinners or parties with the kids. When he died at age eighty-five, I found his phone among his belongings. I jokingly told Charlie, "We should consider burying it with him." He responded, "Heavens, no. He might call." It was nice to be able to laugh over a situation with which we had dealt successfully. We were glad we had set boundaries years earlier so we did not have regrets now.

Myth: We are not a normal family.

Adam was the luckiest man; he had no mother-in-law.

MARK TWAIN

Think of a situation in which you have felt guilty. Can you recall a time that you said "Yes" when you wanted to say "No"? Use the wheel to clarify your own feelings, then practice saying "No." And remember, these types of problems with in-laws, out-laws, and other extended family are more normal than abnormal. I find that most couples have at least a few of these issues to work out at some point in their marriage.

I am reminded of a cartoon that showed a support group meeting for an organization called "Adult Children from Normal Families." The room was empty.

I am frequently asked, "What is normal?" Especially for those of us who grew up in chaotic families, it is hard to know. I really do not know if "normal" exists, but in twenty-plus years of counseling couples and families I have found one common denominator that seems to predict the optimal functioning of a family: *healthy families operate along generational lines.*

By generational lines, I mean that members of each generation tend to be connected to people of their own age. They have appropriate boundaries with parents, children, and extended family members. Thus, grandparents have their own lives, as do the married couple and other family members. They do not look to their children to entertain them or live for them. They do not interfere in their grown children's lives or with the parenting of their grandchildren.

The married couple primarily talks with *each other* rather than with one of their parents or other family members about problems. They focus on each other and their "new" family, not their family of origin. They support each other in assuring that the extended family does not interfere with or dictate their lives.

The children have a peer group and pursue their interests and activities within that group. They interact with their parents on important issues and know they will not be allowed to conspire with grandparents or other family members to combat their parents' authority. Aunts, uncles, and grandparents may play important roles in children's lives, but as the children grow up their primary relationships are with their parents and siblings.

You can visualize these dynamics in the following diagram:

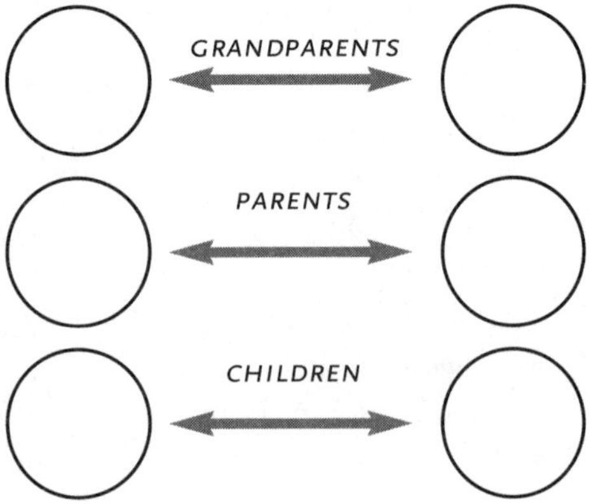

As the model indicates, family members connect most closely with their own generation, operating along generational lines. The model represents an ideal, a framework for "normal" that can work for marriages and families.

For troubled families, it is very different. Unhealthy families are embroiled in turmoil. They confuse boundaries, priorities, and generational lines. The wife may talk mostly with her mother, or the husband goes hunting each weekend with his father and friends. Aunt Edna may call repeatedly, giving advice and dictating how things should be done. Or, as the children grow, one parent may use the oldest child as a confidant, even talking negatively about the other parent.

The following diagram illustrates these confused dynamics:

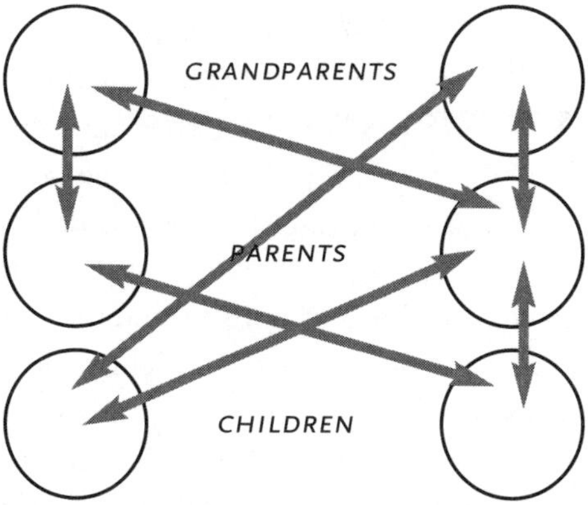

If the diagram looks messy and confusing, that's because it is. It depicts a grandfather depending on his son, a grandmother over-involved with her eldest grandchild, the father favoring his youngest child, and the mother complaining about her husband to everyone but him. Consequently, the grandparents are neglecting to build and maintain their marital relationship, the parents ignore theirs, and the children resent each other. Misunderstandings abound and there is no end to conflict because everyone gets involved in everyone else's business.

Family life becomes a lot happier and marriages a lot stronger when the dynamics are clear and boundaries established. Realize that energy going out of the marriage is energy not available to you and your spouse.

How is your family operating? Are your in-laws or extended family a source of conflict in your marriage?

One of the traps I frequently see existing for couples is the mistaken belief that they can please everyone. While specifics vary, problems ensue for a couple when one or the other or both of the spouses focus on trying to meet everyone's needs but their own. We learned about this firsthand one very cold Christmas in Wisconsin.

Myth: I must please everyone.

I'm not sure of the key to success, but the key to failure is trying to please everyone.

AUTHOR

It was our first holiday season after the birth of our son, and the weather had turned especially bitter, with windchills down to 45 degrees below zero. Both sides of the family eagerly asked us to bring the baby and celebrate Christmas Eve with them and the relatives. We were scheduled to be at one house at 3:00 P.M., another at 6:30 P.M., with a final stop at 9:00 P.M. I repeatedly changed the baby, nursed him, crammed him into a snowsuit, and dragged him to the next house with equipment and diaper bags in tow. As the day wore on, the baby became increasingly crabby, Charlie and I were snapping at each other, and the car did not want to start. After we left for the third stop, Charlie and I looked at each other and asked: "Why are we doing this?"

We knew the answer—to please everyone. We had promoted a more sensible arrangement (one day with each family), but neither extended family agreed. Both my family members and Charlie's insisted their plans took precedence, and neither wanted to miss the baby's first Christmas. We said "Yes" in fear of hurting someone's feelings, attempting to please everyone. Ironically, no one felt really happy that year . . . especially us.

We were smarter the next year. A month before Christmas, Charlie and I sat down and talked about what we wanted for the holidays. We agreed we wanted time together alone as a family and time with both families. We also agreed we did not want to run around in a frenzy to gratify everyone, as we had the previous year. We decided we would spend Christmas Eve with Charlie's family and Christmas morning by ourselves. We would then join my family later on Christmas Day for an evening meal and visiting. It has been that way ever since—no problems, no turmoil. Is everyone happy? I don't know; I don't ask. It works for us.

When racing around trying to make everyone else happy, you suck the energy from your relationship with your spouse. You create mushy boundaries that cloud your priorities and leave you exhausted. You find that the harder you try, the worse it gets. The answer is not to do more, it is to do something different.

Work as partners to redefine your roles with family members. Agree on an approach for holidays and special occasions that works for the two of you, not one that leaves you stressed and angry. Talk with family members with compassion and understanding so feelings are not bruised. More often than not, they will understand. They have probably faced some of the same dilemmas in their own relationships.

Myth: I must fix all the problems.

All happy families resemble one another; every unhappy family is unhappy in its own way.

LEO TOLSTOY

I recently received a phone call from a nursing colleague who was upset that her family relied on her to solve all their problems. This is not an uncommon predicament for those in the healthcare profession for, as you might expect, helping professions tend to attract very helpful people to their ranks. Arlene described her dilemma this way: "*All* my family members call me with their problems. I try to stay out of things, but I'm the one they call."

"Give me an example," I said.

"Well recently my mom called and was very upset because my brother used her charge card without permission."

"What did you do?" I queried.

"I encouraged Mom to talk with my brother and explain her feelings. I told her to ask my brother to pay the charges. I also urged her to be clear not to do that again in the future. What do you think? Was that good advice?" she asked.

"Great advice," I responded. "The problem is the whole matter was none of your business."

"What?"

"This was an issue between your mom and your brother. They are certainly old enough and capable enough to work it out for themselves."

"I never thought of it that way," she reflected.

"When I am in those situations, I always ask myself, *Whose problem is it?* Does this problem really involve me? If not, I politely excuse myself from the discussion."

"But my family counts on me to help with their problems," my friend insisted.

"That is because you have trained them to do so, by listening and being on call for them. You can also train them to handle their problems themselves and not rely on you."

"But they might feel hurt or get mad," she protested.

"They might. But you really aren't doing them any favors. In fact, you may be making things worse."

"How do you figure?"

"You may be sending the subtle message that they cannot handle their own problems, or you may be stopping them from getting the help they really need. Sometimes, when we listen to people's problems, they get just enough relief that they don't make any real changes."

"I think I know what you mean," my friend said. Sometimes I feel Mom doesn't really want to change her approach with my brother; she just wants to complain about him. She lets him take advantage of her, then complains to the rest of the family."

"Out of fairness to your mom and the rest of the family, you need to let them know your rules have changed. Tell them you have full confidence in their abilities to solve the problem and that they don't need you. Then tell them you would really rather not hear about issues unless they involve you. With practice, it will get easier. And pretty soon they will stop asking."

"I'll try, but I think it will be hard."

"Yes. Any time you change behavior, it is very difficult," I suggested. "It may be helpful to identify what *you* get out of it when you get involved."

"Get out of it? Nothing. Absolutely nothing but grief and turmoil."

"Well, you get something out of it or you probably would have stopped by now. Sometimes 'helpful' people get hooked into these situations because we feel good about ourselves when we can be helpful. We feel like a hero—the one with all the answers."

"I know what you mean. Sometimes I temporarily feel good, like I'm the one who can solve the family problems. But a lot of times they don't listen to my advice anyway."

"Right."

"They just want me to listen."

"Right. Years ago, I adopted a philosophy about advice. I refrain from giving it, even when asked, unless I'm paid for it."

"That would make it interesting," said Arlene laughing.

"Sometimes when people get something for nothing, they put no value on it. They are just wasting your time complaining. When people invest, they pay attention."

Arlene called about six months later and reported that the situation with her mom and the rest of the family had improved tremendously since she stopped providing "drive-through therapy." Ironically, her brother mentioned to her that he felt closer to her because she had stopped trying to be the know-it-all and behaved more like a sister.

Myth: My family history does not affect me.

The family you come from isn't as important as the family you're going to have.

RING LARDNER

Ask yourself, "Whose problem is this?" before you jump into any family situation. If it does not involve you, stay out. Solving another's problem is a hopeless undertaking and, if you are not careful, you will be the one blamed if things do not improve. Remember, if you stand in the middle when arrows are flung, you will more than likely be the one who gets hit.

Couples often are very surprised by how much of their family history follows them down the aisle. They thought they had escaped the problems by leaving home, establishing their own lives, and marrying, only to find out that remnants from their past haunt their relationship and their serenity. They discover that boundaries with family can also mean emotional borders that need to be established.

CASE STUDY: Melissa and Alex

Married only six months, Melissa and Alex came for counseling with no major problems, just confusion. Melissa's parents were divorced when she was thirteen years old, due in part to her father's alcoholism. Alex's father died when he was three years old, leaving his mother with three children to raise. Alex's mom became an alcoholic and was verbally and physically abusive to Alex and his siblings.

Both Melissa and Alex are deeply committed to their relationship yet scared and uncertain how to make it work. "There has not been a successful marriage in my family for generations," Melissa began. "Both of my parents have been married a number of times, none of the marriages particularly happy."

"I don't remember ever having a happy family life," interjected Alex. "Most of my childhood was spent in constant turmoil living with my mother's drinking and all the problems it caused. Even now, she has difficulty managing her life."

"We just don't feel like we have any role models, anyone to turn to when we need advice or assistance," said Melissa. "We really can't ask our parents."

"I don't know why you would want to, based on what you have shared about your families," I said. "One of the secrets of creating a happy marriage is looking at and spending time with happy couples. You need to find new role models who can be helpful to you."

"That makes sense . . . but where do we find them?" asked Melissa.

"Connect with people in your neighborhood and through your church. You have taken steps by coming to counseling and reading about marriage," I said. "It is too bad you didn't have the role models in your family, but that doesn't mean you can't learn the tools for marriage now."

■ ■ ■ ■ ■

Both Melissa and Alex were visibly relieved to hear that they could study marriage and make it work. I assured them that the skills for creating a good marriage could be learned, as "statistics show that even a small dose of training before marriage can positively affect marital satisfaction and outcome."[5]

Alex and Melissa's concerns are not unusual. Research indicates that children of divorced parents often struggle in their marriages. "Without any guidance and family history, their own marriages begin without an internal compass for telling them which way to turn when difficulties arise."[6] There is a higher probability of divorce among children from divorced parents.[7]

Children from broken marriages do not learn from their parents the skills in problem solving, compromise, and commitment so necessary for a long-term relationship. They see marriage as a slippery slope that often leads nowhere. They enter adulthood anxious about love, marriage, and commitment. They approach marriage with fear because they are afraid of failing and being hurt. Commitment is difficult due to this fear of failure, thus setting in motion a vicious cycle, with fear leading to difficulty in making commitments. A lack of commitment leads to failure.

Issues for children of divorced parents include this fear of commitment and an internal hurt over what they did not receive while growing up. They know full well what was missing: laughter, attention, family vacations, a model for a loving relationship. But they find themselves falling into the same traps, the same problems, not knowing where to find the right resources to help in building a happy, healthy marriage.

Children of divorced parents often have a fantasy that their parents may get back together and they will again be part of an intact family. They may worry about one or more of their parents and feel responsible for their happiness. Well into adulthood, they may still grieve over the loss of the family that was shattered and the inability of the two people they love most to live together harmoniously.

Talking about their feelings and personal history is one way to leave some of the baggage behind. It is also very helpful to go for some counseling or on a marriage retreat to establish the "new family" while letting go of the old. It is critical that children of divorced parents understand that their script is not yet written. Their marriage does not have to fail.

> Myth: I always expect the worst.
>
> **It is so much easier to grieve a loss of what we had than it is to grieve a loss over something that never was.**
>
> CHERYL RUGG

An interesting dynamic that occurs frequently with children from divorced parents is the sabotaging and testing they do in their own relationships. Raised on the roller coaster of conflict that characterizes troubled families, they have been conditioned to anticipate the worst and not trust the best. They brace themselves even when all is well for "the other shoe to drop."

I remember waiting for doom shortly before my wedding. Charlie and I were happy and excited about getting married; everything was falling into place with nary a glitch. As the wedding day drew closer, I became increasingly anxious—and not because we were getting married. Rather, I was sure something would go wrong. I became convinced that Charlie would be diagnosed with a fatal disease or killed in a freak accident before the wedding could ever take place. I just knew something would go wrong because, in the past, it seemed like it always had.

After our seamless wedding, I realized that I looked for problems because that was what I was used to. I would pick fights over nothing and imagine issues where none existed. I really had very little experience with the status quo; it had been years since I had enjoyed a stable family life. I began to question whether I was addicted to the roller coaster of crisis and problem . . . and, in fact, I was. In my efforts to understand my addiction, I learned a lesson from the rats.

Perhaps you recall some of what you learned in Psychology 101. You were probably introduced to human behavior and conditioning by observing rats. Consider the following experiment:

- Build two identical boxes and put a rat in each.
- In Box A, give the rat a food pellet every time he hits the buzzer with his nose or foot.
- In Box B, give the rat a food pellet only some of the times he hits the buzzer with his nose or foot.

QUIZ

1. Which rat will learn to ring the buzzer first?
2. Which rat will keep ringing the buzzer the longest after you stop giving it the food pellet?

Answer: Rat B in both cases.

The rat that gets the pellet only some of the time tries harder because it is never sure when it will receive the pellet. After all, it has waited in the past and the pellet eventually came. It has learned that by just trying, at some point in time it will get the food pellet.

In psychology, this is called intermittent positive reinforcement. It is the strongest reinforcement that exists: for rats *and* for people. It is also the hardest behavior to extinguish once learned. Even though the pellet, or reinforcement, stops, the rat continues to try because it is so used to waiting. It will continue trying until it is exhausted.

Consider gambling. If you have ever played the slot machines, you know periodically you win at least a few coins. So you keep playing. You believe the big win, or in the case of rats, the food pellet, waits just around the corner since you are already getting the crumbs. If you do happen to have a big win, you probably will, like most players, simply put the coins back in to wait for an even bigger win.

You can be assured that those who run the gambling casinos know all about intermittent positive reinforcement. They know if they can keep people coming back to play, they will eventually get all their money.

Consider other addictions, such as alcohol. Most alcohol abusers seek the "high" or "buzz" they are used to feeling when they drink. They tend to have "euphoric recall"—they remember the good times but not the disasters, like when they drank until they got sick or in trouble. They continue to seek that high, the pellet, even when there may be long periods without positive consequences to their drinking.

What does all this have to do with people and relationships? A lot. Intermittent positive reinforcement is the strongest influence on human behavior that exists. It can be a positive influence, such as honoring one's spouse, or a negative influence, such as when a spouse is verbally or physically abusive. The seeds of negative dynamics are planted in childhood when one or both parents are not regularly available. A child experiences a "come-here, go-away" relationship with the parent, much like the rat waiting for the pellet. The parent may be overly critical, too busy, or simply emotionally not available. The child tries harder and harder, occasionally getting his or her needs met, but the attention given is inconsistent.

Children with their needs for approval and attention unmet often have little insight into the origins of their feelings. Not infrequently, they may find themselves in relationships in which their needs remain unmet, and they may be more likely to tolerate verbal or physical abuse.

Ironically, if you were raised with inconsistent affection because of divorce or an absent parent, you are more inclined to reject exactly the kind of consistency you need. You may view a nice guy or nice girl as boring or uncool. You actually may be addicted to the roller coaster and excitement of an "addictive" relationship, which resembles the uncertainly of not knowing when the pellet will arrive. Even when you find the nice one, you may sabotage the relationship in an unconscious effort to mirror your previous experience.

CASE STUDY: Amanda and Steven

Amanda and Steven came to counseling because they were unable to agree on a wedding date or how to proceed with wedding plans. Engaged for two years, they live together in a rented house close to their jobs. Amanda works as a fundraiser for a large non-profit organization. Steve is a salesman at a furniture outlet store. While Steve is eager to get married, Amanda feels hesitant and unsure. She reports she was devastated as a teenager when her parents divorced and has "lost faith" in marriage.

"Just because your parents got divorced doesn't mean we will," Steve began. "We can work things out. I love you."

"Love isn't enough. I know my parents loved each other

but they couldn't make it work," Amanda stated sadly. "I wouldn't want to do that to my kids."

"It sounds like the divorce was very hard on you," I said.

"Yes . . . I didn't really understand that anything was wrong. I was always very close to my dad, but after the divorce, I hardly saw him," said Amanda. "He just didn't have time for me after a while."

"Did you ever try to talk with him about your feelings?" I asked.

"No. Shortly after the divorce, he showed up with a new girlfriend. He was eager to have me meet her and like her. But I felt like he not only left Mom, he also left me. Now, I seldom see him. It's like he started a new life and I'm not a part of it. He's remarried and has a two-year-old."

"How do you think all of that has influenced you and Steve?" I asked.

"Well, I've lost faith in marriage. I'm just not sure how I feel about things . . . how I feel about being married to Steve. Sometimes I think things have changed."

"But what has changed about me?" Steve asked.

"Well, nothing really, but there are times when I just notice things. Like the other day, I purposely left a bag of garbage sitting by the door to see if you would take it out. You walked right by it. You just leave everything up to me."

"I didn't know why that bag was sitting there. You've never done that before. It hasn't been part of our routine."

"It sounds like you were testing Steve," I offered.

"I guess in a way I was. I wonder whether he will notice things in our relationship," said Amanda.

"Amanda, it's hard for me to 'pass the test' when I don't even know I'm being tested," said Steve. "It's like you set me up to prove I will let you down."

"Maybe I do," said Amanda sadly. "I worry that this won't work out, and I will get hurt again."

"But that's not fair," said Steve, starting to get angry.

"It's not fair to you, Steve, but I think the more you understand these feelings, the closer you and Amanda will get to solving the problems. The wounds from broken families run deep. They leave scars for all the family members. It will take time for Amanda to trust the relationship with you. Her trust needs time to build," I said.

"But I've never given her any reason not to trust me," Steve protested.

"No, you haven't, but others have," I told Steve. "We bring our previous experiences into relationships and may expect similar outcomes.

"What would help you feel more confident with Steve, more trusting and secure?" I asked Amanda.

"I don't know. I think I need reassurances that he loves me and is committed for the long-term," said Amanda.

"But I do that," said Steve.

"You may have to reassure her even more, especially after she has contact with her father. It is likely that those times reopen some of the old wounds and feelings. That is an especially good time for you to make it clear that you will make every effort to ensure that history will not repeat itself in your relationship."

"I'm happy to do that," Steve informed me, and then he turned to Amanda and stated: "I love you and am committed to doing anything for our relationship."

■ ■ ■ ■ ■

It took several sessions for this couple to fully understand the impact of her parents' divorce on Amanda and their future relationship. Amanda had difficulty trusting again after seeing her father leave and separate from her. The severe hurt that remains from her feelings of abandonment is difficult for her to reconcile. Although she did nothing wrong and the divorce was not her fault, the actions of her parents forever changed her life.

Partners who come from broken homes commonly deal with such residual hurt and insecurity in their marriages. Developing the ability to understand and a willingness to do the extras to help each other feel loved and secure is essential. As time goes on, the wounds become less of a problem, although the old hurt may fester in some form for the rest of their lives. Divorce in a family affects the most important relationships a child has, all the more reason to put extra effort into marriages.

EVALUATE YOUR FAMILY BOUNDARIES

Happiness is having a large, loving, caring, close-knit family in another city.

George Burns

How are the boundaries in your marriage? Take the following quiz to evaluate.

1. We frequently argue about issues and incidents involving our families.

   True False

2. My spouse believes I spend too much time with my parents/sisters/brothers.

   True False

3. I dread the holidays because of the demands on our time and feeling the need to "please everyone."

   True False

4. Family members frequently call me when they have problems.

   True False

5. I feel like we take most of the responsibility for our parents.

   True False

6. I often feel torn between my spouse and my family.

   True False

7. When I say "No," I feel guilty.

   True False

8. I feel responsible for the problems of others in my family.

True False

9. I frequently find myself in the middle of a conflict between two other people.

True False

10. At times, I am emotionally cut off from members of my family.

True False

11. My family has arguments and conflicts that never get resolved.

True False

12. We often have family members who become scape-goats for problems.

True False

Scoring: How many "true" responses did you have?

0–1: Excellent. You are focusing on your marriage by having respectful boundaries with family.

2–5: Very good. Making progress. Look for opportunities to further define your position with the family.

5–9: Good. Discuss boundaries with your spouse. Practice saying "No" more often.

10–12: Get working. Carefully evaluate the changes you and your spouse need to make to deal more effectively with family. Use the following tools to enhance your abilities and support each other as you make changes.

BOUNDARY TOOLS

Every man sees in his relatives, and especially in his cousins, a series of grotesque caricatures of himself.

H. L. MENCKEN

Your ability to set appropriate limits with family members is crucial to building your marriage. Setting limits gets easier with practice. Try a few of the following techniques:

TOOL #1 Serve them cold. Refrain from being angry, emotional, or argumentative. State your "No's" in a firm, cold, and robot-like way. Use a pleasant, affirming voice with a direct approach to "No." Discuss your limits when you do not have a heated issue to resolve. Serve them cold.

TOOL #2 Don't over explain. You *can* say "No" without giving a reason. You know how? Just say "No." Do not provide a lot of information and do not feel you have to justify your decision. That only makes you look defensive.

TOOL #3 Less is more. Stop discussing it already! And do not draw other people into the issue. That creates attention and brouhaha over the issue. You do not need everyone else to evaluate your decision. And you do not have to prove your point to anyone. You have the right to say "No."

TOOL #4 Use the broken-record technique. "I'm so sorry, I simply can't" is a handy phrase. When pressed for a reason, repeat the phrase. When asked, "Why?" repeat the phrase. Get the picture? You will be surprised how quickly people understand that your "No" is firm.

TOOL #5 Stay out of the middle. Ask yourself the question, "Whose problem is it?" before getting involved in any family difficulties. Use the previous techniques to politely yet firmly say "No" to requests for advice, scapegoating, or rescuing.

TOOL #6 Expect to feel worse first. It can feel awkward to say "No" if you are not used to it. Some people may also attempt to punish you psychologically for asserting yourself (i.e., try to make you feel guilty). With practice, it will get easier and clearer.

TOOL #7 Practice outside in. Setting limits is hard. Practice with people and relationships that are less important to your sense of well being. It is much easier to say "No" to a telemarketer than to your mother-in-law. Practice with little "No's," and identify the big "No's" you want to tackle in the future.

TOOL #8 Limit the guilt by understanding how limits can help. We actually help others when we set limits and boundaries. The information assists them in making decisions and choices without confusion about what actions we will take.

5 You're Going Out Again?

STRATEGY 5: LET GO OF THE SINGLE LIFESTYLE

When I was single, I went *out*. Going out was fun. I met lots of people and partied carefree. In my single days, the discos were all the rage. I would dress in bell-bottom pants, a midriff top, and brown leather boots that laced to the knee. I could tie a boot with one hand by holding both laces and weaving my hand back and forth across the boot—much to the amazement of my acquaintances. It was not uncommon for my friends to have a couple of drinks and yell, "Hey let's ask Barb to tie her boots; it is really neat." We were easily amused in those days.

I have always loved to dance, and in my single days I became prolific in walking the Stroll, grinding the Bump, waving the YMCA, and navigating the line for *Saturday Night Fever.* When I was broke, I would enter dance contests and do the Hustle for a dinner coupon or gift certificate—I was a female John Travolta.

These are the kinds of things people do when they are out—party, dance, drink, and hang out. And all kinds of people are out—from amateurs like me to professional lounge lizards with their gold necklaces gleaming through their open, silk shirts. Funny, Charlie once told me that any guy wearing a gold chain around his neck could not be trusted.

Myth: The party life can continue forever.

Life's heaviest burden is to have nothing to carry.

UNKNOWN

Single life was busy and I was not worrying about anyone but me. When I was in nursing school, I would drop off my dirty clothes at a Laundromat to have them washed, ironed, and returned the same day. It was expensive, but I felt that I had no time to do it. No time? I was living alone, no house, no kids, no elderly parents, and the laundry was too much. I was only responsible for myself, but I was busy going out.

Single life is "doing your thing" without a care in the world, making plans on a moment's notice—a free spirit, unattached.

After a decade or so of partying, I was increasingly weary of the single life. I began to notice that a lot of the people out were really not all that happy, especially those out all the time. And after a while, the whole scene began to look pretty superficial and empty. I knew I would never find what I was looking for in a bar, since the main thing you find in bars are people who like to drink.

Now, I am not saying that everyone who is living the wild single life is a loser. I *am* saying the scene is, hopefully, something you grow out of. After a while, the bar scene gets old. Bell-bottoms, bare midriffs, and leather boots look rather funny on people my age, even if they *are* back in style.

Part of having a successful marriage is letting go of the single lifestyle, and not in a begrudging, sullen manner, or arguing with your spouse like a spoiled child being dragged by exhausted parents out of Chuck E. Cheese's. Rather, letting go is best achieved with the positive excitement of embracing something new and realizing that the single life is just one chapter of hopefully a long life—not the end of your journey. Letting go is most effectively achieved when you feel ready to be done with being single—been there . . . done that . . . time to move on.

At some point, the couples—or more often one of the partners—who come to see me becomes quite insistent that they should be able to do "what I've always done." Emphatic that their lives should not have to change just because of marriage, they insist: "This was who I was when we met. I want to do everything the way I did when I was single." And I explain that if you want everything to be the same as when you were single, you should have stayed single.

Myth: I'm going to do what I have always done.

When I was a child, I spoke as a child . . . I thought as a child; but when I became a man I put away childish things.

1 CORINTHIANS 13:11

Marriage is different. It requires different thinking and different actions. And you don't get different by doing everything the same.

A few years ago, I traveled to Israel on a tour with my mother. Before we started, a very wise tour guide warned the group of thirty that there would be times when the trip would be an ecstatic experience and everything would be perfect and other times that would be challenging and disappointing. "Don't expect everything to be like the United States," he warned. "The rooms may be small, the food not to your liking, and the toilets different from what you are used to." I stared with mild apprehension as I realized that there probably would not be a whirlpool in my stateroom. "However," he continued, "that is the nature of traveling. And remember, if it is exactly like home, than you might as well stay home." *Good point.*

I tried desperately to keep his words in mind one afternoon as I squatted over a hole at a public toilet wiping myself with a material that could best be described as wax paper—not very absorbent, I can assure you.

While wax paper in the bathroom is not usually a part of marriage, marriage *is* a different state of being, a separate karma. It requires a change to "couples-think" instead of just thinking about oneself. The single life is basically selfish and self-centered—wanting what you want when you want it. That *may be* okay when you are single, but it doesn't work when you are married. You have to remember that you have a partner.

Myth: Drinking is not the problem.

One drink is too many for me and a thousand not enough.

BRENDAN F. BEHAN

Drinking is a part of the single scene. Too often it also extends into married life. I frequently see couples that have a pattern of arguing and fighting after one or both of them begin drinking. They may fight about the drinking or fight about something else, but it is clear that alcohol ignites the glowing embers of anger and resentment like gasoline on a campfire. What starts as a minor disagreement or misunderstanding takes on a life of its own, until the point of the argument is lost in a maze of accusations and dramatic behavior. In relationships, excessive drinking precipitates fights and arguments.[1]

Well, what about drugs, you ask? Yes, I know, people use drugs that also cause problems in marriages, drugs like marijuana, cocaine, hallucinogens, and prescription pain medication. And, yes, these present problems. I am focusing on drinking, though, because alcohol remains the number one drug of abuse in America. And unlike many drugs, it is legal.

As an aside, I repeatedly warn my clients about incarceration issues, especially those who expend a great deal of energy trying to convince me that marijuana is not harmful. I tell them: "Well, there is at least one problem: You go to jail if you are caught with it."

In addition to being legal, alcohol use is socially acceptable, widespread, and an enormous problem. Currently, nearly 14 million Americans—1 in every 13 adults—abuse alcohol or are alcoholic. Many more adults engage in heavy drinking or risky behaviors that cause problems. Approximately 53 percent of men and women in the United States report that one or more of their close relatives has a drinking problem.[2]

The consequences of alcohol misuse are serious and many. Heavy drinking increases the risk for a number of cancers and other diseases. It also increases the risk of death from automobile crashes. In 2000, America experienced the largest percentage increase in alcohol-related traffic deaths on record. In 2000, 16,653 people were killed in crashes involving alcohol, representing 40 percent of the 41,821 people killed in all traffic crashes.[3]

Some of my clients are quick to argue with me and insist: "But drinking is not the problem." I tell them, "Perhaps. But you seem to have problems when you drink." (For further information about whether drinking is a problem for you, please see the MAST tool in the Appendix.) Then they give me their reasons, excuses, and justifications for drinking, all of which I have heard before: "I was celebrating my new job." "I just lost my job." "The Packers won." "The Packers lost." (I know, the team may change based on location; however, Charlie insists the Packers are the only team worth talking about.) If asked about my personal favorite reason, justification, or excuse for drinking, it is this one: "The bartender over-served me." Regardless of the excuse, those who drink seldom want to consider the possibility that alcohol could possibly be a problem.

I review with clients the definition of social drinking—two to three drinks.

"You mean an hour?" they ask. *No, I mean a drinking episode.*

Their voices rise in amazement: "Are you kidding? I'm just getting started when I finish off a six-pack." *That might be part of the problem.*

I explain to them that social drinking does not mean getting drunk. It means the ability to stop at two or three drinks and having control over one's behavior. I stress that it is important that they look at what happens *when* they drink. If the drinking is causing problems, then they are a problem drinker. If they are having a problem with their spouse's drinking, then there is a drinking problem.

The widespread acceptance and use of alcohol hypnotizes us into believing it is just fine to drink to excess. We believe it must be safe. After all, the government allows it. It is advertised and promoted everywhere. Why, everyone drinks!

Myth: If everyone does it, it must be okay.

I like whiskey. I always did, and that is why I never drink it.

ROBERT E. LEE

I remember a visit several years ago to Yellowstone Park. Warning signs were posted at the entrance and throughout the park cautioning visitors about the dangerous buffalo that wander freely in the park. The signs made it clear that buffalo are wild animals—unpredictable and dangerous.

In a recent tragedy in the park, a man had placed his young son on the back of a buffalo to take a picture. The buffalo reacted violently and gored the boy to death and severely injured the father. (This might be a good time to review "Shit for Brains" in Chapter 3.)

I was sharing the tragedy about the buffalo with another park visitor when he interrupted, "That's nonsense. They wouldn't have the animals roaming free if they weren't tame and friendly." My thought was that this guy probably also believes the tobacco executives who insist that nicotine is not addictive.

Alcohol is like the buffalo wandering free. It is convenient to be complacent about the risks and problems associated with alcohol misuse since alcohol is easily available and socially acceptable. It cannot be emphasized enough that the misuse of alcohol presents a real danger to individuals, marriages, and the community.

Myth: I can stop drinking anytime I want!

Even though a number of people have tried, no one has ever found a way to drink for a living.

JEAN KERR

Now I have to admit that I am biased about the issue of drinking and marriage. I have seen the carnage that drinking wreaks both personally and professionally. I do not think my parents' marriage would have crumbled without the help of the bottle. And most of the time when I see "crazy" families in my office, alcohol fuels that craziness.

Likely no one sets out to be an alcoholic or to have a drinking problem, and no one makes a conscious decision to ruin one's own health, trash one's family, estrange one's spouse, and create angry children. No, the effects of alcohol misuse sneak up on people and slowly change from that of pleasant companion during social occasions to a serious problem for the user. That line is difficult to identify, locate, and accept for most people.

Drinking is like an insidious illness that slowly grows and spreads throughout the family. It creates a fog of denial that makes the real problem difficult to see and recognize. A cloud envelops people when they drink, and they do not see the symptoms clearly, even when they are apparent to everyone around them. I truly think my father was befuddled and confused when he learned that Mom no longer wanted to live with him and his bottle. After all, it wasn't *that* bad, was it? And it wasn't, not for him. He was inebriated most of the time. The rest of us had to live sober with his drinking. It was like having an elephant in the room and everyone just stepped around it.

When I was a young girl, we had a wonderful lady in the neighborhood, Ms. Lila, who lived alone in a modern ranch home on the other side of the block. Widowed and lonely, she would allow the kids in the neighborhood to play in her yard and pick her fresh rhubarb. On Thanksgiving mornings, we would crowd into her TV room to watch the parades in color, since she was the only one in the neighborhood with a color TV. Though the announcer's face was orange, the parade horses purple, and the sky green, we thought television was marvelous and watched spellbound for hours.

One day several of us were sitting in Ms. Lila's sunroom when she noticed small bruises developing on her arms and legs. We all laughed as she showed us because they were in such funny shapes and patterns. It never occurred to us that it could be anything serious. Three days later, she was dead.

We soon learned that those little bruises were actually the beginning of a slow hemorrhage throughout her body, which would eventually affect every organ. The platelets in her blood, which are essential for clotting, were drastically reduced due to bone marrow damage from an antibiotic she had been taking for an ear infection. A rare complication, the drug-induced thrombocytopenia killed her.

We could not believe it. She had been healthy, happy. The ear infection was a minor, insignificant illness; the bruises appeared to be nothing serious. Little did we know this would be a lethal illness for her.

This is what I see in families with a lot of drinking. Long before major symptoms appear, minor problems surface that appear insignificant. The symptom may seem funny even, a joke, a misunderstanding about what time to come home, an incident with the police when stopped for speeding, a missed day of work. But the drinking takes its toll over time and slowly destroys all the best parts of family life and personal sanity.

Sometimes my clients describe "Jekyll and Hyde" personalities in themselves or their spouses after drinking. A change in personality or mood can be so dramatic that it confuses those around them and leaves everyone "walking on eggshells" and worrying that they may do or say something that will ignite an argument. Sometimes irritability remains long after the immediate effects of the alcohol are gone. The family describes feeling confused, angry, and scared. Family members do not know what to do to make things better and somehow feel that they may be at fault.

Myth: I'm not moody . . . my spouse is hard to live with.

I made a commitment to completely cut out drinking and anything that might hamper me from getting my mind and body together. And the floodgates of goodness have opened upon me—spiritually and financially.

DENZEL WASHINGTON

I remember coming to the dinner table as a child. As soon as Dad arrived, all laughing and talking would stop and a hush would fall like a heavy curtain. We were apprehensive about speaking, joking, or fooling around because we were never sure of the barometer level of Dad's mood, which may help to account for the fact that I weighed sixty-nine pounds when Dad left, even though I was in the sixth grade.

One night I knocked my half-full glass of milk with my elbow and watched in horror as the white liquid trickled across the table and onto the floor with loud, plunking drips. I slowly raised my eyes and saw my two brothers and sister exchange fearful glances while we waited for the inevitable explosion of anger from my father. After a pause of several seconds that seemed like an hour, he threw his head back and let out a huge belly laugh. I sat there stunned—it felt like someone had reached over and slapped me on the face. I waited . . . thinking that this was a cruel joke, a fantasy, a test. Why, just last night, he was a raving lunatic because we were out of butter. Watching him out of the corner of my eye, I slowly wiped up the mess.

A big problem in living with someone who drinks or uses is that you never know what their reaction to the slightest movement or event will be. I describe this to my clients as "come here, go away." Sometimes you are welcome and loved; the next minute you find yourself

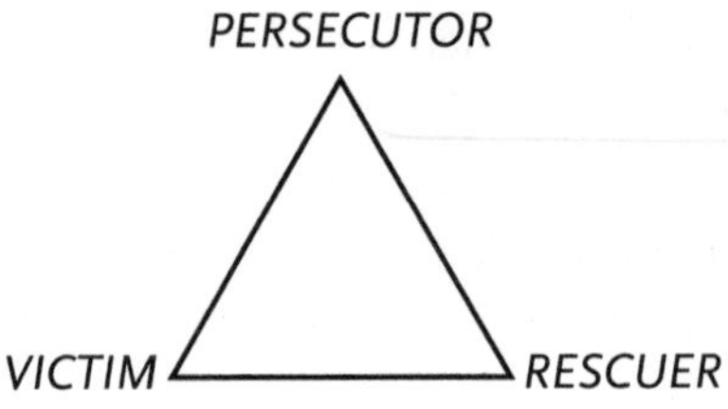

pushed away with an angry blast. It is very bewildering, very "crazy"-making.

In a house with drinking, you never know what is coming next. You walk on eggshells hoping none will break. You try to guess people's moods; the effects of chemicals can change behavior so rapidly. It took me years to understand that Dad's mood changes were a product of his addiction. It was he, not me.

Myth: I don't play games.

No snowflake in an avalanche ever feels responsible.

STANISLAW J. LEC

I explain to my clients how alcohol affects disposition by lowering a brain chemical called serotonin. Acting as a depressant, it shortens the fuse for anger and frustration. I let them know that alcohol loosens inhibitions so that people say and do things they would never say or do when they are sober. And when people do not think about what they are saying, it is easy for trouble to result.

Standup comedian Louie Anderson lamented about drinking: "You know, friends are nice until they have too much to drink. Did you ever notice that you can have a best friend, five drinks is their limit . . . they have seven. (Then) . . . they turn on you. All of a sudden they get this look and say, 'I'm mad at you.'"[4]

As any bartender can tell you, it happens all the time.

I often see a pattern of recurring and predictable behavior in households with a lot of drinking. I call it the Triangle Game. (This pattern of behavior is also often seen in households without drinking when one or both partners have been raised in alcoholic families. For more information on Adult Children of Alcoholics, please see Further Resources at the end of this book.) The beauty of this game is that when it gets boring, everybody just changes roles. It looks like this:

Imagine the husband coming home after an evening drinking. His wife is angry because she prepared dinner and waited over two hours for him to arrive. She feels very mistreated by his behavior (Victim) and views him as a no-good, not-to-be-counted-on creep (Persecutor). He, in the meantime, has had a great time connecting with some old friends. He forgot all about the dinner but is in a great mood and is eager to get home to see his wife and maybe convince her that intimacy tonight would be a great idea.

As he walks in the door, his wife is standing in the doorway with her arms crossed. "Where have you been?" she demands, raising her voice. "You missed dinner and left me waiting."

He feels misunderstood and angry. After all, he should have the right to stop for a drink with his friends occasionally. He works hard. He deserves it! What the hell! He believes he is being treated unfairly (Victim), and his wife has a real problem (Persecutor). They argue and yell for a while, and his wife starts to cry (Victim). He later feels sorry for her (Rescuer) and takes her in his arms while vowing that he will never do it again.

The next morning, the wife feels bad that she was so hard on her husband (Rescuer) and goes to apologize. They have completed the cycle, only to begin again the following week. The game never ends.

If there are children in the household, they quickly learn the routine and join the action. They yell at Dad for making Mom cry (Persecutor). Or they go hug Mom in support of her ongoing problems with Dad (Rescuer). They may just hide in their room feeling misunderstood and ignored (Victim). The game continues with all family members participating. As I said, it never gets boring because family members can just switch roles.

Consider the following couple.

CASE STUDY: Jeff and Barbara

Jeff, a vice president for a large advertising firm, and Barbara, a full-time homemaker, came to treatment due to marital problems and Barbara's drinking. Well-dressed in a three-piece suit, Jeff is Harvard educated, sophisticated, and extremely articulate. He has climbed the corporate ladder at his company and is currently responsible for several divisions and subsidiary corporations. Well-known in the community, he is active on boards and participates in fund-raising projects. He presents as energetic, cheerful, and outgoing.

Barbara's demeanor is in sharp contrast to her husband's. She moves slowly into the room and asks permission to take a seat. While well dressed in designer clothes, she looks tired, with facial creases excessive for her age and sad, watery eyes. Her thinning, drab, brown hair is styled loosely to her shoulders, which slump forward as she sits.

Jeff explains he is committed to his marriage, but finds that Barbara's drinking is a major problem. He acknowledges that they entertain a lot due to his position and that drinking is an important component in his business.

"We *have* to entertain our advertising clients," he explains. "They expect that kind of treatment or they will take their business elsewhere."

Barbara describes how she works hard at being the "corporate wife," but feels unappreciated and ignored most of the time. With her husband working long hours, she is frequently alone and is expected to take care of the planning, food preparation, and details necessary for personal and corporate guests to have a good time. Ashamed, she admits that she "drinks too much," but finds that it eases the loneliness and helps her feel more comfortable when there are so many important people at an event.

"It wouldn't be so bad if she would just have a few drinks," Jeff interrupts. "But she gets drunk. It is embarrassing. I need her to help me entertain these clients."

I questioned them both as to the extent of the "entertaining" for business and pleasure and learned that it was just about every weekend. There often were other events during the week such as community fundraisers and official dinners that also involved drinking. While Jeff and Barbara were not spending their lives in the bars, their lives revolved around drinking events.

I gently cautioned Jeff that it might be difficult for his wife to limit her drinking with their lives structured this way.

"But why do I have to change my life because she has no willpower?" he asks in an angry tone. "You don't understand. We don't want to change anything else in our lives, just Barbara's drinking."

As Barbara glared at Jeff, I explained that it is impossible to do everything the same and expect different results. While they both see the effects drinking has on Barbara, it is important that they see that their lifestyle is a part of the problem. It is very difficult to have so much of married life revolve around "entertaining" and alcohol and not have drinking become a problem. I explained that both of them would need to look at themselves and possibly make some changes.

"But this is not my problem!" interrupted Jeff. It was clear that he viewed Barbara and her drinking as the difficulty (Persecutor) and himself as the embarrassed husband (Victim). He did not view alcoholism as a family illness and was reluctant to look at what changes he may need to make. I worried that he would consciously or unconsciously sabotage any efforts Barbara made to recover.

Jeff dropped from treatment a short time later. Barbara eventually became active in Alcoholics Anonymous and subsequently separated from Jeff.

■ ■ ■ ■ ■

Watch for the game-playing at your house. It will mask the real issues and muddy the solutions. How do you stop it? You just stop playing. You refuse to jump into a role or say the "same old things." In other words, do anything different from what you would normally do. The game will crumble, making it easier to find new solutions to old problems.

Myth: I can do it by myself!

I do not care to belong to a club that accepts people like me.

GROUCHO MARX

I routinely suggest additional resources for clients. Too often they tell me, "I can do it by myself"—whatever "it" is. Sounding like a two-year-old with their hands perched defiantly on their hips, they make it clear they know all the answers and do not need help from anyone. They view accepting help as a sign of weakness or incompetence, which is certainly not the case for them.

I tell them: "Wise people learn from their mistakes. You don't need to make all of them yourself. You can learn from others, others who have been there and have found some answers."

Some of the best places I know for learning are self-help groups like Alcoholics Anonymous (AA) and Al-Anon, which is a program for family members. Present in most U.S. cities and around the world, both programs utilize a twelve-step program for recovery that has worked for millions of people. (Information on Alcoholics Anonymous or Al-Anon in your community is available in the white or yellow pages, or see the information in Further Resources at the end of this book.)

Deceptively simple, the twelve-step program can actually be a program for living. With a spiritual base, a twelve-step program helps you learn how to let go and trust in a power stronger than you that will change your life. The twelve-step program works not only for drinking, but also for resolving many other problems. In fact, the basic format of the program is used for Overeaters Anonymous, Gamblers Anonymous, and other self-help groups.

My clients argue: "I don't want to go to meetings. I just don't feel like it." Then I share with them the old AA phrase: "Take the body and the mind will follow. Just get there . . . sit in the back, and listen." The twelve-step program will help you find miracles in your life, including self-understanding, forgiveness, and personal strength to help you make the changes you need.

Myth: They are just a friend.

I have steak at home. Why go out for hamburger?

PAUL NEWMAN

I often tell clients the story of the man trapped on the roof of his house during a terrible flood. He prayed and prayed for help. Suddenly, a boat came floating by with a woman urging him to climb aboard. "No," the man replied. "I have faith in God that he will protect me and save me. I will wait here." And he continued to sit on his roof.

About an hour later, another boat came by with passengers pleading with the man to come aboard. He again responded, "No. I trust in the Lord to save me."

The water continued to get higher until the man stood on a small patch of roof, losing his footing on the slippery roof. A helicopter suddenly appeared and lowered a rope for him to climb aboard. Again he refused, confident that God would save him. Within minutes, he drowned.

When he arrived at the Pearly Gates, he asked God: "Where were you? I prayed and prayed for you to save me."

"Well, I sent two boats and a helicopter," replied God. "What more did you expect?"

Self-help groups are the lifeboats and helicopters that can take you to safety. And, yes, they really work. Do not keep standing on the roof by yourself.

Most people do not set out to have an affair. They do not wake up one morning and think, "Gee, I would really like to find some hot tail, mar my reputation, destroy my marriage, and end up with enormous legal bills." No, I think most extramarital encounters occur somewhat by accident. People find themselves in compromising situations, attracted to another person, only to discover too late that they are making choices with dire consequences.

Now I know there are some folks who are out there "cruising," or "looking for action," but I don't find that typical. I did, however, have one client who came to see me because her husband had more than fifteen extramarital relationships in seven years of marriage. She wanted to know if she should leave him. I felt like saying to her, "Are you crazy?" Again, this is not typical.

What is typical is people putting themselves in tempting situations—like going for a few drinks with a co-worker who "really understands" them, or discussing all of life's problems with the helpful neighbor or acquaintance at the bar. A risky lifestyle of long work hours, a heavy travel schedule, and single behavior can make infidelity easy.

I warn clients about compromising situations. I urge them to practice vigilance and make sure they are not sending mixed signals, which can result from wearing provocative clothing, "innocent" flirting, sharing confidences—all are "green lights" that may be interpreted as someone looking for sexual intimacy.

I let them know that this is dangerous territory. It is a minefield, and they shouldn't be surprised if giving off such a signal turns into trouble.

When we were in Israel, we rode a bus up the road that borders Jordan. Peering through the window, I could see large warning signs on the rocky, dismal landscape that cautioned visitors that there were many buried land mines in the area. We never stopped the bus. We knew it wasn't safe, and no one felt the need to test it. We believed the signs and did not have to step on a mine for proof that they were out there.

Myth: I am working long hours for us.

He who is wrapped up in himself makes a mighty small package.

SOURCE UNKNOWN

Like land mines, there are signs of trouble before infidelity occurs. Wise married couples watch for danger signs and work to avoid the minefields. And when they feel terribly attracted to someone else, with a sexual urge that they absolutely cannot control, they run home to their spouses and make passionate love long into the night.

Part of the single lifestyle is doing what you want, when you want and not reporting to anyone or anyplace. This approach to personal life often extends to work and career. It is very common for people in their twenties and even thirties to put 200 percent into building their career or climbing the corporate ladder. In some respects, this is probably good—"pay your dues" while you're young and unencumbered.

It can become a problem, however, when you partner with someone else. A hectic schedule with long work hours and multiple demands can leave little time and energy for building a marriage or raising a family. And Americans are working harder and longer than ever. According to a new report from the United Nations International Labor Organization (ILO), "Workers in the United States are putting in more hours than anyone else in the industrialized world."[5]

The ILO statistics show that in 2000, the average American worked almost one more week of work than the year before, working an average of 1,978 hours—up from 1,942 hours in 1990. Americans now work longer hours than Canadian, German, Japanese, or Australian workers.

What are we working for? Not vacations. Typical American workers have an average of two weeks of vacation, compared to four to six weeks for their European counterparts.

Are typical American employees working for happiness? According to regular surveys by the National Opinion Research Center of the University of Chicago, no more Americans report they are "very happy" now than in 1957, despite near doubling their personal consumption expenditures. Indeed, the world's people have consumed as many goods and services since 1950 as all previous generations put together, yet report that they are not any happier.[6]

Are they working to give their family what they need or want? I tell clients: "I have news for you. Your spouse would like more time with *you,* and your kids would be happy in a tent with a flashlight. Do *not* think you are doing it for them."

There are many costs in working so hard. People tend to cut back on sleep and time with their families. A recent survey found that almost a third of people working more than forty-eight hours a week said that exhaustion was affecting married life.[7] Nearly a third admitted that work-related tiredness was causing their sex life to suffer, and 14 percent reported a loss of or reduced sex drive. They also complained that long hours and overwork led to arguments and tension at home. Two out of five people working more than forty-eight hours a week blamed long hours for disagreements and said they felt guilty for not pulling their weight with domestic chores.

The line between work and play has become blurry. While technology was supposed to give us more time, for many it has resulted in an ever-expanding workday, with no boundaries between career and relaxation. People return home after full shifts to voicemail, faxes, e-mails, and phone calls—called "technology tethers" by C. Leslie Charles.[8] It is easy to become a slave to technology, believing that we must "be in touch" at all times. Charles would argue that frequent interruptions only intensify an artificial sense of urgency and time compression, creating stress in our lives.

Happy couples control their time together, making sure work does not slowly rob them of opportunities for connectedness and intimacy. They use technology to simplify their work, not extend it. And they work at being happy with what they have instead of always wanting more.

Several years ago, Charlie was traveling extensively for his job. As he packed one Sunday to go to Denver, we noticed that our cat, Figaro, had left a deposit on Charlie's pillow, which was sitting by his suitcase. Concerned that she must be sick, I took her to the veterinarian the following morning and had $235 worth of tests run. The veterinarian called me into his office to discuss the results.

"The good news," he began, "is that your cat is not sick. All her tests came back normal."

"Well, then, what is wrong?" I asked.

"We believe she is depressed."

Now I'm thinking, *She's depressed? I'm the one who should be depressed. I just ran up a $235 bill for a cat that isn't sick.*

"Depressed?!" I said out loud.

"Yes," the vet stated firmly, and then he asked, "Have there been any significant changes at home recently?"

"Well, my husband is traveling a lot more."

"That can do it," he said. "Cats are very sensitive to these things."

"Well, what am I supposed to do about this? Put her in a self-help group where she can communicate her feelings?" I asked sarcastically.

The doctor did not laugh. Instead, he looked at me as if I was actually a causative factor in Figaro's psychological problems. He went on to suggest: "Perhaps additional attention would be helpful. If she doesn't improve, we can try some antidepressants."

Antidepressants for a cat? Now, I don't know about you, but my thinking was that if the cat needed antidepressants because we were working too hard and gone too much, than maybe it was time to reevaluate work and not drug the cat.

It was time for a talk with Charlie when he returned from Denver. We decided we would modify our work schedules, and we have periodically evaluated our schedules ever since. We recognize that sometimes spouses and children react much like cats.

WHAT ARE YOUR PRIORITIES?

The willingness to accept responsibility for one's own life is the source from which self-respect springs.

JOAN DIDION

Evaluate the focus of your life:

1. Do you go out with your friends, minus your spouse, more than once per month?

   Always Sometimes Never

2. Do several months go by without an outing with your spouse?

   Always Sometimes Never

3. Do your leisure activities center around the use of alcohol?

   Always Sometimes Never

4. Does alcohol need to be present for you and your spouse to have a good time?

   Always Sometimes Never

5. Do you or your spouse have "flashes of aggression" when drinking?

   Always Sometimes Never

6. Do others disapprove of your drinking?

   Always Sometimes Never

7. Do you feel guilty about your drinking?

   Always Sometimes Never

8. Do you find it difficult to find time for exercise and relaxation?

   Always Sometimes Never

9. Do you often forget or postpone family time due to work at the office or other commitments?

   Always Sometimes Never

10. Are you preoccupied with thoughts of work, even on weekends or vacations?

    Always Sometimes Never

11. Do you feel guilty if you don't accomplish something?

    Always Sometimes Never

Scoring: How many "never" responses did you have?
9–10: Excellent. You are clear about the priorities in your life.
7–8: Good. Keep working. You will reap results by changing your behavior.
Fewer than 6: Time to reevaluate. Take a look at how you are spending your time and your priorities. Utilize the following tools to continue building your marriage.

BUILD A FAMILY LIFESTYLE

You cannot escape the responsibility of tomorrow by evading it today.

ABRAHAM LINCOLN

TOOL #1 Develop the "partnership-think." Sit down at least once per week and plan the schedule together for the week. Coordinate time so that responsibilities are covered but you still have time to be together. Avoid surprises that lead to confusion or misunderstandings.

TOOL #2 Schedule a "date" at least once a month. It does not need to be expensive. A lunch out, a budget movie, a walk in the park, or window-shopping provide time together to talk. Rotate the responsibility for planning so there are surprises and events to look forward to.

TOOL #3 Build friendships with other happy couples and avoid couples who are not happy. Find people who like to do some of the same activities and build a regular schedule of getting together. Get together to do something active, like skiing or golf, or do something as simple as playing cards. These get-togethers can provide a source for a supportive network, helping to assure a happy marriage.

TOOL #4 Limit drinking. Limit your drinking to two to three drinks per episode and no more than two episodes per week. Periodically evaluate whether activities are becoming alcohol-centered. And stay out of the bars.

TOOL #5 Attend community outreach programs and support groups. Valuable programs are available in most communities for little expense. Check out free programs at hospitals and associations. They provide information and support that is invaluable.

TOOL #6 Break the overtime habit. Train your boss that you are certainly willing to put in extra hours in a pinch, but do not make it a regular part of your lifestyle. Make it clear that your family is the priority and that balance is important. Few employers will openly disagree, and they will have renewed appreciation when you do put in the overtime.

I make you laugh
and you make me cry,
I believe it's time for me to fly.

"Time for Me to Fly" by REO Speedwagon

6 We Never Do What I Want to Do

STRATEGY 6:
CREATE COMMON INTERESTS AND ACTIVITIES

We hung out at airports a lot when we first got married. Charlie was an expert sky diver and jumped out of "perfectly good airplanes" all over the country. I used to joke that he was "good to the last drop," a saying he did not find amusing. I actually tried jumping myself a few times, but he begged me to stop, saying something about my landings being like a sack of bricks.

But everything changed when our son was born. We quickly discovered that a drop zone was not exactly the greatest place to entertain a baby. He did not enjoy the jet noise, sleeping on the ground, or cold formula. It readily became apparent that unless you are actually involved in the skydiving experience, it is a very boring sport. After several weekends of airport inactivity, I begged Charlie to do something else.

"Let's go to the zoo or something," I suggested.

"Nah. Why don't we just go out to the airport for a little while?" he asked.

"We never do what I want to do," I whined.

"But I thought you liked watching skydiving and all the excitement!" Charlie responded in surprise.

"I do," I explained, "but not every weekend and, anyway, things have changed. I think we need to find some activities that we can mutually enjoy."

Charlie agreed. We both knew we were into a new phase and some of the things we used to do just didn't fit our present life experience very well.

It became even more complicated when we had our second child. With both of us constantly exhausted, most of the hobbies and sports we once enjoyed fell by the wayside. We tried to get out together, to find time for just the two of us, but it was hard to arrange. Even when we did manage a few hours of respite, we found ourselves blankly staring at each other and feeling completely "fried," with each of us wondering how we ever married such a boring, unexciting, and aging partner.

Charlie and I knew that time together was critical, but we were unsure of how to routinely make it happen. After looking at many options, we decided to get season tickets to the Repertory Theatre. The Rep has a professional acting group located in downtown Milwaukee that presents a variety of plays in an old, historic theatre with great atmosphere. Centrally located, the theatre provides easy access to fine restaurants and cocktail lounges for an aprés-show rendezvous. Attending the Rep is a great way to get away from the day-to-day routine and serves as an excuse to dress up and act like people of leisure.

We found that spending money on the tickets ensured that we would attend, even though it was easier to stay home—and it *was* easier to stay home. To go out for an evening usually involved tears—mine, or one or both of the kids'—a burnt dinner, lost tickets, a car without gas, nothing to wear, or all of the above. We had to get the children fed, bathed, and in pajamas. We had to locate, bribe, and feed a sitter. While communicating emergency phone numbers, we tended to the cats and fed the lizard before walking out the door. It seemed at the time like more work than it was worth, but we forced ourselves to go. We knew we would have a great time once we got out—even if the production stunk.

One evening, I recall vividly, the play was an artsy presentation of race relations in the 1800s. Although relevant and profound, it was quite boring, difficult to follow, and hard to understand. Charlie and I struggled through the first two acts feeling good about our commitment to culture. Then during the third act, the man sitting next to me, dressed in a raccoon coat, started to snore loudly.

Charlie leaned over and said, "Be careful. His coat is alive. I can hear it."

I started to giggle and then choked back a laugh as the snoring got louder. I knew that I dared not look at Charlie, for he was certain to have a twinkle in his eye, which most definitely would prevent me from containing my amusement. Alas, I looked at Charlie and my giggle turned into a muffled laugh, which made him guffaw as well.

We were like two naughty children laughing in church. It became all the funnier because we were supposed to be quiet. We began to laugh so loudly that we had to leave the theatre. To this day, we talk about *that* evening, *that* play, and *that* raccoon coat. We had a great time even though the play was lousy.

The best marriages I see are ones in which couples focus on spending time together. These spouses are like great roommates: pleasant to be around, willing to compromise, and eager for fun. Always ready to try new activities, they enjoy their lives and their time together. The energy that surfaces from shared hobbies and activities brings spontaneity and excitement to the marriage, even when the activity itself flops.

As one couple put it: "Even the bad times are good. If the movie stinks, we laugh about it and enjoy ourselves anyway."

Couples with strong marriages recognize that activities may change over the years, but commitment to discovering together does not. As partners, they are open to trying new things and having new experiences, and they laugh together even when everything seems to go wrong.

Couples frequently insist that they do not have the money to spend time together. I review with them the many activities that do not cost a lot of money, such as walks in the park, coffee on the patio, or a budget movie. And occasionally splurging on a special activity to boost the marriage is something I urge as well. When you can afford it the least, I tell clients, is when you need it the most. Special days, like birthdays and anniversaries, are also good times to splurge.

Myth: We cannot afford it.

Modern man is frantically trying to earn enough money to buy things he is too busy to enjoy.

AUTHOR

We have always tried to make our anniversary very special. In the early years, we collected coupons and went to the best restaurant we could afford. Each year, I would insist it was too much, but interestingly enough we never missed the money.

Two years ago on our anniversary, we decided to do something really special. We made reservations to play golf at Black Wolf Run in Kohler, Wisconsin. The community of Kohler, as a matter of interest, is the home of the famous Kohler toilets, bathroom fixtures, and faucets—

the bathroom display building alone is worth a visit. But back to the Black Wolf Run course. It was the site of the Women's Open Championship in 1998. *Golf* magazine ranked it among the "Top 100 Golf Courses You Can Play." Originally carved by glaciers, the course offers sweeping panoramic views of the Sheboygan River Valley.

With names like "Burial Mounds," "Gotcha," "Jackknife," and "Hell's Gate," each hole presents a challenge and a puzzle. The sand traps number more than fifty and resemble the Mohave Desert in their ability to intimidate golfers. For us, survival became an issue. On some holes, like number fifteen, the sand trap goes so deep that we had to descend six steps to reach the bottom.

For two south-side Milwaukee hackers, who were used to lugging around our own equipment, we found the course to be especially extravagant. Attendants greeted us with a cart, carefully loaded our clubs, and drove us to the clubhouse to check in. At the end of the round, they wiped down each club before removing the bag to load in the car. Friendly and courteous, the attendant politely laughed as my husband pointed out: "The ones with all the mud belong to my wife."

This kind of attention does not come cheap. A round of eighteen holes of golf with a cart cost $179 a person, or $358 for the two of us—a lot of money on our salaries. Certainly this is more money than we have to spend on a regular basis, even on an irregular basis for that matter. I feel guilty recalling this—it seems too extravagant, too wasteful. After all, there are still starving people in Africa, and we could play a county course for $22 a round.

Still, I remember every minute of that anniversary. Charlie and I talked, laughed, let the sand fly, fished balls out of the river, and spotted a deer with twin fawns. We fought for space in the cart when it poured on the thirteenth hole, then finished the round in misty sunlight with a rainbow shining over the hills. We have both worked throughout our married life, and we barely distinguish one day at work from another, but we certainly remember *that* day.

Recently, I saw a young woman who had been married about ten years. She was very depressed because her husband had filed for divorce. Although she did not want to divorce, she also felt little was left of the marriage. She shared with me: "We never developed a life together. We didn't go out. We didn't take vacations or even long weekends. We always felt there just 'wasn't time.' We prided ourselves on being practical and not wasting any money."

She found it ironic that *now* they had to spend thousands of dollars to obtain a divorce and determine the custody of their children. I had told her in an earlier session that I had once played at Black Wolf Run with my husband. A fellow golfer, she now asked me about that day and whether I had really enjoyed it. After I described the course and the cost, she observed: "Black Wolf Run is cheaper than hiring an attorney." Yes it is.

Myth: I am too busy for you.

It is not so much what you plan that is important. Often the unplanned is what makes it memorable.

AUTHOR

Couples often complain that they are too busy to invest the time to be together. Yet in the next breath they will tell me of their dissatisfaction with how the marriage is going. I talk to them about the principle of input equaling output, suggesting that great results cannot be expected when the effort going in is minimal.

I share with them my early days in the speaking business. I recollect how I eagerly put in a business phone line, advertised in the yellow pages, and bought a desk.

Then I sat and waited for the phone to ring—I waited a long time. Since I had put in the minimum effort in launching my business, that was exactly what I was getting back—an occasional speaking engagement for a minimum amount of money. What idiocy it was on my part to expect great returns from minimal efforts.

Fast forward to the year after starting my business—when I worked twelve hours a day on promotion, advertising, writing, networking, and other activities to promote my services! My phone has been ringing ever since.

Marriage works the same way. You get out of it what you put into it. If you are always too busy, too tired, or too stressed to spend pleasurable times with your spouse, the rewards will be meager. If the bulk of your interests and passions lie outside the marriage, the relationship simply will not grow. If work, money, and possessions become your top priorities, your marriage will reflect this. If, however, you work together to discover shared interests, create new ones, and spend time together, your marriage will be the best part of your life.

Shared interests are the key. They give you things to talk about, plans to discuss, and memories to laugh about. They bond you to each other as you build a network of friends who share the same interests. They provide common goals on which to build your partnership and marriage.

CASE STUDY: Paul and Michelle

Seeking counseling after eight years of marriage, Paul and Michelle have two small children, ages five and eight. Michelle is a homemaker and tutors part-time at the children's school. Paul works as a tool and die maker for a manufacturing company. He frequently works overtime, often in excess of sixty hours a week. In his spare time, he trains his two horses and travels to regional horse shows.

"We just don't seem to have much in common," Michelle begins. "Paul wants to spend every weekend at the horse shows."

"Well, you can come, too. But you just don't seem interested," says Paul. "I love working with the horses. I would do it full-time if I could afford it. Instead it's just an expensive hobby."

"That's another issue—the money for these horses. Now he wants to buy a special trailer for $35,000."

"That trailer is for *us*. It has a sleeping section and even a small kitchen. We could live right at the shows."

"*You* could live right at the shows. I have no interest in it. This is *your* passion, not mine. I would much rather move to a bigger house close to the kids' school."

"How long have you had the horses?" I interject.

"I had one before we were married and bought another one three years ago. The new mare is a dream come true for me. I have always wanted a horse of this caliber. She earns ribbons and gains recognition across the country. I wish I had even more time to work with her," says Paul excitedly.

"More time? You are out there three and four nights a week and every weekend. As a family, we never have time to do anything together," protests Michelle.

"What about the kids?" I ask. "Do they enjoy the horses?"

"Well, my oldest daughter likes to go to the shows. She is a good rider and has won a few ribbons," Paul pipes up.

"But they get tired of it, too," says Michelle. "They want to do something else once in a while, like play with their friends or go biking. I wouldn't mind if this horse thing happened occasionally, but it goes on all the time. It consumes all of the spare time that we could spend together."

"Do you do anything else together?" I ask.

"We sometimes go to the movies," says Paul.

"Not really," interrupts Michelle. "When was the last time? I bet it was more than a year ago."

"I guess you're right. I work long hours, then work with the horses," Paul agrees. "I love what I'm doing. I'm living all my dreams."

"But I don't feel that I'm a part of your dreams," she responds.

Indeed she is not. Paul's passion in life is clearly the horses. His hobby consumes his spare time, energy, and resources—and Michelle is not a significant part of any of it.

Paul and Michelle stopped coming after a few more visits. Michelle contacted me several years later to report she went back to school to earn her college degree. Paul was still training horses but spending more time with her and the children. They forged a compromise that appears to be working. The long-term success of their marriage will depend on their ability to find other things in common as the children grow and leave home.

■ ■ ■ ■ ■

Having such a consuming interest creates difficulties in a marriage if one's partner does not also share the same interest. Now, before I get hundreds of letters from couples who insist they have nothing in common, but that their marriage is just fine, allow me to emphasize something else. It is a lot more fun if the passion in your life is a passion in your marriage. I *have* seen couples with nothing in common do well, yet I am guessing they have a great deal of money and can fly to Morocco for romantic getaways. If you are not booked for Morocco in the near future, give some thought to building up your common interests.

Myth: We talk all the time.

About the only thing that comes without effort is old age.

UNKNOWN

Almost without exception, my clients will state that marriage and family are the most important facets of their lives. Yet, "the average couple married ten years or more spends only thirty-seven minutes a week in close communication."[1]

Experts say many couples "spend most of their waking hours earning money to purchase more possessions, but do not take time to build a better marriage."[2] Couples focus on the large house, the new car, and the fancy furniture—rather than relationship-building. In two-income households, the situation can be even more dismal. In one-quarter of all two-income homes, the spouses work different shifts. In such households, couples experience poorer health, get less sleep, have fewer friends, and have less leisure time to spend with their mates. Their rate of divorce is slightly higher than the national average.[3] They simply do not have time to devote to each other and the marriage.

Myth: My life is perfectly balanced.

The time to relax is when you don't have time for it.

SIDNEY J. HARRIS

It is possible to "go the extra mile" with separate shifts, extra hours, night school, and the like in the short run, but it is suicide for a marriage in the long run. Charlie and I noticed early in our marriage that we argued a great deal more when we did not spend time together, and before long, the smallest thing irritated or annoyed us. We were not balancing the annoyances with leisure, fun, and passion.

It is much easier to give your spouse "the benefit of the doubt" if you can draw on numerous positive experiences at a time when a negative one occurs. And you create positive experiences by sharing interests you both enjoy.

So how *are* you doing with your time? Are your priorities clear? The eight sections in the *Wheel of Your Life,* pictured below, represent balance. Looking at the center of the wheel as 0 and the outer edge as 10, rank your level of satisfaction with each life area by drawing a straight or curved line to create a new outer edge. The new perimeter of the circle represents the *Wheel of Your Life*. How bumpy would your ride be if this were a real wheel?

Now look at a copy of the balance wheel completed by Paul, the horse trainer from the previous case study, on the next page. He is happy with career, health, personal growth, and recreation and extends the perimeter of the wheel to the outer edges in these areas. But his marriage, his time with friends, his financial resources, and his spirituality have all paid a price. The ride with this wheel would be very bumpy.

Balance is not something you achieve like a trophy that you display on a shelf. It is always changing and needing periodic attention and adjustment. Often just when we get one section of our lives operating smoothly, some other area gets out of balance. It is important to periodically take a snapshot of your balance and adjust the wheel.

We all have the same amount of time each day—twenty-four hours. How you spend that time is up to you. Consciously or unconsciously, you make decisions that structure your life in a certain pattern, a certain flow.

That structure has a lot to do with your stress, your happiness, and your marriage.

When you move to a home farther away from where you work, you decide that some more of your time will

Wheel of Paul's Life

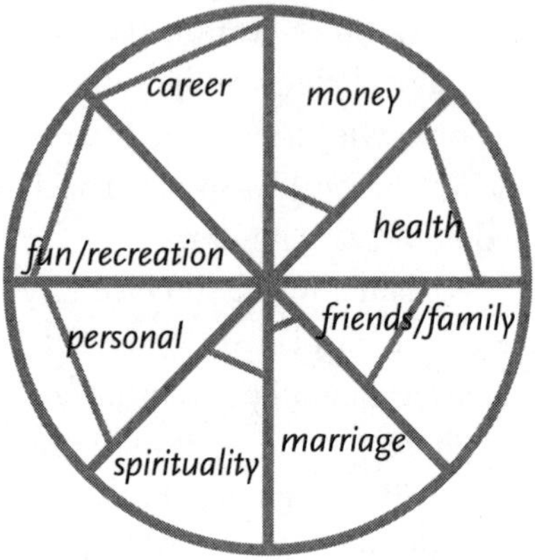

be spent commuting. When you take on the extra assignment at work, you decide that more time will be spent working. And when you try to have a perfectly clean house while the kids are little, you decide that you will spend a good deal of your time scrubbing.

Periodically review how you spend your time. Remember, time is a non-renewable resource—you only get so much. Are you spending your time the way you want?

In Mitch Albom's best-selling book *Tuesdays with Morrie,* Morrie discusses his views on marriage with Mitch:

> "If you don't respect the other person, you're gonna have a lot of trouble. If you don't know how to compromise, you're gonna have a lot of trouble. If you can't talk openly about what goes on between you, you're gonna have a lot of trou-

ble. And if you don't have a common set of values in life, you are gonna have a lot of trouble. Your values must be alike.

"And the biggest one of those values, Mitch?"

"Yes?"

"Your belief in the importance of marriage."[4]

Myth: We have nothing in common.

Half our life is spent trying to find something to do with the time we have rushed through life trying to save.

WILL ROGERS

Believing in the importance of marriage and making it a priority binds two people together with a common purpose and vision. Like a rudder to navigate through life, the vision provides a compass for your decisions. It will guide your decisions regarding what job to take, how many things you really need, and how you spend your time. As other forces tug on your marriage, it will guide the two of you to recommit to each other and refocus your efforts.

CASE STUDY: Ellen and Shawn

Ellen and Shawn have requested an emergency session due to sudden changes at Shawn's place of employment. He has just been notified that, due to downsizing, he will have to transfer to Denver within sixty days or be out of a job. A computer programmer, he has worked for the company for the last seven years and had believed he was in line for a vice president position. This downsizing has come as a surprise. Ellen and Shawn feel stressed and unsure of what to do.

"We just bought our house nine months ago and now we have to move . . ." Shawn begins. "I really don't want to go. We had hoped to start a family this year. Ellen was going to cut back at work. We had things all planned out."

"I'm trying to be positive," Ellen speaks up. "But, I'm not sure about this job for Shawn or the future of this company. How do we know that we won't make the move only to get downsized again after we relocate? And our families are here. I really wanted to keep our roots here."

"Do you two see any upside to moving? Could this be a new opportunity, a chance for a better position, a better lifestyle?" I ask.

"Well, that's another thing. The job is actually outside of Denver. I will either have to commute about forty miles a day or live in an expensive suburb. I'm not excited about doing either. We like the house we have. It's close to Ellen's job and provides easy access to all the things we like to do," Shawn states firmly.

"We purposely bought less house than we could afford," adds Ellen, "so we wouldn't be 'house poor' and not have money to do other things. Also, I want to stay home with our kids when we start a family."

"It doesn't seem like the two of you want to go," I reflect. "You sound clear about your plans and the vision you have for your life together."

"Yes, we thought we were, but this has turned everything upside down. I feel like I have to go. I have to be the 'good company employee,' although I really don't think I would have trouble finding something else here," Shawn says confidently.

"But look at all you have invested in the company," interrupts Ellen. "What if you can't find something else here? Maybe we should make this move and take a risk."

"Both of you are clear about what you are looking for at this point in your lives: a house you can afford, a short commute, and family as a priority. Before making a decision, check out opportunities here and see what's available. It may sway you in one direction or another."

"But the company managers are putting pressure on me for a decision," Shawn objects.

"Stall them. Tell them this is a big move and you need more time to sort it through. Take a couple of days off and check out the job market. It won't take you long to know what's out there," I purport.

Shawn called about a month later and announced he had landed a position with a local company for more money and with greater flexibility. The new position, Shawn believed, also held better potential than his job with his former employer because this new employer was expanding and growing. Shawn reported: "I knew it was the right fit a few minutes into the interview."

Shawn was able to know that this new job was a better fit because he and Ellen knew what they were looking for in their lives.

■ ■ ■ ■ ■

Know what is important in your life and know your priorities. Discover and rediscover common interests that will bind the two of you together. Constantly evaluate whether some new interests or activities might be added. And if you really enjoy something, make it an annual, monthly, or weekly activity.

WHAT ARE YOUR COMMON INTERESTS?

You love what you find time to do.

AUTHOR

This exercise is designed for you and your spouse to do together. Take the opportunity when you are having coffee or spending some time out together to identify interests you currently do together and ones that appeal to you both for the future. Circle all activities you and your spouse currently do together, even if only occasionally:

Watching TV	Going to Movies	Reading
Painting	Shopping	Photography
Darts	Pool	Remodeling
Scuba Diving	Sketching	Sky Diving
Biking	Swimming	Plays/Theatre

Walking/Running	Roller-blading	Kite Flying
Car Races	Sporting Events	Concerts
Camping	Traveling	Golf
Tennis	Cross-Country Skiing	Fishing
Collecting	Horseback Riding	Motorcycling
Boating	Cooking	Craft Shows
Weight Lifting	Playing Cards	Board Games
Bowling	Dancing	Hiking
Hunting	Museums	Art Shows
Snowmobiling	Ice Skating	Gardening
Snorkeling	Bird Watching	Landscaping
Downhill Skiing	Model Building	Water Skiing
Others: ________	______________	______________

Scoring: How many activities and interests do you have in common?
More than 25: Excellent; 20–24: Very good; 15–19: Good, look for new opportunities; 10–14: Fair, evaluate what could be added for the two of you; Fewer than 10: Identify new activities you would both like to try.

BUILD INTERESTS TOGETHER

People who cannot find time for recreation are obliged sooner or later to find time for illness.

John Wanamaker

Use the following tools to enhance the interests and excitement in your marriage. Grab a calendar and sit down with your partner to envision, plan, and implement activities designed to grow your relationship.

TOOL #1 Schedule a date night. Make regular events

together a part of your routine. Ideally weekly but not less than once a month, schedule activities that you both enjoy. If you have children, have at least two or three regular babysitters you can call. Tip them well so they are eager for your business.

TOOL #2 Spend time with happily married couples. Invest in your own marriage by building a network of friends also committed to their marriages. Go skiing, camping, or picnicking with other couples or families. Get tickets to sporting events and plays together. Consider a "dinner club" in which different couples host a dinner party. Not only do you spend time together, you also establish a network with happy people.

TOOL #3 Get physical. Consider combining time together with exercise. Walking, biking, tennis, golf, and hiking provide benefits for the relationship as well as fresh air and exercise. It will energize your body, your spirit, *and* your marriage.

TOOL #4 Plan a yearly family vacation. Consider it a must. The memories you gain are priceless. Vacations do not have to be costly or extravagant; many families go camping or rent a small cabin. Consider taking a vacation right where you live and take day trips to areas of interests. All of these provide a break from the routine and give the whole family a chance to bond with each other through enjoyable experiences.

TOOL #5 Try new things. Want some excitement in your marriage? Then try something new. It does not have to be jumping out of airplanes, though that is exciting. It can be getting up early and watching the sunrise while drinking a cappuccino, or roller-blading by the lakefront, or playing Frisbee golf. Talk about things you have always wanted to try together, then experiment and play with them.

TOOL #6 Laugh more. Look for the humor in everyday activities instead of "saving" your laughter. The more you look for humorous situations, the more you will find them. Humor is an attitude, an approach to life. When things go astray, ask: "Will this make a great story later when we tell it to our friends?" If the answer is yes, then it is not too serious.

7 I'm Going to the Hardware Store, Honey

STRATEGY 7: KEEP A PART OF WHO YOU ARE JUST FOR YOURSELF

It's not hard to tell when Charlie needs some time to himself. He flies out the door yelling: "I'm going to the hardware store, honey." I do not even bother asking, "What for?" Charlie can spend hours at Farm and Fleet just looking, hanging out with the power tools, and talking with the other guys from the neighborhood.

Last time he visited the hardware store, I asked Charlie to pick up a thermos for me. He returned with the thermos, a table saw, and a shiny red ax! Since he does some woodworking, I could understand the table saw . . . but an ax? As I questioned the purchase, my daughter stalked around the house pretending to be Jack Nicholson in *The Shining.* After all, we live in the city with mature trees and we order wood already split for the fireplace. "Why the ax?" I inquired.

"Because I needed one," was Charlie's reply.

Later that day, he was out back chopping on an old tree stump, whistling while he worked. I realized that the new tool was simply a sign of autonomy, a chance for Charlie to have something for himself.

We all have this need for autonomy, the need to feel in control of our own lives, the freedom to keep some part of who we are just for ourselves. Autonomy is the reason the business executive plays in a band on the weekends, or the busy homemaker studies stand-up comedy and appears at the local comedy clubs. Autonomy is the basic need to have something dear to our hearts that expresses who we are and helps us grow. It often does not make financial sense or even seem sensible to others, but it is essential for our balance, personal growth, and development. It is also critical for a happy marriage.

Autonomy, which literally means "self-law," is the ability to feel in control of one's life and to maintain personal independence. Closely aligned with freedom, it encompasses self-determination and the quest to run one's own life. Without autonomy in a marriage, people feel trapped, hen-pecked, and controlled. Resentment builds as frustration increases. Self-esteem plummets when the excitement one finds in life feels smothered.

The quest to be autonomous and independent is universal and begins in childhood, much to the chagrin of most parents. I remember clearly when my daughter, Stephanie, decided at age three that she wanted a kitten. She approached her dad with a well-thought-out list of reasons.

"Absolutely not," he yelled. "There is no way that we will have another cat in this house. We already have one. That's enough."

"But that one isn't *my* cat. I want one for me, one that will sleep on my bed and play with me," Stephanie exclaimed.

"No!" Charlie stated emphatically. "I said 'No,' and that's final. If another cat comes into this house, I will move out."

A few minutes later, Stephanie came out of her bedroom with a small brown suitcase, handed it to her dad, and said, "I'm going to miss you, Daddy."

She got the cat the next week.

Autonomy is an essential human need. As the counterpart to common interests, it is a critical element for a happy marriage. Wise couples actively work to find the balance between the two. While contented partners are devoted to each other, each partner has other interests and his or her own friends. Even in the best marriages, wise partners do not hitch all their dreams to one person. Unexpected things happen in life in unexpected ways. You need to know that you are complete as a person and able to manage your life.

Some couples, especially early on in their marriages, have this ridiculous idea that all their spare time needs to be spent together, and they leave behind any interests that they do not both share. This is *not* a good idea. The happiest marriages I see are those in which both partners have outside interests, friends, and activities.

Women often find autonomy and companionship with groups of other women. For over forty years, my mother played cards the first Tuesday of each month with an assembly of women from the neighborhood. The "card club" would rotate houses so that each member "hosted" the get-together about once a year. The preparation was always the same no matter who was the hostess: lemonade and beer, chips and pretzels, a new pack of playing cards, and a wood carrying case filled

Myth: We should do everything together.

Constant togetherness is fine—but only for Siamese twins.

Victoria Billings

with blue, white, and red poker chips carefully stored by color.

The first thirty to forty minutes of the "meeting" were spent exchanging information, amusing stories, and the latest adventures in marriage and child rearing. If all preceded smoothly, the pack of cards would be opened and the playing would begin. Table talk and laughter rippled through the house as they played games such as "500," "Rummy," or "Shit on Your Neighbor."

Through the years, this group shared the joys and heartaches of marriage, child rearing, careers, and the changing roles of women. Most importantly, perhaps, the group provided support in a very uncertain world. At some gatherings, the cards sat unopened and the chips remained neatly stored in their wood container due to more pressing matters. This certainly was the case when Esther's husband died of a sudden heart attack at age thirty-eight, leaving her with an eight-year-old son to raise. And there were no cards the night Connie announced, at age thirty-six, that she had been diagnosed with advanced leukemia.

Husbands were not invited to these get-togethers. I doubt they would have wanted to come anyway. These gatherings were for women only and provided support for almost half a century.

Men have similar get-togethers, like hunting or fishing trips or attending sporting events together. A male gathering might involve the weekly golf game, an annual opening day with the local team, or a hunting trip to Alaska. These get-togethers provide an opportunity for men to share a sense of camaraderie, to get a break, and to gain new perspective.

This balance between time together and autonomy is one of the critical challenges in a marriage. The need for autonomy requires understanding, communication, and a willingness to acknowledge that no one person, no matter how perfect, can fill all your needs.

> Myth: There is no way to balance.
>
> **It is the common interests that make marriages enjoyable, but it is the little differences that make them interesting.**
>
> AUTHOR

There is the old story about a newlywed couple. Shortly after the wedding, the wife becomes upset that her husband wants to continue on a bowling team and asks him to quit. He agrees to do so if she will give up her quilting class. She agrees to forgo the quilting class if he will stop playing softball on the weekends. They continue with these kinds of compromises and then realize, after five years: "You are not the person I married." As my teenagers would say, "No duh!" All of the exciting things that had made your spouse interesting and fun have been set aside.

It is easy for "time for yourself" to get lost, especially when careers and children are young. It can feel like there are not enough hours in the day. There is always another load of wash, another project at work, the yard to rake, and errands to run. The children have to go to the doctor, the mother-in-law needs help, and the bathtub has overflowed. It seems impossible to meet everyone's needs, let alone have time to do something for yourself. When there is extra time, the tendency is to do more of the same—extra hours at work for extra money, another PTA committee, or more childcare. Yet the ability to maintain your own interests and build new ones is critical for you and your marriage.

The ability to know what you want and how to get it is more complicated in a marriage. There are conflicting needs, limited resources, and sometimes ego threats that get in the way. You cannot both be out doing your thing when there are small children at home. You cannot both go to graduate school at the same time and still pay the mortgage. And sometimes what you used to be able to do is now impossible.

CASE STUDY: Matt and Laurie

Matt and Laurie, married five years, came to treatment due to increasing conflict over "outside" activities and decisions in their marriage. Matt is a very successful partner in a computer consulting company and Laurie works part-time as a social worker for a local agency. They have two children, Aaron, age five, and Jennifer, age two. They are avid cross-country skiers and have skied in numerous cross-country events—until the last few years.

"I don't have time to train anymore," complains Matt. "All I do is work, at the job and at home. I am not able to pursue my training like I once did."

"Well, I can't either," says Laurie defensively.

"I know, I know. Neither one of us is able to do the things we used to do. It's very frustrating. I used to train all weekend, even in the off season."

"What do you do now instead?" I ask.

"Well, we try to spend time with the kids. And there is always so much to do around the house," Matt laments.

"I just don't think we can run our lives the way we used to when we had no responsibilities," said Laurie.

"What do you mean?" I ask.

Laurie responds: "Well, we always vowed that children would not change our lives. We wouldn't be like other couples we knew. We would keep doing all the activities we always did and not let the kids interfere with that. But that's not the way it worked out."

"That's right," interrupts Matt. "We tried, for example, to take the kids biking. We bought two of those expensive trailers so they could sit in the back. We went exactly five miles and Jennifer was crying and Aaron wanted to go home. Now they put up a fuss whenever we get the bikes out. They want nothing to do with it."

"That was eight hundred dollars we could have saved," adds Laurie with a chuckle.

"We've tried to take them cross-country skiing with us too, but they only want to go a short way and then play in the snow," Matt observes. "I feel so tied down. Sometimes I feel like I have to ask permission to do the things I want, like I have to ask my mother."

"I'm not your mother," replies Laurie. "It's just that we have to coordinate what we are doing now. You can't just disappear and bike fifty miles and leave me with two kids and no help. Our lives just don't work the same way they used to."

"Well, I think you two have discovered part of the answer," I said.

"What do you mean?"

"Things aren't the same. You have two children, both of them at tough ages. You will only be frustrated and angry if you try to run your life like you did when kids were not in the picture. A two-year-old and a five-year-old do not want to train for competition: they want to play. They don't want to be left with sitters, they want to be with you. How can you change your life so you can still incorporate some of what you like to do and have it work in this new phase of your marriage?" I ask.

"Well, I've suggested that we get involved with downhill skiing again," Laurie shares. "There are a number of hills close by that cater to families. I think the kids would be much more interested in that, and we could do it as a family."

"But I would still miss cross-country. It's been a part of my life for a long time," complains Matt. "I miss the old days of training each weekend and going with friends to the events." He looks at Laurie and sadly states: "We used to do it together."

"Yes, that's very hard," I empathize. "This is one of the difficulties as our lives change and evolve. What worked well in one part of our lives does not work as well in another. Part of the solution is finding the joy in each phase with the children while still managing to carve out some time for your marriage. How could you do some cross-country skiing and make it work for your family?"

"You know, some of the hills have cross-country trails as well as downhill trails," Laurie offers.

"You're right. I didn't think of that. We could take the kids to the ski hill and switch off a bit so we both get time to get some cross-country skiing in," Matt says hopefully.

"And many hills also have ski schools for kids and other family activities that allow the two of you to ski together. While it is a bit of work to deal with all the equipment, travel, clothes, etc., I think you all would enjoy it once you got out there," I say encouragingly.

"I would be thrilled to get a chance to do what I love," Matt responds.

■ ■ ■ ■ ■

While not the way "it used to be," Matt and Laurie were able to work out a system for skiing and outside activity that included the family *and* individual time. By entering in periodic ski races and competitions, Matt was able to enjoy cross-country skiing without feeling that he was abandoning his family to train and participate. And much to both of their surprise, their kids loved the sport and quickly became very accomplished skiers.

Myth: There is no time for me.

Your life cannot go according to plan if you do not have a plan.

AUTHOR

Sometimes clients insist that no matter what they do, there is absolutely no extra time in their lives for individual activities. They go to great pains to convince me that their situation is simply different from anyone else's I have ever seen in the office. There is *not* a solution for them.

At this point, I share with them a story about my children when they were very small. The youngest was two at the time, and I frequently felt overwhelmed and exhausted. Some days I was so busy dealing with spilt juice, lost cats, and toothbrushes put down the bathroom drain that I had no time for a shower. Such was the case one fall afternoon. I was attempting to feed my toddler an early dinner. As most mothers know, feeding a toddler is time-consuming, as you actually have to spoon the food three times. You spoon the food in the mouth, wipe up the chin, and put the same food in again. If you repeat the process once more, you have accomplished *one* spoonful of food.

So I was sitting with my toddler spooning, still in my bathrobe, when my sister walked through the door. Dressed impeccably in a navy blue three-piece suit, she had just completed a board meeting downtown. She took one look at me and declared: "I think you have lived on the south side too long." We laughed, but I realized something about how I was living my life. I hardly took the time to dress some days. I was burned out with the kids, fried with housework, and desperately needing a break.

That night when Charlie got home from work, I confronted him with my frustration. "I never go anywhere," I started. "You go to the Y, you see your friends, and on Sunday you have time to watch the Packers."

"Well, there's always time for the Packers," he joked.

"No, I'm serious. I need a break from the kids. I never get to do anything for me. It isn't fair. I'm always stuck here. I don't get to go anywhere."

Charlie took me into his arms and said, "But who's stopping you? I would be happy to take over and give you a break . . . but you don't make plans. Any time you want to get out, just let me know and I will work around it."

I'm rarely speechless, but I was then. It was true. He never discouraged me from doing anything I wanted to do, let alone stopped me. It was me holding myself back. I felt that I had to give everything to the children, to the family, without saving a slice of life for myself. Even worse, if I did take time for myself, I felt guilty, like I should be doing something else. After all, I had so much to *do.* I had become a Dorothy Doormat, taking care of everyone else but me.

This is not uncommon, especially for women. We are trained to be the caretakers and nurturers. We give and give until we are burned out and resentful. Women often become the emotional caretakers in the family, tuning into everyone's wants and needs but their own.

According to researchers, women are "wired" to have a greater ability to connect with the emotions around them. Recent research by Raquel Gur and her husband, Ruben Gur, Ph.D., focused on the brain scans of volunteers who looked at photographs of actors depicting various emotions. Both men and women recognized happiness when they saw it, but women were much quicker to identify sadness. "A woman's face had to be really sad for a man to see it," Ruben Gur says. "The subtle expressions went right by them, even though their brains were working harder to figure it out. When it comes to reading emotion, men just don't get it."[1]

Perhaps because of this ability to read emotion, wives generally manage family activities, including relations with extended family. They arrange holiday and birthday celebrations, anniversaries, and family visits. Wives take on the primary role in managing the social life of the couple and family.[2] Call it intuition, or simply care-taking, women get so involved in caring for others, they forget to care for themselves.

Men, on the other hand, are more likely to overdo at

work. "Men have been socialized to place 'work' at the center of their lives, while 'love' is at the center of a woman's."[3] Programmed as the "provider," men often report feeling the pressure of making a living and paying the bills. They may feel they have no time for self-care or relaxation, fearful that if they slow down the economic well-being of the family will suffer. They become the Melvin Milquetoast in the workplace, only to experience stress-related illnesses such as heart disease and chronic fatigue.

Both men and women need a break, but they do not necessarily have to leave town to get that break. You can give each other space and give yourself permission to make your personal well-being a priority. Allowing each other to "do one's thing" will contribute to freshness and happiness in both of your lives. An important question to ask yourself when you are feeling like a Dorothy Doormat or a Melvin Milquetoast is: "What is stopping *me* from doing the things I want?"

- **Is there something you have always wanted to try?** Whether a new sport, art project, or hobby, consider trying it this year. It is easy to say you don't have time, but if you are watching at least two hours of television a week, you have time. We make time for what is truly important.
- **What did you used to do that you miss?** What is stopping you from doing it now? Stop putting off some of the things you really want to do because you have a case of the "shoulds" spinning in your head. You know the ones: "I should wait until the kids are older; I'll do it when I retire; I shouldn't take the time."
- **Creativity breeds creativity.** The creativity unleashed by spending some time focusing on yourself or trying something new can actually help you in

other areas of your life. I have often noticed that "writer's block" seems to go away and the ideas return when I do something else creative or get some physical exercise. Your creativity will spur creativity in your life and your marriage.

- **Stop the excuses.** You can always find excuses—too much snow, the bridge is out, the Packers won, the Packers lost. An excuse is simply a way to get others to partner with you in avoiding. In fact, as you verbalize your excuses, you will find that people will actually give you more excuses to use. What is the best way to get started? Get started!
- **Negotiate some space.** Do both you and your spouse a favor by agreeing that autonomy in your marriage is important and needs attention. Talk about what you would like to do and what feels fair. Trade off time away and support each other so you both can feel good about taking time to take care of yourselves.

Sometimes clients know they need to make changes but are unable to muster the energy or the confidence to get started. I suggest to them that this is one of the best benefits of having a spouse. Marriage provides you with a built-in cheerleader who can encourage, motivate, and applaud your accomplishments. "After all," I tell them, "you have to have someone in your life who contradicts your high school guidance counselor."

I tell them about my senior year in high school and the requirement that all students had to conference with the guidance

Myth: There is no way out of my rut.

There are high spots in all of our lives and most of them have come about through encouragement from someone else. I don't care how great, how famous or successful a man or woman may be, each hungers for applause.

George M. Adams

counselor before graduation. A gray-haired woman who lived behind a massive mahogany desk, she had a folder for each student with the names spelled out in all caps on the file tab. Inside each folder were copies of the SAT scores, recent academic records, letters of recommendation, and any disciplinary actions a student had incurred. Each student was given exactly twenty minutes to review the file, receive the "official" guidance recommendations, and exit with a three-bullet-point plan.

I remember my meeting as if it happened yesterday. I sat waiting in the hall with a line of students, eagerly anticipating my turn to hear the recommendations. I knew I had done well on my SATs. I was a good test taker and, frankly, I thought they were easy. I tried to anticipate what she would say. Maybe she would recommend a prestigious school in Boston, or even a school abroad. She might even suggest a special assignment with the government or an international agency in Switzerland. My mind was spinning with dreams—so many possibilities awaited me. Finally it was my turn.

I confidently walked to the seat next to her desk. Leaning forward, I waited for the words of wisdom that would change my life.

"You did fairly well on the SATs," she began.

I was beaming inside. I knew it. I just knew I did well on those tests. I sat there confident in the knowledge that she saw great talent in front of her. What would she recommend? Harvard? Perhaps skip college altogether and go directly into some kind of graduate program?

"However," she continued, "you really haven't done very well in high school."

"I didn't apply myself," I quickly explained. "I was bored with a lot of the work."

"Well, that may be; however, I really don't think you are college material."

I sat there stunned. *What? What does she mean, "Not college material"?*

"Really," she continued, "the only thing you show a real talent for . . . is . . . eh . . . typing. Look at this," she explained as she pointed to a column of grades on the academic report: "You got all As in typing."

"Typing was easy," I meekly explained.

"That's my point," she asserted with some excitement. "You would be *perfect* in a steno pool. Perhaps learn some shorthand. There will always be a need for a good stenographer in the world. Here is a plan for you."

She handed me a sheet of paper with three bullet points: *Typing, Shorthand, Filing.* "Oops, our time is up. Best of luck to you."

I walked out of the office feeling defeated and angry. I had received no encouragement on which to build any dreams or goals. I was left, in my mind, with only negative messages: "You can't do it. You will never do it. You are not college material."

Most of us receive negative messages like these at some point in our lives—maybe from a parent, a teacher, or a guidance counselor, or maybe just from ourselves. We begin to believe things about ourselves that are not necessarily based in fact. Maybe we do poorly in one math class and decide that we are not very smart. Possibly we were slow in one race and decide we are not athletic. Perhaps we feel shy at a gathering of strangers and decide we are not "people persons." The motto "I can't" becomes ingrained in our minds and we limit ourselves, our goals, and our lives.

An encouraging spouse can help you overcome these messages. He or she can give you a positive voice when all the negative voices remind you of your perceived shortcomings, life failings, and lack of basic talent. A motivating spouse can urge you on when the voices tell you to quit, and he or she can comfort you when the journey is slow.

By the way, I *did* go to college. In fact, I have three college degrees. It was Charlie who encouraged me to go to graduate school. He was the one who said I would make a great psychotherapist. His words have always been: "You can do it."

There will be times in your life when setbacks and discouragements make it difficult to keep your energy flowing. At these times, you need the magic of encouragement. Encouragement provides the fuel for success. The voice telling you that "You can do it!"—this is a gift you give each other in marriage. It costs nothing and it is an easy gift to grant to someone you love.

CASE STUDY: Ron and Denise

Ron and Denise came to treatment shortly after Ron began graduate school at the local college. Working full-time at the post office, Ron is pursuing an advanced degree in computer science in hopes of leaving his job and beginning a different career. Denise works as a teacher at the local high school. Both feel stressed, tired, and worried about their finances.

"I just think this is too hard," Ron begins. "Maybe I should wait until the kids are older to return to school. I'm working during the day and gone four evenings a week."

"But this is what you always wanted to do," argues Denise. "And you only have another year and a half to go until you graduate."

"I know, but a year and a half is a long time," Ron comments. "It's just not fair to you and the kids."

"It isn't fair to *you*, if you don't pursue this goal," Denise says emphatically.

"It sounds like the two of you are in agreement that Ron should go to school," I observe.

"Yes, we both agreed on it before I started, but my mother and sister think I am shortchanging the family," Ron confides. "They often call to check on us and feel there is too much stress and tension in our house."

"I think they're just jealous that *they* haven't gone on to school," counters Denise. "And your mother is convinced that the job at the post office is the best you will ever do. What's right for her is not necessarily right for you."

"I know . . . but maybe they are right," Ron says. "I worry about the money and the time spent away from you and the kids."

"There will always be people in your life who do not agree with your plans and dreams," I suggest. "Surprisingly, sometimes they are people very close to you. Perhaps they disagree because they don't understand your dreams, or they may even find change threatening. The important issue is whether the two of you agree. If you do, don't let others sway you from your goals."

"Are there some scheduling adjustments you can make to have home life flow a little smoother while you go to school?" I ask.

"Well, I've been debating whether to change to thirty-two hours a week for this last year. Then I could take some afternoon classes and still be home in the evening. It would be less money, but I think we could manage for one year," suggests Ron.

"I think that would be great," adds Denise. Then I would have more flexibility with my job because you would be home. We couldn't save any money for a year, but I believe your education is an investment for our future."

Denise and Ron are both positive about Ron's vision and their plans for the future, but they are letting outside influences affect their situation. Ron in particular is sensitive to the comments made by his family and has lost some of his momentum as he second-guesses his decisions and actions.

This couple benefited from outside support and some additional tools to use in providing encouragement to each other. Ron finished school and was able to obtain a much better job with higher pay and more flexibility. The results were well worth the extra investment.

■ ■ ■ ■ ■

Encouragement is the magic that allows people to reach new heights, attain new goals, and become the best they can. In successful marriages, partners offer large doses to each other on a regular basis.

Encouragement cannot be overrated. Few things cost as little yet go as far as words, looks, and gestures that boost your spirits and motivate you to greater effort and new achievements. Encouragement builds your confidence and self-esteem. It helps you believe in yourself and your abilities. It builds support for your vision and your partner's dreams, yet encouragement is often misunderstood.

Myth: Praise and encouragement are the same thing.

A minute of encouragement during a failure is worth more than hours of praise after a success.

AUTHOR

Praise is not the same thing as encouragement. Praise is awarded for a job well done, an achievement. It is given for completed tasks as a reward for the effort. This is one of the primary problems with praise; those who need it the most are least likely to get it. We all remember the kid in the front of the class who raised his or her hand and knew all the answers, but it was the struggling, discouraged child in the back of the room who needed the attention.

Praise is based on external evaluation and external control, often by an authority figure or parent. It usually involves "winners" and "losers" and creates a climate of competitiveness. The recipient may feel worthwhile only if he or she is "on top," which may be at the expense of others. The same people may "win" over and over again, while others become discouraged and resentful.

Praise can actually be discouraging. We can become over-reliant on the opinions of others, undermining our self-worth. We may become more hesitant to make decisions and take actions on our own, unsure of whether our decisions and actions will earn praise from those around us. Praise produces dependency at a time when we want to be autonomous and self-directed.

Encouragement is given for effort or improvement. It focuses on assets and strengths. It sends the message: "You don't have to be perfect, effort and improvement are what is important." Encouragement makes it clear that your contribution counts and is appreciated. Encouragement fosters cooperation and trust. Unlike praise, encouragement can be given at any time, especially during those times when you or your spouse is struggling. The special language of encouragement can make a big difference.

The more you practice giving encouragement in your marriage, the higher both of you will soar in achieving your goals. The marriage will feel like a haven from the world, a place to renew and rejuvenate, and a source of strength, inspiration, and support to pursue your dreams. Costing nothing, a daily dose of encouragement fuels your goals one by one and helps to make dreams come true.

WHAT IS YOUR VISION?

A goal is a dream with a deadline.

NAPOLEON HILL

1. Project yourself into the future, any time from tomorrow or several years from now. Imagine two days in your life that would be ideal days for you. Imagine a picture of what your life would be like. Write down the details.
   - ✔ What would you be doing?
   - ✔ Where would you be working?
   - ✔ Who would you be with?

- ✔ How would you be spending your time?
- ✔ How would you be earning a living?
- ✔ What would you be doing with your free time?
- ✔ What hobbies and sports would you be pursuing?
- ✔ What new interests would you want to explore?

2. Looking over these two ideal days, what changes would you have to make to give life to what you envisioned today?
3. What changes could you make tomorrow to move you closer to your ideal?

ENCOURAGEMENT TOOLS

Nine tenths of education is encouragement.

ANATOLE FRANCE

Encouragement has a special language all its own. Because encouragement focuses on effort or improvement rather than results, it can be given at any time to your spouse and to yourself. Try practicing using the following tools to support your efforts and to incorporate a regular dose of encouragement into your marriage.

TOOL #1 Phrases of encouragement:

- "I like the way you handled that problem."
- "It looks like you enjoyed that project."
- "Since you are not satisfied, what could you do to improve the situation?"
- "How do you feel about your efforts?"

TOOL #2 Phrases of confidence:

- "I have confidence in your decisions."
- "That is a tough problem, but I am sure you can handle it."
- "I know you will figure it out."
- "You have handled situations like that before."
- "I know you can do it."

TOOL #3 Phrases that emphasize contributions and appreciation:

- "Thanks, that was very helpful."
- "Thanks, I really appreciate ________, it makes the day go smoother."
- "I need your help with ______."

TOOL #4 Phrases that focus on effort and improvement:

- "It looks like you put a lot of effort into that."
- "It looks like you gave that project a lot of thought."
- "I can tell how much progress has been made."
- "This definitely shows improvement."

Attempt to make a conscious effort every day to use the language of encouragement with your partner and yourself. Practice the kind of positive thinking that translates into positive action. First, we act the way we want our lives to be and then, one day, we find we are not acting.

8 If You Really Loved Me, You Would Know What I Like!

STRATEGY 8: ASK FOR WHAT YOU NEED AND WANT

I remember my first wedding anniversary. I hinted for a month before the big event. Anticipating a piece of jewelry or maybe a special dinner, I could not wait to see how Charlie would surprise me. You can imagine my astonishment when I unwrapped a box containing vacuum cleaner bags.

"Vacuum cleaner bags?" I gasped.

"Yes," said Charlie proudly. "The first year is paper. I thought it was perfect."

Perfect? He thought this was perfect? I was hurt and angry. *How could he give me vacuum cleaner bags? How did he have no idea what I wanted? I had given hints for a month.*

Later, he informed me: "I cannot see into your head. If you wanted something, you should have asked."

"If you really loved me, I would not have to ask," I pouted.

"Who made that rule? I can't read your mind," he responded.

Myth: I have a glass head.

If you wanted flowers, you should have married a florist.

CHARLIE OATMEAL

"But I gave you hints for weeks. Remember, I showed you the newspaper advertisements for the jewelry sale at Boston Store," I said.

"Oh, that's what that was for? I just thought you liked the ad," he responded.

"If you really loved me, you would have known what I was thinking," I replied, petulantly.

"I love you, but I have enough trouble knowing what *I* am thinking. I don't know what *you* are thinking or what you *want* unless you tell me," he said firmly.

I learned something that first year. The best way to get what you want is to ask for it. And the clearer you are about your needs and wants the more likely they will be met.

I know, I know, having to ask for what you want is not romantic. Your partner should just magically be aware of your wants and needs. This is the fantasy of the glass head, which is based on the assumption that other people think and feel the way you do. Yet other people do not see the world the way you do . . . *even if they love you*. They cannot see into your cranium, your brain stem, or your gray matter. If you do not verbalize your wants and needs, your partner can only guess about them. It does not matter how much your spouse loves you or how much he or she may try, your partner will not be able to "read" you always.

Why we get into the glass-head game, I do not know, but this malady seems to be a common one. It is evident in the talk of married people:

"You should know how I feel." *No, it is clearer if you explain your feelings.*

"I thought you knew what I like." *Have you talked about it before?*

"If I have to ask for it, it doesn't count." *Says who? Who made up this rule? Your partner still has to make the effort once he or she is aware of what you want. That counts, as far as I'm concerned.*

"Surprise me." *Be careful. You may get vacuum cleaner bags.*

Myth: I can read your mind.

Assumptions are the termites of relationships.[1]

HENRY WINKLER

Your head is not made of glass and neither is your spouse's. A good rule of thumb in marriage is not to expect that your husband or wife will guess what is happening with you. Verbalize. This, of course, means the two of you have to communicate.

Worse than the glass-head believer is the mind reader. Mind-reading partners create a new meaning for every word. They do not worry about what is being said; they "figure it out" based on their knowledge of their partners and their presumed background in psychology. They have a tendency to disbelieve what is said. They know better. So they frequently "correct" their partners by telling them what they really mean.

CASE STUDY: Ken and Laura

Ken and Laura sought premarital counseling because they were having "communication problems." In the process of planning their wedding and reception, both were experiencing frustration and confusion.

Ken, quiet and reserved, works as an analyst for a local insurance company. His parents divorced when he was three years old, so he spent most of his childhood going back and forth between houses. His parents have both since remarried and moved out of the state.

Laura, a legal assistant for a large law firm, comes from an intact family. Her parents, thrilled over the upcoming wedding, were making every effort to support the couple in their decisions. They expressed concern, though, that the wedding would become too costly and urged the couple to make wise decisions regarding the caterer, menu, number of people, etc.

So Laura began the counseling session stating, "This whole wedding thing has ended up being more work than we thought. I just can't seem to get Ken really interested in all the planning."

"I'm interested," he offered. "I just don't know much about it."

"You just don't *want* to learn. Sometimes I don't think you really care whether the day is special or not," Laura said accusingly.

"Of course I do," assured Ken. "I would just rather not have such a big event because I'm afraid the real meaning of the day may get lost."

"I think you are afraid your parents will say or do something to embarrass you!" Laura said.

"Laura, I am not clear how you arrived at that conclusion from what Ken said," I interjected. "I heard him express a concern about the event becoming too large. I didn't hear him mention his parents."

"Well, I know that is in the back of his mind," she responded.

"How do you know that?" I asked. "Has he told you that in previous discussions?"

"Well, no," Laura replied. "I just know that it was really hard when Ken was growing up to deal with his parents' divorce and then to have to accept new step-parents. His parents would often argue and embarrass him. I bet he worries about that happening at the wedding."

"No, I'm really not worried," said Ken. "I really don't care *what* they do or say. This is *our* day and my focus is on you."

"I thought you were concerned about them," said Laura, noticeably relaxing. "That's part of the reason I wanted a lot of people at the wedding, so we would be less likely to have to deal with any conflict between your parents."

"Whatever gave you that idea?" Ken asked. "I got over being embarrassed by my parents long ago. Besides, they both have mellowed a lot since they remarried."

"Well, I just thought—" Laura began.

"Next time, ask me," Ken stated firmly.

■ ■ ■ ■ ■

It is critical to believe what your partner is saying and not to make assumptions. Assumptions can lead to wrong conclusions and guessing can lead to mistakes. Communication is confusing enough without attempting to read minds and responding, quite possibly, based on inaccurate information. Stay focused on what your partner says, and believe the words you hear.

> Myth: I am a great listener.
>
> **One of the hardest things to do in life is to listen without the intent to reply.**
>
> UNKNOWN

When we establish the importance of honesty and saying what we mean, we are likely to take more care in our communication with one another.

Most people believe they are good drivers—it is always the other guy who messed up in traffic. In the same way, most people think they are great listeners. Yet often what a couple describes as communication is really two monologues in duet. Neither individual listens. Each focuses on what to say next, not on what their partner is saying. Each listens to bits and pieces while carefully planning his or her next comment.

Listening is not the same as hearing. People hear many things without really concentrating. Listening takes effort. "The verbal content of the message spoken and heard comprises only 7 percent of the communication transmitted. The tone of voice conveys an additional 33 percent. The other 60 percent is expressed by body posture, gestures, and facial signs."[2]

To communicate meaningfully, focus on the person, not just the words. Effective communication involves a number of skills. It means being open to the feelings behind the words. It means taking time to clarify confusing statements. It often involves asking questions to glean more information. And it may involve repeating what you heard to clarify the message and to offer information back that lets your spouse know he or she has been heard. Active listening is a lot of work.

CASE STUDY: Christopher and Tammy

Married seven years, Christopher and Tammy came to counseling because of constant arguing. With two small children, ages six and four, both Tammy and Christopher acknowledged it was difficult to find time to talk without interruptions.

"What do you argue about?" I asked.

"Anything!" Tammy said, chuckling. "We seem to start a conversation and pretty soon we are arguing about a minute detail. I don't think Chris listens."

"Yes I do," said Chris. "It's just that she wants to talk when I'm in the middle of something."

"You are always in the middle of something," Tammy replied. "When is a good time to talk?"

"Well, someone has to do some work around the house," Chris suggested.

"Oh, are you saying I don't do my share? Well listen, buster, I chase these kids around all day. What do you do? Watch TV!" shouted Tammy.

"So now I don't deserve to watch TV!" said Chris, raising his voice too.

"I think I get the picture," I interrupted.

After a moment of quiet, Tammy stated: "That's exactly what happens."

"It is interesting how you two started by discussing how you want to communicate better, yet you ended up fighting about housework and TV," I noted. "Neither of you are trying to hear actively what the other is saying. Rather, you anticipate an argument and gear up for it."

"Yes, that is it," agreed Tammy while Chris nodded his head.

"Let's try again," I suggested. "Tammy, you stated that you do not feel that Chris listens to you."

"That's right," she said. "When I try to talk to him, he turns away or watches TV. I don't feel like I have his full attention."

"If you did have his full attention, what would he be doing?" I asked, wanting to get specific behaviors for Chris to try.

"Well, he would look me in the eyes as I am talking. Maybe he would nod his head or add to the conversation," Tammy responded.

"Do you think you could do that?" I asked Chris.

"Sure," said Chris. "I do listen to her. But if this helps, I am willing to try. I think it would work better if we agreed on good times to talk, too," he added.

"What do you mean?" I asked.

"Well, I would love to sit down and talk when I *first* get home, to unwind and connect," said Chris. "But sometimes Tammy waits until I'm into a TV program or reading the newspaper. Then I'm distracted."

"What do you think?" I asked Tammy.

"Sure." Tammy agreed instantly and then said to Chris, "I always thought you wanted to relax first, so I waited until later when you were watching TV. It really would be better to talk when you first get home because the kids are usually napping at that time."

■ ■ ■ ■ ■

By focusing on behaviors and agreement, this couple was able to move away from blaming and move toward listening and problem solving. Both were willing to commit to talking for a minimum of five minutes a day, with each promising to focus primarily on listening. Each agreed to use new listening tools that included repeating what was actually said by the other before responding. This not only slowed down the discussion, but also allowed more time for listening. It really forced each of them to concentrate on what the other was saying. As they experienced success in their communication instead of frustration, they became more committed to really listening to each other.

Myth: I do not have to listen if I am not interested.

Before marriage, a man will go home and lie awake all night thinking about something you said; after marriage, he'll go to sleep before you finish saying it.

HELEN ROWLAND

As I have indicated, my husband Charlie is a Green Bay Packers football fan. And Charlie is not just an everyday Packers fan—he is an avid, obsessed, crazy fan who has followed the team for thirty years. Each Sunday, as the Packers windsock blows on the front porch, he sits in his Packers jersey with his Packers coffee cup and cheers his team. Through the Packers' glory years, as well as those laced with embarrassment and humiliation, Charlie has never wavered from his loyalty.

Charlie not only watches the games, the pre-game shows, and the replays, he also monitors the progress of the team on a daily basis. Draft choices, training, injuries, coaching—all activities are evaluated and discussed. The sports page is the first thing he reads in the morning and the NFL wrap-up is his final activity of the day.

Football? I have no interest in it at all. As I mentioned in Chapter 7, I do not believe a couple has to share everything. I cannot understand why football is so popular or what the special attraction of the Packers is for my husband. It is clear though—Packers' football is important to

Charlie. So I listen to his analysis of "what was wrong with the last play" and "the coaching mistakes," and I attempt to look engaged. I follow the saga of quarterback Brett Favre's thumb injury and the special problems of handling the ball when the temperature is below 10°. I listen to Charlie discuss the team's approach—"sitting in the pocket, having the good mixture, and hitting early and often." I seldom have a clue what he is talking about, but I listen.

I know there are times he does the same. I highly doubt he is interested in my free sample bag from the Clinique sale. While he attempts an expression of interest when I show him fabric swatches for drapes in the dining room, I doubt he is really excited. And his feigned enthusiasm about choosing borders for the bathroom is just short of hilarious, but clearly he tries.

Myth: I cannot keep communication on track.

If one person says you have a tail, you can ignore it. If three people say you have a tail, you had better turn around and look.

AUTHOR

Good communication, or a good connection, means *trying* even though you are clueless—even if you do not care about the topic. You pay attention and attempt to connect because you are committed to the relationship and to each other.

In attempting to understand the world from the other person's perspective, you are demonstrating the ability to empathize. Empathy is one of the most important characteristics of a mature, committed relationship. The ability to see the world through someone else's eyes is *to walk a mile in another's moccasins,* to paraphrase a popular Native American expression. It is important to make the distinction that being empathetic does not necessarily mean you agree with another's point of view. It simply means that you *understand* and can even *feel* where the other person is coming from. And we all really want to feel understood.

I love the beginning of the movie *The Fugitive*. One of the opening scenes shows Harrison Ford's character in a bus accident, with a train barreling down the track toward the bus. He narrowly escapes through the bus window, only to see the train coming off the tracks and plowing through the earth toward him. With only a fraction of a second to escape, he manages to jump out of harm's way. Still, the viewer is not sure where the train will go, whether the hero will be injured in the process, or what the final outcome will be.

Experiencing excitement like this is great at the movies, but I would rather not experience it at home. The roller coaster of arguments that go nowhere, the fights with no end, and the piles of unresolved issues sap energy and time. They block trust, destroy intimacy, and erode a marriage.

Several communication behaviors that partners engage in resemble a train wreck. These behaviors "derail" a discussion, barrel nowhere, and invite disaster. You know when you are derailing because you feel like you are having the same fight over and over again. Or, when you argue, you are left feeling unsure of what you were arguing about in the first place. You start on one subject and end up at another destination—just like a train off its track.

Some behaviors characteristic of communication that is derailing include the following:

- **Defensive body posture or tone** As soon as your partner starts to talk, you feel your defenses going up and you feel yourself becoming almost eager for the battle. You may cross your arms, look away, or use other gestures to push away what your partner is saying. As you brace yourself, your face shows an attitude that suggests to your spouse, "Go ahead . . . make my day!"

- **Eye rolling** This technique makes it clear to your partner that you do not value what he or she is saying. It is hardly worth your time! An obvious put down, this behavior makes it clear you are not listening. It is impossible to have good eye contact or connection with your spouse if you are rolling your eyes.
- **Tongue clicking** Reminiscent of your third grade teacher, this behavior is designed to make your partner feel small and foolish. It conveys the thought: "Only an idiot would be saying those things and presenting that opinion." Designed to shame and interrupt, it is received about as well as it was in third grade.
- **Head shaking** This goes well with tongue clicking. It is a technique intended to push away the words of your partner and communicate your disagreement, even before his or her sentence is finished. Once you start shaking your head, usually you are no longer listening. Then your partner may waver in presenting a position. He or she knows you will not validate anything about to be said, as you are poised to disagree.
- **Sighing** You are bored and you want to make sure everyone knows it. This technique did not work well for Vice President Al Gore in the 2000 Presidential Debates, and it will not work for you. Your partner will resent it. Sighing indicates that you are not interested and that you can find a million other things more fascinating. Stifle the sigh; it only derails.
- **Cutting others off** Designed to "stop them cold," cutting people off makes it clear you have only been waiting to "have your say" and are not interested in what they wish to share. By interrupting, you make sure you get your chance to drive your point home. The discussion becomes more of a battle of "who is right" and "who is wrong" than "how can we agree."

The discussion shifts from understanding each other to declaring a winner and loser.

- **Yelling and screaming** This is a natural outcome of cutting others off. When people feel they are not being heard, they tend to speak louder. And as you and your partner get louder, it becomes clear no one is listening. Instead, it becomes a contest to see who can yell the loudest. Like pouring gasoline on the train wreck, emotions start to ignite, and someone is likely to get hurt. The derailment is proceeding at full speed now and will soon end at an unplanned destination.
- **Cursing** This is another way that you or your partner can "up the ante." Swearing adds to the drama of the discussion. It fuels the smoldering train wreck until feelings of anger and resentment erupt.
- **Name-calling** This is a natural follow-up to cursing, since so many curse words are derogatory labels. This technique is often used when one of you feels you are losing the argument. By adding name-calling and labeling, you can "get back" at your partner. It makes it possible to hurt that person, as he or she has hurt you. While the childhood chant, "Sticks and stones may break my bones, but names will never hurt me" has a nice ring to it, don't believe it for a minute. Names *do* hurt and so do words. Hurtful words hang in the air; you cannot take them back.
- **Sarcasm** Often used by folks who fancy themselves "intellectual," sarcasm is nothing more than a camouflaged insult. Designed to hurt and confuse, it derails the communication because your partner has to pause and wonder what you really meant. Of course, he or she is simply supposed to know. The partner is left feeling like a moron! It is a lot clearer if you say what you mean and mean what you say.

- **Emotionality** Excessive tears and sobbing may feel like a nice release, but they can stop communication dead in its tracks. Your partner will not want to be totally honest with his or her feelings in the face of your tears. Some of the tough stuff just needs to be discussed without the immediate "sob response" that tends to shut things down.
- **Door slamming** Dramatic and loud, door slamming gets attention—sometimes more than intended. One young couple was having an argument when the wife dramatically slammed the door of the apartment and stormed into the hallway. The noise startled the neighbors, who all peeked out their doors and up and down the hallway. The woman stood sheepishly by the door waiting to get back in her apartment. She did not use this technique again.
- **Suitcase-pack** More drama. This technique brings the commitment right into focus, with the message: "This is so bad, I am leaving." It erodes the foundation of the marriage because your partner does not know whether you are serious or just being dramatic. Taking off with your suitcase makes it impossible to work things out, and sometimes your partner may call the bluff and leave too. One woman who frequently did the "pack the suitcase and leave" routine came back to find that her husband had moved out. He left not a clue as to where he went. So keep the luggage in the attic if you are not going on a real trip.
- **Pouting** Another third-grade derailment technique, pouting involves building a fortress around yourself. You put up the walls and make it clear that no one can get in. With practice, good pouters can make life difficult for those around them. This time, the train is off the track and you have blocked the road so the

repair crew cannot get to the site of the accident. Pouting can stretch a routine argument into a battle lasting for months.

Clients routinely tell me that they wish they were closer to their spouses, although they often build concrete walls that keep them separate. These walls are called *defense mechanisms,* and they do just that—defend and protect us.

Myth: It is not me that blocks the communication.

No one ever listened themselves out of a job.

CALVIN COOLIDGE

Defense mechanisms are necessary in order to function in the real world. It would be very hard to conduct business, fight off aggressive salespeople, or negotiate a car deal if we did not use some defenses. Designed to protect our inner core, defense mechanisms are necessary for healthy functioning and survival.

They can become a problem, however, in our intimate relationships. With your spouse, it is important to let the defenses down and allow the walls to crumble. When "stuff" is in the way, it is impossible to feel close and connected.

Some of the most common defense mechanisms include the following:

- **Denial** Interestingly, many people can list the things their spouses do wrong, but they have to think for a moment about their own contribution to the problems. Denial makes you unaware of your own behaviors. You cannot see in yourself what others see. Like the emperor in the story *The Emperor's New Clothes,* you are blinded by the obvious and cannot view yourself clearly. Ideally, your spouse can be a very important mirror for you. He or she can be that special person who provides constructive feedback and coaching—a mentor to help you reach your goals.

- **Projection** This defense works well with mind reading. Instead of listening to your spouse, you simply "project" your feelings onto him or her. You decide what he or she thinks, feels, wants, or intends without checking out your assumptions. Even if what comes back is different from what you thought, you use your crystal ball to declare what he or she *really* means. Spouses who use projection spend a lot of time interpreting and analyzing how their partners feel rather than listening to what their partners actually say.

  I am reminded of the story about the sixth grader who comes home from school and asks his mother, "Where did I come from?" Mother launches into a detailed discussion of human reproduction, sexuality, and childbirth—to the confusion of her son. "Mom, I'm not interested in all that," he says finally. "It is just that Billy is from Detroit and I was wondering where I'm from."
- **Manipulation** As if communication is not confusing enough, you may say one thing when you mean another, or what you say is a shading of the truth in order to get your needs or wants met. Sometimes manipulation does work, but your partner may feel tricked or used in the process. Like the couple who is driving home and the woman insists they get off the freeway to get gas at Exit 92. After filling up, she insists that they stop at a casino that just "happens to be closeby." Not totally honest, she attempts to get what she wants by manipulating the situation *and* her spouse.
- **Censoring** Perceiving yourself as a bit of an expert, you have strong opinions on how the world and

other people *should* work. You use "shoulds" and "shouldn'ts" for how people feel, think, act, believe, and behave. When things are not working according to your rules, you spout the "should" philosophy to prove your point. The problem is, you can be right and still be so very wrong. I believe my teenager *should* keep his room clean, but his room looks like a bomb exploded in it most of the time. I think my husband *should* remember every birthday and holiday. Guess what? He does not. Censoring implies a critical judgment of others, as if we are the authority. People are annoyed and resentful when they are censored. As one spouse put it: "Quit shoulding on me!"

- **Passive/aggressive** Pretending you do not care about a decision or an event, you agree with your spouse, only to become angry and resentful after the fact. For example, a husband asks, "Where would you like to go for your birthday?" "I don't care," the wife replies. The next week when they are out to dinner, she says, "What is so special about this? I eat everyday. I thought you would make more of an effort for *my* birthday!"
- **Rescuing** Another technique that prevents honesty in relationships is letting your spouse off the hook for things that are his or her responsibility. A husband may feel embarrassed when his partner is given negative feedback or a wife may make excuses to others for her partner's behavior or action. These people have no need to be responsible for their actions because their respective spouses rescue them and justify what they do. Rescuing prevents you from seeing your partner accurately and giving honest feedback.
- **Stamp collecting** This technique seems to be a specialty area for women, but men are known to do it too. You may keep a running list of "issues" you have,

without ever letting issues go. You may stockpile these issues so you have a warehouse of ammunition for the next argument that can be brought up in the heat of battle. You use your ammunition at such times—not to solve anything, mind you—just to bolster your side if you are losing ground. If necessary, you can produce a list that includes forgetting to pick up Aunt Ida for the family picnic six years ago, bouncing a check back in college, and denting the car last spring. Enough already! You likely have enough new issues to argue over without pulling out a laundry list from the past.

- **Over-controlling** Believing you are usually right, you find it difficult to let go of an idea, method, or plan. You expect your partner to go along with what you say and want. You may even get impatient when he or she fails to go along with you or to do it your way. Of course, *your way* is right. From how you place the toilet paper roll with the sheets on top, to sorting laundry, to sanitizing the bathroom, to parking the car, it is your way or the highway. Over-controlling is likely to get you nowhere.
- **Defensiveness** You immediately feel attacked when your partner attempts to give you feedback, no matter how gently. You take criticism personally and feel your spouse is just being too tough on you. If your partner disagrees with you, you feel attacked and wounded. Others describe you as "too sensitive," but you cannot seem to help it. The shield goes up, preventing you from taking in any new information that just might be helpful. Interestingly, compliments ("What an attractive dress!") are often treated the same way. You consistently respond in a predictable way: "You like this dress? You can't like this old thing! This is nothing special!"

- **Rationalizing** You are able to find ways to justify any of your actions, beliefs, or behaviors that your spouse does not agree with or like. Good with words and analysis, you can spin a response so well that your spouse gives up and tells you that you are right. You pride yourself on your intellectual abilities without understanding that you simply "feel through your head," instead of through your heart. Sadly, it keeps your spouse and others at arm's length. He or she wants to be connected to your heart, not married to your brain.
- **Shutting down** The old silent treatment puts an end to communication quickly. No matter what your partner says or tries to say, you make it clear you are not listening. You refuse to engage, either verbally or through body language. You use your silence to punish. As it takes considerable effort to maintain the silence and live together, the wall gets higher and thicker. A time comes when you would like to resume communication but you have no idea where to start. The wall of resistance is too high and your partner has long ago given up wanting to scale it.

Use of these defense mechanisms and derailing behaviors may result in a communication disaster for you and your spouse. Accomplishing something positive is unlikely. Rather than resolving the problems you had, more problems surface. The walls prevent you from connecting at a feeling level and understanding each other's point of view.

Observe the use of derailing and defense behaviors with the following couple.

CASE STUDY: Jim and Susan

Married six years, Jim and Susan were court-ordered to take counseling after a domestic altercation ended in violence.

While neither party was seriously injured, both received citations for disorderly conduct and for pushing each other. Reportedly, neighbors called the police due to the yelling and screaming coming from the apartment. Jim, a salesman for a car dealership, worked long hours and frequently came home exhausted. Susan stayed home full-time with their two-year-old daughter, Angela.

Both presented as angry and discouraged, with little insight into what was wrong in their marriage.

"I'm glad someone called the police," Susan started. "It was getting out of hand. That is not good for Angela. Why do you have to raise your voice so much? You are so angry and mean," said Susan as she began to cry. (Emotionality)

"Me? You're the one who started it," Jim replied. "I think you are jealous because I can raise my voice and be assertive (Projection) and not act like a sniveling mouse like you." (Name-calling)

"This dialogue is not very productive," I interrupt. "Why don't you tell me how this incident started."

"Jim came home in a bad mood. His job is very hard and his boss doesn't appreciate him," (Rescuing) said Susan. "He started complaining about the way I did the laundry and kicked the wash basket across the floor."

"She doesn't do it right," said Jim. "She puts the whites in with the blue jeans and doesn't turn the shirts inside out so they won't fade. She should know how I like my laundry done! Everyone knows you don't just throw clothes in." (Censoring)

"Why don't you do your own laundry if you are unhappy with her efforts?" I asked.

"Because she is home all day, and a good wife should be able to do the laundry," Jim said, getting angry.

"My best just isn't good enough," said Susan sobbing. "He complains about my cooking, how I handle Angela. Even at our first anniversary, he stormed out of the room because the steak was not cooked right." (Stamp collecting)

"Things would work fine if you would just do what I say.

I know a lot more about running a house than you do," said Jim. (Over-controlling)

Interrupting the session, I had both Jim and Susan review their behaviors and defense mechanisms. With the focus on themselves rather than the "other person," both could see how their defenses were derailing their efforts. Since a small change could lead to a big change, they each focused on one area to work on for the next week. They were also asked to discuss everyday events for five minutes each day. The next week, they were both amazed at how the amount of conflict in their relationship had lessened.

"I don't know if it's just because we are both trying, but we didn't have a real argument all week," said Susan. "We actually sat down and laughed at what the kids were doing."

"We mostly talked about little things, but it was a lot more relaxed," said Jim. "I just hope it can last."

"That is entirely up to the two of you," I said. "You have the power to determine how you will treat each other. This is a good beginning, and you can build on it."

■ ■ ■ ■ ■

With encouragement and commitment, this couple was able to stop the use of defense mechanisms that interfered with their intimacy—one wall at a time.

HOW IS YOUR COMMUNICATION?

A happy marriage is a long conversation, which always seems too short.

ANDRE MAUROIS

1. Which derailment techniques do you use? Check all that apply:

- ☐ Defensive body posture or tone
- ☐ Eye rolling
- ☐ Tongue clicking
- ☐ Head shaking
- ☐ Sighing
- ☐ Cutting others off
- ☐ Yelling and screaming
- ☐ Cursing
- ☐ Name-calling
- ☐ Sarcasm
- ☐ Emotionality
- ☐ Door slamming
- ☐ Suitcase-pack
- ☐ Pouting

Out of this list, pick the two that are the most problematic for you. These will be the two that you concentrate on for future communication.

2. Which of these defense mechanisms do you use to build walls between you and your spouse? Check all that apply:

- ☐ Denial
- ☐ Projection
- ☐ Manipulation
- ☐ Censoring
- ☐ Passive/aggressive
- ☐ Rescuing
- ☐ Stamp collecting
- ☐ Over-controlling
- ☐ Defensiveness
- ☐ Rationalizing
- ☐ Shutting Down

Pick one primary defense mechanism that builds a wall between you and your spouse. Agree that you will support each other in your efforts to reduce the frequency and intensity of using this defense.

COMMUNICATION TOOLS

To keep your marriage brimming, with love in the wedding cup, whenever you're wrong, admit it; whenever you're right, shut up.

OGDEN NASH

TOOL #1 Focus on your two derailing behaviors. Have you found that you yell too much? Consider putting a dollar in a jar each time you raise your voice. Do you tend to pout when you are upset? Ask your spouse to hug you when you get into this behavior. The key to changing behavior is to do anything different. If you do something different, you will get different results. Review progress on a weekly basis. For most couples, if you get rid of your two primary derailing behaviors, you will increase the intimacy in your marriage by 70 percent and reduce the conflict by 90 percent.

TOOL #2 Identify your primary defense mechanism and agree with your spouse that you will tear down that wall. Remember, this is the time to take your own inventory, not evaluate your spouse's behavior. It is easy to see the faults in others; it is much more difficult to confront your own. What is the defense mechanism that most gets in your way? Describe it to your partner and commit to making a concentrated effort to reduce and diminish its use.

TOOL #3 Agree to talk, uninterrupted, five minutes each day. This means the TV is off, you are not reading the paper, and you are focused on what your spouse is saying. This may sound simple, but it actually takes commitment and follow-through. Many couples are amazed at the improvement when they commit to talking every single day.

TOOL #4 Ban "always" and "never" from your vocabulary. These are fighting words. Since it is unlikely that statements are *always* true, because you do not always do something considered negative and it is unlikely that you have never done something positive, the immediate response is to become defensive and retaliate. Always and never invite an argument and pour gasoline on any conflict. Charge a dollar each time one of you uses these words to fuel an argument.

TOOL #5 No museum pieces. Let the past stay in the past. If you have an old issue that has to be discussed so you can put it to rest, schedule time and discuss it. Then let it go. Agree that you will not bring up old issues when you are arguing or problem solving.

TOOL #6 Throw away the crystal ball. No matter how smart you are, you cannot read minds—and do not expect your spouse to either. The best way to ensure your message and feelings are known is to express them. Take at face value that your spouse is saying what he or she means.

Sometimes I feel like I've been
tied to the whipping post. . . .

"WHIPPING POST" BY THE ALLMAN BROTHERS BAND

9 Why Can't You Fill the Ice-Cube Tray?

STRATEGY 9:
EXPRESS FEELINGS TO EACH OTHER

Standing by the large picture window in our living room watching Charlie leave for work one summer morning in the early years of our marriage, I reflected on how easy it was for him. He just showered, grabbed a cup of coffee, pecked me on the cheek, and bolted out the door. He was going to a large, downtown company to TALK WITH ADULTS. He would have a morning coffee break, with time to read the paper. He would not have to eat spaghetti or toasted cheese sandwiches for lunch. In fact, he would be able to actually *finish* his lunch with no one bursting into tears. Watching him drive away, I remember sighing as my three-year-old yelled from the bathroom something about the cat being in the toilet.

Talk about the grass being greener. Charlie's life looked easy, even fun. I pondered my reflection in the bathroom mirror. A tired woman peered back at me, dressed in a faded pink bathrobe with spit-up on her right shoulder. I scanned our modest flat and inventoried the sink piled with dishes, the dirty clothes bulging from the top of the hamper, and the books strewn across the floor in front of the bookcase—the result of a recent "search and destroy" mission by our son. I felt little energy to tackle the day and was convinced it had to be easier to be employed.

I was able to recover somewhat by the time Charlie returned home around 6:30 that evening. Appearing exhausted, he flopped in front of the TV and picked up the evening newspaper. As I raced around the kitchen attempting to get barbequed chicken, tater tots, and steaming carrots on the table, our two-year-old found a screwdriver and successfully removed the back of the stereo. Filling the water glasses for dinner, I reached in the freezer and found we were out of ice cubes.

"I wish you could at least fill the ice-cube tray!" I hollered over my shoulder.

"Well, you're home all day . . . is that too much to ask?" he replied.

"I'm not the one who uses the ice," I barked. "I'm not your mother, you know. Can't you do anything for yourself?"

"Listen, I work all day," Charlie said defensively.

I continued on my tirade: "What—and I don't? How easy do you think it is to chase after these kids, never getting a break, stuck with all the messes around here?"

"Messes, you want messes?" Charlie responded. "You should see what I walked into this morning. Four PCs were down, my best technician gave his notice, and the boss says we are paying too much in overtime. Believe me, I am not sitting around sipping a cup of coffee watching *Good Morning America*."

"And who gets to watch *Good Morning America*? You have no idea what goes on around here," I shouted.

"Well, it doesn't look too hard to me. You get to play with the kids, go to the park, and read *Curious George* books. Sometimes I feel like all I do is work," Charlie said and then sighed.

"At least you accomplish something at work. I face the same messes over and over again. I just barely finish the laundry or cleaning when I have to start all over again," I lamented.

At that point, Ken ran laughing into the room, pushing his sister in a walker.

"How much trouble can these great kids be?" asked Charlie smiling. "I wish I had more time to spend with them. The work at the office never ends, and I rarely see anyone smile all day."

"Well, it's not all smiles here either," I responded. "It is a lot of work that is never finished. I feel like I'm everyone's maid."

"Well, sometimes I think *I'm* just a paycheck," Charlie snapped.

And the argument continued. Both of us were so eager to prove our own point and make it clear we had the worst of the deal, we really did not listen to what the other person was saying. Certainly neither of us stopped to think about the other's feelings.

When I share this story with couples in therapy, they usually nod their heads and say they know that argument. They glare at each other with a "See, I told you so!" look. They miss the point. The point is not who is working the hardest, or whose day was worse, the point involves feelings.

Understanding each other's feelings is the beginning of true intimacy. I routinely talk with couples about the danger of just hammering on and on from their own respective points of view. I make it clear that they should try to understand first, then try to be understood. I warn them of the dangers of listening only to the words spoken without connecting to the feelings behind the words. And I caution them about the potential for relationship disintegration when feelings are ignored.

Myth: You should know how I feel.

You can jump off a cliff to prove you are right, but you are still dead when you get to the bottom.

AUTHOR

Feelings are at the core of conflict in a relationship. However, too often in a marriage each of the spouses appears eager to batter the emotions of his or her partner over matters of little consequence. I am amazed how intensely a couple will argue a point to prove that he or she is right and the other is wrong.

I emphasize the importance of focusing less on who is "right" and more on what is being felt. Recognizing that each partner may have his or her feet stuck in the mud of "being right," I stress that it is not necessary to even agree with a partner's feelings. I instruct the couple that all each of them needs to do is acknowledge the reaction of his or her spouse and express understanding.

The quicker the focus is on the feelings part of a conflict, the faster an issue will be resolved. By using the techniques presented in the last chapter to break down defenses, you will understand feelings more quickly. Feelings are not right or wrong, they just are. An argument is not lost if you understand your partner's feelings, and you will broaden your own viewpoint and open yourself up to more love and understanding.

You may have a tendency to confuse feelings or use complicated words to describe them: "I am not angry really; I am a little frustrated and aggravated." I call that *feeling through your head*—taking an intense feeling, squishing it into a little ball, and then forcing it into a cubbyhole in your brain. Feeling through your head is trying to intellectualize something that is really visceral, something deep inside.

Feelings do not exist in your head; rather feelings are in your gut, your throat, and your chest, and they can wrap around your stomach until it hurts so bad you cannot eat. Feelings can choke you at the base of your diaphragm and make it difficult to breathe. Feelings can cause your temple to pound while your arms and legs feel weak and shaky. Feelings are often difficult to locate, difficult to name, and difficult to explain to someone else.

Still nothing feels as intimate between two people as sharing, exploring, and understanding each other's feelings. The connection between two hearts and souls—this is the true intimacy in marriage, and it is that bond we are all looking for in this world.

The problem is that many of us are not all that good at it. A training program for understanding and embracing feelings may not have been a part of our growing up years.

I have found it is a lot easier to express feelings if you keep it simple. In Alcoholics Anonymous and Al-Anon, the philosophy of *KISS* is stressed. KISS stands for Keep It Simple, Stupid. Emphasized in the KISS viewpoint is the need to refrain from making things overly complicated. A psychodrama workshop is not required—nor primal scream therapy—in order to express what is inside. Simply learn the basic feeling words and practice using them.

Consider using the following words to describe *your* feelings:

MAD SAD GLAD SCARED
ASHAMED HURT

- **Mad (Angry)** Feeling frustrated? That is probably mad. I know we hate to admit that we are mad. Dogs get mad, not us, so say *just a teeny little bit angry,* but give it a name. People seem to have a lot of trouble with anger, either stuffing it so deep inside that it chokes them or letting it explode in a scary way like a bottle rocket on the Fourth of July. It is possible to express anger appropriately, but it takes practice. Anger is no more a negative emotion than any other feeling, but most people have very little training using anger for positive growth.

- **Sad** Sadness to many is easier to express than anger. Sadness is more socially acceptable and less frightening. Women in particular seem to feel more comfortable with feeling sad. I know women who cry when they are angry, sob when they are sad, and hold back tears when they are happy. I happen to be one of the latter, so I do not dare watch *Old Yeller* with mascara on. So with women, strong emotions are often reduced to sadness and tears.

  In contrast, since many men have been taught that tears are not "manly," you rarely see sadness expressed by them publicly. Often male sadness gets transformed into anger, which is perceived as more macho and thus more acceptable. Are you beginning to see how confusing this can all be?
- **Glad** How often do you share feelings of happiness with your partner? Do you even acknowledge feeling happy to yourself? Sometimes I ignore or push away glad feelings instead of relishing them. I may even try to talk myself out of them, pondering why I would be so happy today. After all, the car needs new brakes and I was just notified that the IRS is going to conduct an audit! But sometimes I feel happy in spite of myself, and it is great to give this expression. It is especially useful to acknowledge glad feelings if your spouse had a hand in creating them. Expressing happy

feelings actually creates more happy feelings. Expressing joy and contentment to each other will bring more joy to your marriage.

- **Scared** Many of us secretly love to be scared at movies or on thrill rides, yet most of us hate to admit it. Fear seems to be an emotion we try to grow out of—since "only little kids get scared." We are taught that being brave is a sign of adulthood and the sign of a "well-adjusted person."

  Yet many arguments in marriages are based on fear and insecurity—fear that your partner may leave, fear that you are no longer attractive, fear that something disastrous will happen. All of us have many fears and insecurities. Even if we push them deep into hiding so no one can see them, they still bubble up to the surface and burst onto the scene at the most inopportune times. Once again, we find ourselves feeling like children under our covers, turning on and off our blinker flashlights, and imagining strange sounds downstairs.

  Fear can drive us to say and do things we really do not mean. It is important to understand this fearful part of each other and provide each other reassurance.

- **Ashamed** People are not all that nice sometimes. It may be hard to admit, but we all say and do things that we later regret—such as asking the clerk at a well known fast-food restaurant if there were "mouse heads" in the chili! I really did that! I had read that a woman found a mouse head in her chili, and thereafter, whenever I took the kids to this particular fast-food restaurant, I would ask the server to hold the mouse head. Finally one day, I noticed that when I said this, I really embarrassed my husband and kids. Ashamed, I realized I should never have said it, and I have not mentioned mouse heads since (except for here, of course).

- **Hurt** Many a quarrel or rift in a marriage begins because of the hurt feelings of one of the partners. Hurtful actions or hurtful words create wounds that are difficult to mend. Sometimes the hurt is inflicted without our realizing it or intending it. We may feel that a partner's hurt is unjustified because it was not our intent, but that misses the point. If your arrow missed the target and accidentally impaled your spouse, the wound is still painful and your partner is hurt. You may not be able to take the hurt away or heal the wound, yet it is important to acknowledge a partner's hurt feelings and to express how very sorry you are.

Myth: Expressing my feelings should be easy.

No one is as angry as the person who is wrong.

PROVERB

Okay, you ask, so how do I do it? How can I tell my wife I am angry without blowing a gasket? How do I tell my husband how hurt I am without sobbing and turning into a blob? The answer . . . practice. Like anything else in life, expressing your feelings takes practice if you want to do it well. In marriage, like parenting, when we do what seems "natural" or instinctive, we may get the worst results. We are likely to do a great deal better when we think about our options, choose our words carefully, and use tools that can help us when times are rough.

One tool that works well in marriage is the "I statement." It looks like this:

I feel __________
when you __________

Fill in the first blank with a word from the feeling list and the second with a behavior of your spouse. For example, "I feel sad when you don't call me during the day," or "I get scared when you are late." These sound and impact much better than: "You never call me!" or "You are always late." Rather than focusing on blame, an "I statement" identifies the feeling of your experience. The "I statement" promotes understanding instead of defensiveness.

To be able to use "I statements" in the midst of conflict, you have to practice using them when there is peace. And when you practice using the "I statement" technique, start with glad feelings and with small issues. It is best not to begin with issues like the charge cards or your mother-in-law. We will get to those. Start with little things—and practice, practice, practice.

> Myth: If I am not mad at you, my anger should not bother you.
>
> **Holding on to anger is like grasping a hot coal with the intent of throwing it at someone else; you are the one getting burned.**
>
> BUDDHA

Anger scares people, and angry people are scary. Sound obvious? I guess it is, but I have seen many relationships absolutely demolished because one or both partners cannot handle anger appropriately. When anger is expressed inappropriately, it is like walking in a minefield. You are never sure when a bomb is going to go off and what part of your heart and soul will be torn apart.

People who have intense anger seem to believe that just because *they* feel it, they have a right to express it. Just because the anger is justified, they can ooze it all over the house. They practically puke anger—on their spouse, their children, and anyone else who gets in their way.

Years ago, I interned at De Paul Rehabilitation Hospital, a drug and alcohol treatment center. We often joked that we could tell the health of the family by looking at the family dog. Clients would bring in pictures of their family all dressed up and smiling for the camera. Huddled and cowering to the side would be the family dog, looking scared and downtrodden. Accustomed to the tension within the family, this poor creature could not fake "happy" for the picture.

Sometimes clients insist that others are responsible for their mood or their yelling. They report that they were not in a bad mood until they came home, or their spouse asked about their paycheck, or their shirts were not ironed properly, or the cat peed on the carpeting, or they discovered they were out of toothpaste. "Who wouldn't lose it?" they ask me incredulously.

I then tell them the story of the New Yorker who buys a newspaper every morning at a newsstand on Madison Avenue, and every morning the clerk grabs his money without so much as a thank you. In spite of this treatment, the New Yorker politely thanks the clerk and wishes him a good day.

One morning his friend asks him, "Why do you continue being so pleasant to that guy? He's rude to you every morning."

"Because I am not going to let someone else determine my mood or my day."

We all have to take responsibility for our moods, our responses, and how we treat others around us. Blame is just another name for avoiding responsibility, and that will keep you stuck—stuck blaming your unhappy childhood, your third grade teacher, the pimples you suffered in high school, and the job you lost when your company closed. Enough already!

Clients try to tell me that when *they* yell, it "doesn't count" because they never hit anyone. They insist they are not even mad at their spouse, the children, or the dog. They just sometimes have bad days and need to vent when they get home from work. Well, here's a newsflash: It feels like puke for the people in the room when they "vent." Whether they are mad at another driver, their boss, or their spouse, the yelling, screaming, and swearing at home all sounds the same. It is a dump—and it is happening right in the middle of the living room. Like fallout from a nuclear bomb, it sprinkles down on everyone and does not dissipate easily. Long after they are done venting and are feeling cheerful again, the fallout remains in everyone's hair, eyes, and mood, and the effects of the fallout do not feel very good. Consider the following couple.

CASE STUDY: Patrick and Melissa

Married almost nine years, this couple came to treatment after Melissa threatened to file for divorce. Pat, a salesman for an office furniture company, is frequently on the road working long hours. Melissa is a supervisor at a local bank and is responsible for the teller and customer service areas. They do not have children, although Melissa has a grown daughter from a previous marriage. The precipitating event that led them to seek treatment involves the remodeling of their house.

Talking softly and slowly, Melissa explained, "We just finished a nine-month remodeling project."

"Yes, nine months of hell!" interrupted Pat.

"We added a master bedroom and bath to the rear of the house," Melissa suggested. "It was a nightmare. We had problems with the plumbing, the electrical work, the foundation—you name it and we had a problem with it. It seemed like everything that could go wrong, went wrong."

"I still say they screwed us," said Pat angrily. "Those guys didn't know what they were doing. I don't know what you were thinking when you picked that contractor."

"Pat, you are raising your voice. Would you please quiet down a bit so we can talk?" I requested.

"That is the way he was for nine months," Melissa

pointed at Pat and continued, "only worse. He was angry every day. He would call me at work and complain about the workmen and the equipment, and question the decision to remodel."

"I told you! It wasn't *you* I was angry at. I was angry at what was happening," said Pat.

"Let me get a little background here," I interrupted. "Didn't you both agree to remodel?"

"Well, it was my idea initially, but Pat agreed once we drew up the plans," explained Melissa. "We both picked the contractor and signed for the loan."

"You helped pick the contractor?" I asked.

"Sure, but I didn't really want to remodel in the first place," Pat insisted.

"But you did agree to it?" I persisted.

"Yes," Pat conceded. "It wasn't that I was angry at Melissa, it was just that the whole project was so frustrating."

"But you took it out on me," Melissa said and then began to cry. "Everyday getting your phone calls at work, dreading for you to come home, knowing that you would be angry about something else. It drained me. It took all the joy out of the project."

"Well, I like the house now," interrupted Pat.

"Yes, but I paid quite the toll to get there," snapped Melissa.

Melissa certainly did pay quite an emotional price for the remodeling project. Pat mistakenly believed that expressing his anger on a daily basis shouldn't affect those around him. I carefully explained to him that he had to learn to deal with his anger differently. Otherwise, the anger would become a wedge between them and block other feelings they both valued. Fortunately for this couple, Pat was willing to work hard with a counselor and learn other responses.

■ ■ ■ ■ ■

Try not to let anger create a cloud in your house. If you find yourself getting easily angered, attend anger management classes or work one-on-one with a counselor. It just might be the best investment you ever make in your marriage.

Sometimes couples attempt to deal with conflict by just avoiding it. It is as if, by ignoring the problems that fuel conflict, the problems will simply disappear and be forgotten. While there certainly is wisdom in letting a few minor problems roll off your back like rain, my experience is that the big issues do not roll very well. Rather, they get stuck about halfway down and then stab you in a kidney or other delicate area. These issues eat at you and build up to the point where everything your partner does will irritate the heck out of you. You eventually may wonder if you can get into the Witness Protection Program and move away—even though you have not been involved in a crime.

Myth: There is no benefit to arguing.

What counts in making a happy marriage is not so much how compatible you are, but how you deal with incompatibility.

LEO TOLSTOY

You may start to feel that you have to walk on eggshells around your partner or you may slip and spew something that has been bottled up for a long time. Although we are wise not to walk around sharing whatever thought or feeling comes to mind—even though it would make for interesting meetings at work—it is important in our intimate relationships to be honest and straightforward with feelings and issues.

We all are likely to know couples that brag about how little they argue, how they agree on everything, how they never have problems. Personally, I dislike people like this. They leave me feeling like a failure, struggling in the quicksand and needing to seek assistance at the self-help section of the bookstore. Then I remind myself that according to the Coalition for Marriage, Family and

Couples Education in Washington, D.C., the number one reason for divorce is "the habitual avoidance of conflict." The ability to deal constructively with conflict is a plus in a marriage. Other researchers also have found that "distressed couples avoid conflict much more frequently than non-distressed couples."[1] Out of struggle comes opportunities for personal growth, and when you are growing, the marriage is too.

Myth: We need to agree on everything.

One of the best hearing aids a man can have is an attentive wife.

GROUCHO MARX

The key is not to avoid conflict but to learn to deal with conflict more effectively. If you are growing, you will always, always have arguments with your spouse. The goal, however, is to make the disagreements less often, less volatile, shorter in duration, and more productive. In dealing with conflict effectively, you have to learn how to express feelings appropriately.

Although dealing with issues head on, expressing feelings, and negotiating a compromise are all important, I routinely warn couples that they will never agree on all issues. Too many couples have the mistaken belief that they must work out every discussion, every disagreement, and every minute point that comes their way. They expend a great deal of energy arguing over the best laundry detergent, the most efficient way to pack the car, the optimal setting for the thermostat, the importance of making the bed with decorative throw pillows, and the personality characteristics of certain relatives and extended family members. They may explore, at length, the *correctness* of each other's personal habits—the importance of flossing, the best toothpaste, and which way the toilet paper goes on the roll.

I have seen such discussions in which each partner

insists he or she is right with remarkable vigor, time, and repetition. The debaters may produce receipts, documents, and spreadsheets to support their positions. Random calls may be made to innocent bystanders with requests at short notice to confirm a particular point of view. A quick check of the Internet may be used to locate research studies or other statistical material that proves, once and for all, the validity of a particular opinion. I perhaps, on occasion, have been a participant in such discussions myself.

A point is reached somewhere between the thirty-seventh and fiftieth discussion of the same issue where partners may as well agree that they will never agree, as this appears to be a fairly safe conclusion. After all, both members of the union have already eagerly promoted their respective point of view comprehensively and convincingly.

> Myth: Being in love means never saying you are sorry.
>
> **I told my husband, "I can only be great in one room of the house, you decide which one it should be."**
>
> JOAN RIVERS

While it may be difficult to let the argument go, and each spouse may wish to hammer his or her point into the ground (like endlessly pushing the elevator call button in hopes that the elevator will arrive faster), at some point it is best to agree that an agreement will not be reached. The partners might then be able to walk away shaking their heads at how bullheaded a spouse can be, how he or she can lack even the resemblance of common sense, and stupidly but smugly smile at the correctness of their personal position. While not a complete victory, it provides for each spouse a reasonable peace and a sense of relief that the battle is over.

Of course, the most magical part of this prolonged arguing to prove one's point is that you discover over time that most discussions do not mean much anyway and likely are of the utmost unimportance in the larger scheme of life. You will find, after several years of marriage, that very little is worth fighting about, and you may even conclude that life is too short to put a lot of energy into trivial matters.

Agreeing to disagree is one of the wisest decisions couples can make.

The following passage is from the best seller *Love Story,* by Erich Segal, which sold 21 million copies.

> I wasn't running now. I mean, what was the rush to return to the empty house? It was very late and I was numb—more with fright than with the cold (although it wasn't warm, believe me). From several yards off, I thought I saw someone sitting on the top of the steps. This had to be my eyes playing tricks, because the figure was motionless.
>
> But it was Jenny. She was sitting on the top step.
>
> I was too tired to panic, too relieved to speak. Inwardly I hoped she had some blunt instrument with which to hit me.
>
> "Jen?"
>
> "Ollie?"
>
> We both spoke so quietly; it was impossible to take an emotional reading.
>
> "I forgot my key," Jenny said.
>
> I stood there at the bottom of the steps, afraid to ask how long she had been sitting, knowing only that I had wronged her terribly.
>
> "Jenny, I'm sorry—"
>
> "Stop!" She cut off my apology, then said very quietly: "Love means not ever having to say you're sorry."[2]

Read by college coeds, tired housewives, and millions of

others, *Love Story* became a mantra and prescription for how love should work. It was made into a movie starring Ryan O'Neal and Ali McGraw (her last decent appearance, by the way). Millions of romantics believed this was the way love should be. After all, the idea that love was sufficient, with no apology ever necessary, was firmly in print and broadcast on the big screen.

But who made up this rule? Does supporting research exist? Is it true that apologies are really not necessary in healthy relationships? I have had hundreds of couples come in for marital counseling quoting *Love Story* and using it to rationalize a personal preference not to take responsibility for bad behavior. Let me be perfectly clear: Being in love *means* saying you are sorry—sorry for things you did, sorry for things you did not do, and sorry for things you may not even know about. You say you are sorry if your spouse is hurt, sorry that he or she is angry and sorry you cannot help more. You say you are sorry the world is such a tough place, that we have to pay taxes, and the car won't start. You say you are sorry that the kids grew up so fast or not fast enough. You say you are sorry when parents are sick and sorry your partner has to work so hard. And you say you are sorry that life is so unfair and then ask what else you can do. In a happy marriage, you move away from "who is right" and "who is wrong" to "who is hurt" and "how can I help." And you *do* say, "I'm sorry" if you think it will help.

HOW DO YOU ARGUE?

Let the wife make the husband glad to come home, and let him make her worry to see him leave.

MARTIN LUTHER

Answer the following questions as honestly as you can to evaluate your own arguing style.

1. Your partner is upset because of something you did, but you don't think you did anything wrong. How do you handle this?
   A. Immediately mention the many times he has done something wrong that upset you.
   B. Storm out of the room yelling, "Of course, I'm the one that's always wrong about everything!"
   C. Ask for more information, letting him know that you want to understand how he felt about the incident.
   D. Immediately say you are sorry, recognizing that he is probably right.
2. You wish there was more romance in your relationship. How do you handle this?
   A. Tell her that she is about as romantic as a cleaning woman or man.
   B. Accuse her of having an affair, since her affection must be going elsewhere.
   C. Tell her that you love her and would love to receive more affection. Give her specific examples of what you mean.
   D. Do not do anything, realizing that you cannot change her.
3. During an argument with your partner, you often:
   A. Bring up as many museum pieces as you can to win the argument.
   B. Say things that you later wish you could take back.
   C. Use "I statements" to explain your feelings and encourage your partner to do the same.
   D. Walk away or try to change the subject.
4. You come home from a long day at work and find the kitchen a disaster with dirty dishes, pans, and leftover food. Your partner was home all day with the kids. How do you handle this?

- A. Immediately label him "Mr. Clean" and let him know that he has to clean up the mess.
- B. Accuse him of being blind to the mess.
- C. Let him know how overwhelmed you feel after working all day and would appreciate it if he would clean the kitchen.
- D. Quickly change clothes and begin cleaning the kitchen. You know no one else will do it.

5. Your spouse forgets to tell you that she has to work all weekend and you made plans to watch football with some old friends. If you had known sooner, you could have made arrangements for childcare but now it's impossible to find someone on such short notice. What do you do?
   - A. Tell her that she is selfish and thinks the world revolves around her and her schedule.
   - B. Say, "I'm in charge here and I'm tired of you trying to run things. I'll stay home this weekend, but you owe me big time."
   - C. Make sure that she understands why you are so upset. Stress that the two of you need to take time to communicate in order to coordinate plans.
   - D. Let her know it is no big deal. You are just sorry she has to work.

Scoring: Add up your As, Bs, Cs, and Ds. Which category is represented the most? Review the following key for your most prominent style.

A. Manipulator—*Winning an argument is important to you and you will do anything to win, yet you lose with this approach. Your spouse will feel manipulated and angry, which often leads to withdrawal and/or defensiveness. Use the following tools to modify this style.*

B. Exploder—*When upset, you tend to lose control, sometimes yelling or becoming verbally abusive. Use the extinguishing techniques to stop this behavior. It may also be helpful to obtain professional help.*

C. **Talker**—*You have the skills to solve problems and use techniques to reveal feelings. Be careful that you listen as much as talk. It may be more difficult for your spouse to open up if you do all the talking.*

D. **Avoider**—*You give in, keep the peace, and avoid making waves. Unfortunately, you sweep more than just problems under the rug, you sweep your feelings too. Practice speaking about your feelings using the "I statements" and work with your spouse to discuss important issues.*

SHARE FEELINGS WITH YOUR PARTNER

The formula for achieving a successful relationship is simple: you should treat all disasters as if they were trivialities but never treat a triviality as if it were a disaster.

QUENTIN CRISP

TOOL #1 Recognize what you are feeling. The first step in sharing feelings is the recognition of our own feelings. Practice throughout the day by taking the time to tune into your feelings and name them. Refer to the simplified feelings list and do not make it too complicated. Say a feeling out loud, then incorporate it in the statement: "I feel ______ right now." This exercise will get you into the habit of talking and thinking at a feeling level.

TOOL #2 Practice "I statements." In building skills or changing behaviors, practice is necessary. For one month, commit to making "I statements" three times a day using the feeling list. Does it feel awkward and silly? Good. Then you know you are doing something differently. If it felt completely natural, it would be what comes naturally.

TOOL #3 Extinguish explosive behavior. Get out the money jar again. Any time your spouse feels you are raising your voice or becoming angry, put a dollar in the jar. You may even want to start with five dollars so it really gets your attention. When the jar gets full, go out for a romantic dinner and talk about your progress.

TOOL #4 Become a parrot. When the two of you are having conflict, practice repeating exactly what you heard your partner say before responding. Allow your spouse an opportunity to correct any language that is not consistent with his or her intent. Keep repeating what you heard until you both agree on the accuracy of what was said. This process slows down the discussion and promotes listening. You will feel validated and heard because your partner has taken the extra time to listen and understand.

TOOL #5 Need some space? Set the timer. Feel the need to cool down or just get out of the conflict for a while? That is fine, but set a time to return to discuss the issues that have led to conflict. Do not return in less than an hour or stay away longer than half a day. Allow each other to leave the conflict, and then think, reflect, and return with a commitment to settle the conflict in a positive way.

TOOL #6 Write down what you believe is the other person's point of view. When you come back together to talk, do not start by talking. Instead, come to the table with a pen and paper. Immediately write down what you believe accurately describes your partner's point of view and his or her feelings. Then read your papers out loud. This exercise helps both parties feel heard and understood.

TOOL #7 Face each other and hold hands. At a time when things are especially tense, it is exactly the right time to work on getting closer. Try this technique. Put two chairs together and face each other. Sit with your knees touching and hold hands. As you look into each other's eyes, express your feelings using "I statements." Agree that neither one of you will break away until you both feel that there is closure in the conversation.

TOOL #8 Repeat what the other person says. As you listen to each other's feelings, repeat exactly what you hear and not your interpretation of the content. If your wife says, for example, "I feel hurt when your mother criticizes me," you would not respond, "So you think my mother hates you." That is not what she said. Practice repeating the exact words and paraphrase the discussion.

Use phrases such as:

"So, I heard you say . . ."

"I understand your position to be . . ."

"You seem concerned about . . ."

TOOL #9 Ask clarifying questions. Use questions to let your partner know that you are really interested and listening to what he or she has to say. Utilize phrases such as:

"Tell me about . . ."

"Explain . . ."

"How do you feel about . . . ?"

"Describe . . ."

TOOL #10 Understand the feelings. What are you feeling? What is your partner feeling? Use the feelings list and identify which words are closest to what you are feeling. Use "I statements" to express your feelings to your partner. Practice when you are not having conflict so that the use of "I statements" works easier when you most need the tool. And try to make more use of the feeling GLAD.

TOOL #11 Offer three solutions to solve the conflict. Can you come up with one or more solutions that would solve the problem and eliminate the conflict? Try to come up with a minimum of three, no matter how far-fetched the solutions seem. Brainstorm with your partner until some solutions become apparent.

TOOL #12 Separate the issue from the person. Just because your partner may appear to have made a dumb decision, it does not mean he or she is dumb. Just because you acted selfishly, doesn't mean you are selfish. And just because you do not agree, it does not make your partner wrong. Focus on solving the issue without shooting the messenger.

TOOL #13 Don't insist on winners and losers, or who is right and who is wrong. If someone has to lose, then the relationship loses. If someone has to be wrong, then the relationship will feel wrong. Focus on understanding, not winning. Understand your spouse first, the issue second.

TOOL #14 It is okay to agree to disagree. There are some issues you will never agree on. That is okay. You do *not* have to agree on everything. You can agree to disagree and stop attempting to convince your partner that your point of view is the right one. The argument is closed, completed, caput. Put it to rest, in the can. Time to move on.

Money? It's a gas.

"Money" by Pink Floyd

10

We Still Have Checks, So How Can We Be Out of Money?

STRATEGY 10:
SPEND LESS THAN YOU EARN

I grew up with hair—lots of hair—that was dyed, tinted, razored, permed, moussed, and spiked. In my house, we created new 'dos with brush curling, finger waves, braiding, straightening, ironing, crimping, and orange juice can rollers. We utilized barber clippers, thinning shears, blunting scissors, razors, shavers, and other defoliators. Hair was very important.

One of my earliest memories of my mother is of her leaning over the kitchen sink squirting malodorous perm solution on colored plastic rods covering my head. Each rod had been wrapped—"not too tight and not too loose"—with a strand of hair lined with perm paper. The strong fragrance of the curling chemicals stung my nostrils and eyes as the cold liquid drenched my scalp and dripped down onto my shirt and hands.

When the timer buzzed, we knew that the perm solution had softened the hair to "take the curl" and the first part of the torture was over. My hair was then towel-dried and the "fixer" applied. Once again, my torso was draped over the sink while the freezing fluid dripped in patterns onto the ceramic tile. Then the final rinse—and each roller was removed. Row after row of perfect S-shaped curls cascaded down my face. The next day at school came the reward—all my classmates noticed my beautiful new "perm" and golden waves.

That was life growing up with my mother, the beautician. We always had the latest hairdos, cosmetics, beauty equipment, and supplies. If there was a new frosting technique, my sister and I were the first to have our hair pulled through a cap with a crochet hook and each strand of hair brushed with bleach formula. When the new eyebrow wax arrived on the beauty scene, we walked around the house on a Sunday night with yellow goop on our brows to prepare our "arches" for the coming week.

The world of beauty was my framework, my upbringing, so I thought nothing of buying a new hot roller kit about a month after I married Charlie. It was on sale and I picked it up for twenty bucks. When Charlie came home and saw it on the table, he was furious. He shouted, "How could you spend twenty dollars on *that* when we barely have enough money this week to eat?"

I stared at him in amazement. I could not believe he was even questioning me on this purchase. Had he no realization of what it took to curl hair? It went without saying that hot rollers were essential. What was I to use—an old iron heated on the stove?

"But how can we be out of money? We still have checks," I joked. "And after all, I can't go to work without fixing my hair. My other hot roller set burned out."

"Well, we can't afford it!" he insisted.

"Can't afford it? That's like saying you can't afford underwear."

"We should have talked about it first. After all, we are married now. And I didn't plan for hot rollers in this week's budget."

Naturally, my immediate impulse was to call oh, maybe fifty of my very closest friends to get *their* opinion on this hot roller discussion. I mean, should one be forced to face the world with hair that looks like it was styled with an eggbeater? I knew full well, of course, whose side they would be on, but I resisted. I also did not call my mother, though my hand trembled over the phone in righteous indignation.

It was painfully clear that I had married the most insensitive, narrow-minded, unsupportive man on the face of the earth. It was obvious that he did not have even a rudimentary knowledge of what it took to be beautiful day after day. I felt like screaming: "This beauty is *not* all natural."

After I recovered from his total lack of understanding about hair and basic beauty needs, I realized that there was some truth in what he was saying. We did need to talk about money. I could no longer do whatever I wanted. We were partners now and needed to agree on spending. But how could we agree? How would we arrive at what was important? We both handled our money so differently before we got married.

Based on my experience with couples I have met in my counseling practice, Charlie and I are not the only ones who struggle with money issues. Conflict over money, especially in the early years of marriage, is very common. It is estimated that at least 60 percent of all married couples have had some degree of conflict over money,[1] and 44 percent of couples say differences in spending styles could prompt them to call the wedding off.[2]

Money means different things to different people. For some, money represents security. The more they have in the bank, the more secure they feel. For others, it is simply a means to an end, and often that end is fun. Their attitude is "spend while the sun shines" because one never knows what tomorrow will bring. And then for some, money is a means of control, a vehicle that allows one to demand compliance from other people. Whatever your orientation, your and your partner's ability to agree about money, expenses, and savings will greatly reduce the conflict in your marriage.

People have funny ideas about money, including what they are willing to do to get it. According to a survey on the Bloomberg Web site, 65 percent of those responding to a survey would live on a deserted island for a year if paid 1 million dollars. Sixty percent would even go to jail for six months for a crime they did not commit for that amount of money. And 10 percent of us would lend our spouse to another for a night. For 10 million dollars, one-fourth of us would abandon our friends, our family, and our church.[3] Clearly, people believe that money can solve their problems and give them happiness.

While 40 percent of married Americans admit to keeping a secret from their spouses, it is not usually regarding an affair or a romantic encounter; it is about money. The most common secret is how much they spend. Of those with a secret, 48 percent said they had not told their spouses about the real price of something they bought. It was not only women who said they had lied to their spouses about prices; the percentage was about the same for husbands.[4] Spending in a marriage is the "great deceit."

Part of the problem with money is that people want more. Americans love money. We are often focused on money. Thanks to fifty-plus years of television, radio, and mass media pushing merchandise at us, we are convinced that MORE will make us happier. We are told that the pursuit of material things will make our lives better and more comfortable. We feel we deserve it; after all, we work hard. We should buy it if we really want it. The idea of delayed gratification gets tossed aside as we pursue the American dream, which too often is simply the pursuit of affluence.

Myth: I want what I want when I want it.

If you know how to spend less than you get, you have the philosopher's stone.

BENJAMIN FRANKLIN

Like two-year-olds stomping their feet, the mantra in many households is: "I want what I want when I want it!" From early on, we learn a pattern of consumption that is focused on "extrinsic values," of obtaining more to make us happy. However, there is increasing evidence that the pursuit of affluence has damaging psychological effects, including severe depression and anxiety.

In a series of case studies dating to 1993, Ryan and Kasser examined the effects of pursuing money and material goods. Focusing excessively on obtaining wealth was found to create a lower sense of well-being and self-esteem. Feeling more insecure and negative about oneself was not tied to how much money a person already had or what age or nationality they were. Everyone who sought affluence as a goal had a lower score for happiness.

The researchers found that people who focused on "intrinsic values" or inner goals experienced a higher sense of vitality, fulfillment, and self-actualization.[5] And the irony was that these people were actually more likely to find wealth because they worked on developing their own talents and personal attributes.

Wealth becomes a by-product of personal success.

In spite of research to the contrary, many people still believe that more will make them happier. "The avarice of mankind is insatiable," wrote Aristotle twenty-three centuries ago, in describing the human tendency to have a new desire as soon as an old desire is satisfied.[6] More than two thousand years later, not much has changed.

Myth: I will be happier with more.

Money won't buy happiness, but it will pay the salaries of a huge research staff to study the problem.

BILL VAUGHAN

For decades, Lewis Lapham has been asking people how much money they would need to be happy. "No matter what their income," he reports, "a depressing number of Americans believe that if only they had twice as much, they would inherit the estate of happiness promised them in the Declaration of Independence. The man who receives $15,000 a year is sure that he could relieve his sorrow if he had only $30,000 a year; the man with $1 million a year knows that all would be well if he had $2 million a year, . . . Nobody," he concludes, "ever has enough."[7]

Now, I know what you're thinking—$1 million or $2 million would be enough for me. Actually, you might even think that $500,000 would work just fine. But the research does not support a magic number at which point we suddenly breathe a sigh of relief, stack our gold deplumes on the closet shelf, and rest assured that our lives and future are financially secure. Quite the contrary, new affluence seems to bring new worries and anxieties, as we hold ourselves up to yet another yardstick.

An example is found in the wild financial years of the mid-eighties, when many New York investment bankers earning "only" $600,000 a year felt poor and suffered from depression, anxiety, and loss of confidence. On less than $600,000, they were unable to keep up with their neighbors, colleagues, and friends. As one broker described his lack of success, "I'm nothing. You understand that, nothing. I earn $250,000 a year, but it's nothing, and I'm nobody."[8]

This is the problem with money and consumption. Each new luxury quickly becomes a necessity and then an even newer luxury must be identified. We become convinced that we must give our children more than what we had. Each year we should have more: more things, more money, and more comfort.

I talk with my clients about the easiest way to truly become rich—have *simple needs.* I give them suggestions for simplifying their lives and trimming their expenses. Often their response is to argue with me about why they *have* to have a cell phone and cable TV. My son tells me, by the way, that we are the *only* family in the whole city without cable.

About ten years ago, we carefully saved our money to buy our first new car. We had always bought used cars or received hand-me-downs from relatives, so the excitement was high when we drove our brand-new Saturn off the lot. The dealer did a good job adding to our exhilaration by taking our picture with the new car amid much fanfare. The car was a beautiful teal vehicle with brown leather interior. It glistened in the lights, with every piece of metal shining.

The third day we owned that beautiful new Saturn, with the odometer at 235 miles, a young man ran a stop sign a block from our house and hit the side of that magnificent teal vehicle, smashing the front panel and the passenger door and shattering the headlight. Emerging tearfully from his car, the other driver quickly informed us: "My dad is going to kill me. I don't have insurance."

Looking at me, Charlie said, "I think we are the ones who should be crying."

Several years later, we bought our next and last new

car. Again within 400 miles, someone talking on a cell phone instead of watching traffic smashed into the back of our car. I told Charlie that from now on I am simply taking a hammer to any new vehicle we buy before bringing it home. That will eliminate the worry over waiting for it to happen.

Myth: Credit cards are convenient.

There is nothing so habit-forming as money.

DON MARQUIS

And, of course, this is the real problem with *more.* More gives you more to worry about and, if you are not careful, what you own will begin to own you. As one friend of mine explained after selling his speed boat: "The two happiest days in a guy's life are the day he buys a boat and the day he gets rid of it."

One way that Americans feed their appetite for material things is by purchasing more than they can afford. The primary method of doing this is through the use of credit cards. It is very common for couples to brag to me about how many credit cards they have and how they are "worth" so much because companies are eager to extend them credit. They truly believe that they are not in financial trouble because they can make the minimum payment on their credit cards each month. I suggest that they just don't get it.

I tell them how my son was flipping through my wallet one day when he was five years old. He came across the leather holders for my credit cards. As he pulled one out, he inquired, "What is this for?"

I explained that it was a credit card and that "you can charge what you want and pay the bill later."

He thought for a minute and responded, "Sounds like you are spending money you haven't earned yet."

Who said kids don't understand the world? At age five, he got it.

Simply said, spending what you have not earned is the major problem with credit cards. Credit cards create an artificial sense of having more than you actually do. They create an aura of spending in which you do not have to think about each purchase, or the merits of pricing, or whether you can really afford it. You are not at your credit maximum, so you must be able to afford it. Right? *Wrong.* Using credit cards indiscriminately is one of the leading causes of financial problems for couples and can quickly lead to debt.

According to Kanner's survey, only 9 percent of Americans have no credit cards with the average person having three or four bank cards and eight to ten credit cards. And while about half of us (49 percent) always pay our credit card balance in full, another 5 percent usually pay only the minimum, with the rest paying what they can afford.[9] People will delude themselves that if they still have "credit" on their card, they must be doing okay. If they can make all their minimum payments, they are not "really in debt."

The problem with carrying any balances on credit cards is that you end up having your discretionary income (the money left after basic expenses are paid) go to interest costs and card expenses. This is the money that could be saved.

To get out of debt and stay out of debt, you must have a cash mentality. Every dollar spent, every purchase, needs to be a conscious one. The best way I know to achieve a cash mentality is to pay with money from your wallet or checking account. Day after day, purchase after purchase, paying with cash forces you to see exactly how much you have left and how each purchase affects the bottom line. It helps you avoid the creeping debt that will rob you of sleep and serenity.

Here are some of the warning signs that you are nearing debt overload:

- You have fewer dollars at the end of the month. This is the money you have left over after paying bills. If you are dipping into your savings or using credit cards to cover shortfalls in your checking account, you are moving into the danger zone.
- Your credit is maxed. Even after paying off high balances with an equity loan, tax refund, or bonus, your cards are quickly maxed again. This indicates that you are living beyond your means.
- You pay the minimum. You are unable to make a real dent in your credit card debt because the best you can do is minimum payments.
- You have no emergency fund. Most experts recommend a short-term or emergency fund of three to six months of expenses. Such a fund is designed to bail you out in case you lose your job, or the car breaks down, or some other unexpected and costly problems occur.
- You cannot sleep. While more difficult to measure, if you are struggling with insomnia because of what you owe, this is a signal you have too much debt.

I urge clients to get rid of their credit cards. If they feel they must keep one for "emergencies," I suggest they leave the card at home in a drawer.

What is the best plastic surgery you can ever do? Cut up your credit cards.

So who should manage the money? Who should make the financial decisions? Many of the "money" arguments I see revolve around the question: Who is in charge? Often the person who feels they *should* be in charge is the one earning the most money.

I grew up in the fifties, when the traditional family consisted of a father, a stay-at-home mother, 2.5 kids, and a house in the suburbs. The unwritten rule was that the father was the "head of household" and knew best about money, finances, and matters of great importance. Indeed, some of you may remember the great TV father of the time, Robert Young, from the series *Father Knows Best*. The framework of the father as the all-knowing financial expert was seen as gospel, especially when men earned substantially more than women.

Myth: The head of household should make the decisions.

I have yet to hear a man ask for advice on how to combine marriage and a career.

GLORIA STEINEM

The picture on earnings has changed dramatically in the last fifty years. The old model of the male being the primary breadwinner just does not hold true anymore. In fact, more than 25 percent of women in dual-career households earned more money than their husbands in 1998. In households where both the husband and wife worked full-time, nearly 31 percent of the women earned more than their husbands.[10]

Regardless of where the money is coming from, most couples these days prefer a sense of partnership regarding finances to a dictatorship. They are interested in planning together and working toward common goals.

I stress to clients that they need to find a way to handle the money that works for them. There isn't just one right way to do it. Some couples pay bills together with a joint account. Others split up the bills and use their individual accounts to pay the bills. Still others prefer to have the spouse most interested or talented in regard to money management handle it all.

Any of these techniques can work just fine. The important thing is to agree at some point on a system and then stick with it. Review finances frequently to make sure your financial goals are on track, and save as much money as you possibly can.

Myth: Let's take out a loan to get out of debt.

There are two ways to be rich, make a lot of money or have simple needs.

AUTHOR

My clients frequently present a plan to get out of debt by borrowing more money, usually by taking a home equity loan. This approach is currently an epidemic.

Years ago, when couples borrowed money on their house in addition to their mortgage, it was called a *second* mortgage. This was not something most people wanted. It had a negative connotation to it—a bad ring. *Second* mortgage. Nobody wanted a "second." It spelled *loser* to most people.

I remember my parents talking about a certain uncle of mine who had taken a "second" on his house due to poor money management. He was viewed as a failure; he obviously had not managed his money well. You would have thought the poor guy was barely peeking out of the gutter based on what the family said about him.

Then, the folks in the lending business changed the name of these loans to "home equity" loans, or lines of credit. Sounds better, does it not? After all, equity is good. "Loan"—bad, "equity"—good. Thus began the boom in equity mortgages that has mushroomed in the last decade. *Now* people almost brag about taking out a second mortgage: "I got a really great interest rate on my equity loan and have been able to consolidate all my bills. I'm actually saving $430 per month!" *No, you have extended your debt.*

Advertising touts the advantages of "getting out of debt" by "consolidating your bills" with a low interest loan. The problem? It is still debt. And most people who consolidate credit card debt without cutting up the credit cards purchase items on credit cards again, leaving them with the loan and the debt.

CASE STUDY: Will and Kristin

Kristin, an attractive, middle-aged mother of two, initially came to see me with symptoms of depression, sleeplessness, irritability, difficulty concentrating, and excessive worry over the future. It quickly became apparent that her symptoms were largely based on the financial picture of her marriage and life. After several sessions, her husband, Will, came with her to discuss the development of a financial plan.

A factory worker of twenty years, Will worked the assembly line at a forging plant. Thin and tired, Will's face was deeply creased from years of hard labor and smoking. While willing to participate in the session, he saw little value in coming for counseling, as he felt that "everything was going okay."

"My wife gets nervous about money," he explained. "We're doing okay. She worries too much."

"Well, let's take a look at net worth," I said.

Together we made a list of all their assets. They had bank accounts that totaled $2,200, car values of $6,400, furniture, and possessions. Though they had been married for eighteen years, they did not own a house, which they attributed to difficulty in accumulating enough money for a down payment.

We then listed all the liabilities they had. They had a car loan for $14,000, credit card debt of $8,000, and back support payments of $3,400 that Will owed from a previous marriage. We tallied up the figures:

Assets	Approx. $9,000
Liabilities	$25,400
Net Worth	–$16,400

It quickly became obvious that Kristin's worries were well-founded. She and Will not only had significant debt, but even more conspicuously they did not have a plan to eliminate their liabilities so they could begin to create personal wealth and financial security.

I referred them to a credit counselor who helped them

restructure their debt to a low interest loan. She also worked with Will and Kristin to establish a budget and savings plan. As a part of that plan, all credit cards were eliminated.

It took several years, but Will and Kristin were able to save enough money to purchase a large duplex. They were then able to lower their fixed expenses by renting the flat upstairs for extra income. This provided "extra" money to begin saving for retirement.

■ ■ ■ ■ ■

Debt is debt, and you do not get out of debt by incurring more debt. The only time I encourage clients to consider a debt consolidation is when it is combined with some financial counseling to help them change their spending habits. They need to learn how to dramatically live below their means and trim their expenses. Often this includes a restructuring of lifestyle, with economical food preparation, discount entertainment, and use of public transportation. I remind them of the saying, "If you do what you always do, you get what you always got." They will not get out of debt by operating the same old way.

Myth: There is an easy way to be rich.

The safest way to double your money is to fold it over once and put it in your pocket.

KIN HUBBARD

I wish I had a nickel for every client who comes to see me wanting a quick fix to his or her long-term financial problems. I call it the "Microwave Syndrome." Like the person waiting sixty seconds for water to heat in the microwave, the client will tap his or her feet impatiently and want financial security now. Clients like this are the folks buying lottery tickets, investing in risky stocks, watching the infomercials, looking for schemes, and waiting for the big break.

People with the Microwave Syndrome tend to be

dreamers, convinced that if they just get the right deal, the lucky break, they will never have to worry about money again. Rather than put together a workable and steady plan to financial health, they spend their time searching for the quick answer to make all their dreams come true. I routinely tell them, "Good luck—you'll need it. If it were that easy, we'd all be rich."

They hate it when I talk that way because for thirty, forty, fifty, even sixty years they truly believed that the streets were lined with gold. They only had to find that gold. After all, America is the land of dreams and riches, is it not? And I suggest, "Yes, there are riches out there for those who work hard and plan carefully."

This type of dreaming has gotten worse with the "infectious greed" of the nineties, the advent of the state lotteries, and the introduction of gambling in many states. Gambling is the poor man's dream. Gamblers believe that next time they will be lucky. The big win is always right around the corner.

I speak to my clients about the gold seekers in the 1800s who came to Colorado by the thousands to discover gold and register their stakes. Full of dreams, they toiled against the elements to find the vein of yellow that would make them rich. While a lucky few did find gold, the vast majority did not.

One group of entrepreneurs did get rich though, regardless of the prospecting success or lack thereof—the merchants who sold the shovels and equipment to all the prospectors. They made money whether the diggers found gold nuggets, dust, or donkey dung. They were the ones who really hit the jackpot. I encourage my clients: *Find a way to sell the shovels.* While not as exciting as standing in a stream and pretending to be Humphrey Bogart, working consistently toward concrete goals will yield better results than chasing get-rich-quick schemes.

Create solid opportunity in your life by obtaining a good education, refining job skills, and working hard. Then start saving and investing your money.

I cannot tell you how many people come to see me insisting that there is no way to save any money because they "barely make it as it is." Having had varied experience with affluence (i.e., some really good years and some really bad), Charlie and I long ago noticed that we simply spend more money when we have it. In fact, some of our best saving years were actually the years when we made the least money. As Charlie once observed: "When we make more money, we are simply broke at a higher level."

Myth: We don't have enough money to start saving.

Why is there so much month left at the end of the money?

JOHN BARRYMORE

There is only one way to save money—get into the habit of saving. How? Easy. *Pay yourself first.* That is, set up automatic withdrawals and contributions that occur before you ever get your hands on the moola.

Most couples find it helpful to start with three basic savings accounts: short-term or emergency savings; mid-term for special purchases like a car, vacation, or house; and long-term retirement savings. If children enter the picture, it is also helpful to set up college accounts, beginning at their birth, to accumulate interest over the long term.

These accounts are easy to set up. Go to the bank and have an automatic withdrawal from your checking account go into your short- and mid-term savings accounts with each paycheck. Start with a small amount, just $25 if money is tight, and increase the amount with each pay boost. Any bonuses or windfalls, like a tax refund, should be promptly placed in one of the accounts.

Find out if your employer has a 401(k) or 403(b) plan

in which you may participate. Many employers not only offer them but also match a portion of your contribution, making your savings grow faster. Because money is put into the fund before taxes, you will hardly miss the money. Again, start with what you can afford, but continue to build the percent until you are at the maximum 15 percent.

A solid savings plan will guide you to financial security and a worry-free future.

WHAT IS YOUR MONEY PERSONALITY?

There is no stronger force in the world than compound interest.

AUTHOR

Take the Retirement Personality Profiler by going to the Savings Council's Web site, www.asec.org, and clicking on Savings Tools. The following money personalities are presented:[11]

Planners (23 percent of Americans) are careful savers and enjoy financial planning. They are willing to take some calculated financial risks to pursue better returns. They believe that a secure future and comfortable retirement is attainable if they plan and save.

Savers (19 percent) are extremely careful with their money and seldom see their finances upset by unexpected events. But they are hesitant to take any risks, which makes them more savers than investors. In the long run, this can substantially affect their returns, and they may not be able to accumulate as large a nest egg.

Strugglers (18 percent) are not impulsive but have many setbacks in their finances. While they may consider themselves disciplined savers, they frequently have unexpected events that send them off course. Low-income Americans are often in this group.

Impulsives (24 percent) believe that it is possible to have a comfortable retirement, and are willing to take financial risks. But they are not disciplined in saving and tend toward impulsive buying with frequent setbacks to their goals. Impulsives tend not to follow through with their plans and goals.

Deniers (15 percent) dislike financial planning and do little planning for the future, even immediate events. They either feel that retirement is too far in the future, or that they will never be comfortable anyway, so why deny what they want now.

Planners and savers are more likely than the other types to save large amounts for retirement and to plan carefully for other financial events, such as buying a house, paying for a college education, etc. What type are you?

CREATE A FINANCIAL PLAN

Watch your pennies and the dollars will follow.

SAM WALTON

TOOL #1 Together establish a budget that is realistic and fair. List all your fixed expenses, long and short-term savings, and other costs of daily living. Do not forget to include some money for entertainment and fun, but know how much it is costing you. Anticipate future expenses, like a new car, education, or a child's wedding, by starting a fund now with regular contributions. Every six months, review your budget and see how you are doing. A computerized money program, such as Microsoft Money or Quicken, can be very helpful in organizing and monitoring your progress.

TOOL #2 Set a dollar amount for purchases. Make an agreement that any acquisition over a certain level will be discussed before buying it. This eliminates surprises or one partner feeling "out of the loop." It will also help you both stick with the budget.

TOOL #3 Set up accounts to "pay yourself first." These accounts should include a 401(k), Roth IRAs, and other retirement plans; college accounts if you have children; house/car/vacation accounts; and short-term savings. Have automatic withdrawals set up to put money in each account every pay cycle. Then pay the bills and any balances. What is left is your discretionary money, or money you can spend however you want. Increase the amounts you deposit in the accounts with any pay raise or special bonus you receive.

TOOL #4 Keep detailed logs of all spending for one month. This will give you an accurate picture of where your money is actually going. Review carefully each expenditure, asking whether there is an opportunity to reduce spending. Work toward establishing your fixed expenses to be as low as possible. The lower they are, the richer you will be.

TOOL #5 Develop a long-term plan for financial security and independence. Plan together for the long-term—focus on future events and retirement. The younger you start, the less money you will have to accumulate due to the power of compound interest. If you do not have expertise in this area, it will be money well spent to meet with a financial planner. Many great retirement tools are available on-line as well.

I can't get no . . . satisfaction.

THE ROLLING STONES

11 We Never Have Sex Anymore!

STRATEGY 11: BUILD INTIMACY OUTSIDE OF THE BEDROOM

There is an old joke that if you put a dollar in a jar every time you have sex the first year of marriage, and take a dollar out of the jar for every sexual interlude after the first year, you will never empty the jar.

I don't know if this is true, but I do know that sex is a common issue for married couples. They come to treatment complaining that their partners want sex too much or too little, too fast or too slow, too kinky . . . or more kinky. They complain of exhaustion, not having enough time, and finding sex to be "one more chore."

I remember joking when the kids were little that I would finally get them to bed and the cat would want to get on my lap. I'd push the cat off, and Charlie wanted to get on. It felt like someone always wanted something from me.

As married couples get busier and busier with the demands of career, children, and establishing a home, many find that the passionate sex they enjoyed early in the relationship has given way to flannel nightgowns, face cream, and a bed filled with children and pets. Too often, it becomes easy for a week, a month, or longer to go by without any sexual intimacy, until one of the partners complains: "We don't have sex anymore!"

Folks in long-term marriages know, however, that sex tends to ebb and flow just like the other feelings in marriage. It is very common for sex to almost come to a halt when the kids are little due to pure exhaustion. Things also slow down when there are illnesses or other problems that siphon energy and attention away from each other.

We learned this firsthand in the spring of 1973 when Charlie had to have a double hernia repair. He was recovering fairly well until the fourth day post-op, at which point he seemed to go steadily downhill. Looking very pale and thin, he was nauseated with frequent bouts of diarrhea and vomiting. I thought it was simply a result of the anesthesia or the stress of surgery. Like any good nurse, I kept urging him to drink more fluids and brought him water on an hourly basis to encourage hydration.

In spite of my best efforts, he continued to become sicker and sicker. I offered him ice water, tea, soup, and any fluids I could find that would sooth his gastrointestinal tract.

Two days later, we were stunned to see an alert flash across the TV screen that the city water supply was contaminated with the parasite Cryptosporidium. Told to boil all water, we learned that close to half a million people were sick and several had died. It was the largest epidemic due to a contaminated water supply that had ever occurred in the United States.

Now it goes without saying that intestinal parasites

do not a good sex life make. It took months for Charlie to recover and even longer for intimacy to return. He blamed me for getting the Crypto since I was the one bringing him water. His anger only intensified when it became clear that I also did not get infected. For years, he told the story to anybody who would listen, claiming, "My wife tried to poison me. She just kept bringing me more and more water." So much for great nursing care.

But the point is that sexual activity in a marriage changes over the years. And I don't mean just a downward spiral. Many couples experience some of the best sex ever after they make the decision to pursue permanent birth control. Some find a real renewal when the kids leave home and privacy returns to the bedroom. There is often an uptick when work slows down or retirement begins.

I remember well the year that I got laid off from my job as vice president of operations for a large healthcare system. At first angry and depressed, we both quickly noticed our sex life improved as we spent more time together. Charlie frequently threatened to call my former boss—a nun!—and thank her for our great sex life due to the downsizing.

Like every other aspect of marriage, a great sex life takes time and attention. Couples have to team up on making decisions that enhance the intimacy in the marriage. Everyday decisions, such as accepting more overtime or taking a promotion, have to be evaluated based on a larger vision of the relationship.

Ideally, sex is not just an afterthought to the whole picture. Smart couples keep it a priority and give it time and attention.

One of the most common myths I hear about sex is that intimacy should be spontaneous, automatic, and exciting like it was early in the relationship. With exotic movie scenes in their heads, or a vision of themselves with Mel Gibson or Halle Berry, clients talk with me about their Hollywood notion of what sex "should" be like. Never mind that *they* don't look exactly like movie stars. I let them know that even Mel and Halle don't look like Mel and Halle first thing in the morning.

Myth: Intimacy should be spontaneous.

Sex is more exciting on the screen and between the pages than between the sheets.

ANDY WARHOL

Clients want the mystery and excitement they see on the big screen. They tell me of their disappointment that the wild passion they hoped for and perhaps even experienced a time or two early in the relationship is gone. They insist they want "that back" but are unsure of how to find it.

I find it helpful to quiz couples about those "early days" when everything was great.

"Would you shower or bathe before the date?" I inquire.

"Of course," they reply looking at me as if I have surely gone mad.

"What about hair and nails? Would you take time with both?"

"Yes, sometimes I would go to the beauty shop, get my hair done and a professional manicure," the woman responds.

"What about shaving?" I ask the man. "Would you go out with stubble or make sure you were clean shaven?"

"Well, of course I'd shave very smooth so I could make out with her," he'd respond laughing.

"Would you dress carefully and apply makeup or cologne?"

"Yes. We always took great care to look our best," they would explain.

"Exactly how long would you take to get ready for a date when the two of you first got together?"

Laughing, they both insist that it often took a better part of a day.

"So, you spent much of the day preening, planning, and preparing for the date?"

"Yes," they both respond, not getting the point.

"Well, what exactly was spontaneous about the sex that evening?" I would ask. "You spent an entire day getting ready in hopes that it would lead to a romantic encounter. This was not spontaneous; it was planned. How much time do you spend now to get ready in hopes of some passionate sex?"

The room is usually very quiet at this point in the session. The clients slowly acknowledge, with nervous laughter, that they often go to bed with a facemask, daylong stubble, torn pajamas, and other items that don't exactly encourage arousal.

Myth: Single people have better sex lives.

Sex. In America an obsession. In other parts of the world a fact.

MARLENE DIETRICH

Great sex, like most other things in life, requires an investment to have great results. One must make an effort to be attractive, set the scene, be in the mood, and attend to the other's needs. It does not just magically happen. It certainly does not occur in the everyday life of pore-minimizing cream and snore strips.

Most married people at times wonder secretly about their sex lives and how theirs stacks up against other couples'. They get into the numbers game, wondering what is "normal," and often asking themselves, "Shouldn't we want it more?"

The popular culture drives comparisons, with a focus on sex as a goal and a trophy. As Gina, a young mother of two, states, "I saw the cover of *Cosmo,* and the idea of learning ten new techniques to satisfy my man filled me with exhaustion. But then I began to wonder if there was something wrong with me."

What's gotten lost with all the media buzz surrounding the swinging single lives of the rich and famous is that, contrary to popular belief, married couples actually have sex more often than their single counterparts. "The average for married couples is six times a month," according to John Gagnon, Ph.D., professor of sociology at the State University of New York, Stony Brook, and co-author of *Sex In America: A Definitive Survey.*[1]

His national sex survey of 3,400 Americans, conducted by researchers at the University of Chicago in 1994, showed that sexual activity for single people is lower than that for married: about once per week, not counting those who are completely abstinent. The main reason for this is that many singles lack a regular sex partner. One advantage of being married is that you only have to roll over when you feel the urge. It may not always happen, but it is easier than "going out looking for it."

Married folks also seem to be a great deal more satisfied with their sex lives, even though the actual act may be of shorter duration. According to the survey, almost 30 percent of women who don't live with a male partner indicate that sex often lasts for more than an hour. For live-in partners, only 13 percent of the women, and only 8 percent of wives reported this. Almost three-quarters of married women reported that lovemaking lasted fifteen to sixty minutes, with 16 percent finishing even faster.

But shorter appears to be sweeter. Not only do married people report that they feel emotionally fulfilled, they also report the highest levels of physical pleasure. Rather than finding monogamy monotonous, 91 percent of husbands and wives say that they are "thrilled" with their sex lives. According to the survey, 42 percent of married women said they found sex extremely emotionally and physically satisfying, compared to just 31 percent of single women who had a sex partner. And 50 percent of married men find sex physically satisfying, compared to 39 percent of cohabitating men.

What researchers are finding is that what makes for great sex is a strong bond between two people. According to Linda J. Waite, Ph.D., professor of sociology at the University of Chicago, "a permanent commitment to one's sexual partner makes a big difference to both sexes' sexual satisfaction."[2] Her research shows that men and women who are committed to a monogamous relationship get the most joy from sex, while those who pursue sex with other partners are less emotionally satisfied in the bedroom.

Sex isn't only about intercourse. Making love in a committed relationship nurtures the development of a soul mate. According to an ongoing study by Gina Ogden, Ph.D., a marriage and family therapist in Cambridge, Massachusetts, "Those who feel a strong spiritual connection with their partner say that as love and trust build over the years, their sexual relationship grows and grows."[3] Ogden has surveyed more than four thousand people, and she has found that sex helps couples share deep feelings, laugh together, and feel accepted. She found that couples that have a close spiritual connection describe a building over the years of greater trust, commitment, and love. As those qualities build, the sex also grows.

The most common dilemma that I hear from married couples is that they have different sexual appetites. That is, one partner is more interested than the other. In twenty years of counseling, I have never heard a couple express exactly the same needs and desires.

Usually, the complaining person is the male. Though,

Myth: We should both feel the same about sex.

Sex is a conversation carried out by other means. If you get on well out of bed, half the problems in bed are solved.

PETER USTINOV

on occasion, I have had a woman in my office emphatically complaining about the lack of interest of her husband, declaring, "Three times a week is simply not enough." Invariably, this woman is married to a man who has the libido of a turtle and just shrugs his shoulders at his wife's "unreasonable requests."

This is not the typical scenario, however. Usually it is the woman who is less interested and expresses personal exhaustion as the main roadblock.

Consider the following couple.

CASE STUDY: Neal and Monica

This couple came to see me after one year of marriage. Both work for a large information systems company that installs software and hardware in local businesses. Ambitious and dedicated, they attend college part-time and are pursuing master's degrees in information technology. While childless, they are hoping to start a family in another year.

Both complain of a lack of closeness. They acknowledge they have little time to spend together due to the work/school demands but insist they truly enjoy each other's company. They have established few traditions and routines outside of work and school, but both indicate that they feel more like roommates than spouses.

Neal, in particular, is focused on money and the goal of financial security before having a family. Monica believes in Neal's goals but questions when they will ever have the opportunity to enjoy life and slow down a bit. Both agree that their sex life has plummeted as they have become increasingly busy with work and school.

"She is never interested anymore," Neal complains.

"Sometimes a month or more goes by and we don't get together."

"Well, we hardly see each other," states Monica defensively. "We are only home together on Friday nights, and we are both so tired."

"What about the rest of the weekend?" I ask.

"We bought a house last year and spend most of the time on the weekends with remodeling and other projects to get the house into shape," explains Neal. "It needs a lot more work than we thought."

"What about Saturday nights? Is there time to catch a movie once in a while?" I ask.

"We're usually too tired," says Neal. "We sometimes rent a video, though."

"What about vacations and holidays?" I inquire.

"What vacations?" replies Monica. "We both have time coming, but we never take it. We are trying to save it in case we have a family."

"Well, your planning and ambition are admirable. You both clearly have your goals in focus and are pursuing them," I explain. "I worry, though, that you are so busy making a living, you are forgetting to make a life."

In the next few months, Neal and Monica began to make changes in their lifestyle that allowed more time for intimacy and relaxation. They discovered they could pursue their goals and still make time for each other. I cautioned them to make changes one at a time and not to feel that they had to overhaul their entire lives.

"It's like when you have a headache," I explained. "You take two aspirins, not the whole bottle. Balance works the same way. Take two aspirins and see if things feel a little better."

Not surprisingly, they found that intimacy and sex improved as they spent more time together. I last heard that they had finished school and were expecting their first child.

■ ■ ■ ■ ■

What does housework have to do with sex, you may be thinking? My clients ask exactly the same thing. But new research demonstrates that men who participate in the household chores have a much better sex life than those who don't. According to a study by John Gottman, Ph.D., women feel more respected and loved by husbands who share in the housecleaning and child rearing.[4] This certainly doesn't come as any surprise to women.

Myth: I shouldn't have to do housework.

No man was ever shot by his wife while doing the dishes.

AUTHOR

I have always been amused by Charlie's requests that involve "we." You know the ones, "Did *we* file the taxes?" "Did *we* make the kids' dental appointments?" "Did *we* call the school to let them know the kids are home today?" Exactly who is *we*? I have a feeling it is *me*.

Sometimes I get back at him with the word "anybody." I wait until only Charlie and I are at home and request, "If *anybody* is going downstairs, can they throw another load of wash in?" "If *anybody* gets a chance, can they wipe up the bathroom?" At that point Charlie is the one asking, "Who is *anybody*? I'm the only one home."

"I know," I answer. "*Anybody* is married to *we*."

While housework was tested in Gottman's study as a separate factor, cleaning really isn't the issue. The husband who does housework tends to be a mutual and supportive partner. This kind of partnering creates great marriages and happy sex lives.

The couples with the most satisfying sex lives work, laugh, and play together out of the bedroom as well as in it. Intimacy is like a second language or a secret code. The couple develops "inside jokes" and what my friend Cathleen calls "boudoir talk" (i.e., talk only meant for each other's ears). Bedroom talk is full of private secrets and humor.

I frequently hear from clients how they want a "soul mate" or a "passion partner." But I tell them, "You don't get it. Intimacy is not one giant orgasm; it is sharing life's daily joys and tribulations. It's about telling secrets after the lights are out and laughing at jokes that no one else on earth would understand. It's about quiet understanding. I call it the Art of Everyday."

The Art of Everyday is the very essence of a marriage. It is what binds two people together and makes intimacy build.

Charlie and I sometimes play a game called "Tell Me Something New." Usually on a Saturday or Sunday morning when we are still in bed, we share some tidbit of information that we have never shared before. Of course, the game has become considerably more difficult over the years. We have been married twenty-three years, yet there are still new things to share. Like the time I skipped school and got suspended. Or the time Charlie accidentally burned down a garage. Sometimes serious stuff, sometimes just fun. We always feel closer after talking.

Myth: Sex isn't important.

If it weren't for pickpockets, I'd have no sex life at all.

RODNEY DANGERFIELD

Build the Art of Everyday into your marriage. Partner on all the household activities and work together. We used to have a rule at our house: *No one sits down until we can all sit down.*

Sometimes, couples come to therapy with a host of difficulties, and then they explain after several sessions that they have not had sex for many years. When asked what the problem is, they simply shrug their shoulders. They cannot describe for me whether they grew apart and were no longer interested in sex or whether the lack of sex seemed to move them apart. While both parties may indicate that they miss the physical contact and closeness, they just aren't sure how to get things going again. Or, after a while, they may have convinced themselves that sex isn't all that important anyway.

While it certainly isn't the most important facet of a healthy relationship, sex does play a role. Sex provides an opportunity for a special closeness that is very difficult to achieve in other ways. It continues to build a bond between two people. Over the years, that bond just grows stronger and creates a special intimacy that makes the marriage solid.

I have rarely seen a great marriage that does not involve sexual intimacy, though I have had folks insist it is possible. In the best marriages couples have sex on a regular basis throughout the years, unless illness or physical problems make it impossible. Even then, very close couples find ways in which to express their love for each other.

A friend of mine has elderly parents who live in the rural Wisconsin countryside. Married over fifty years, they still farm their land each season and raise livestock for market. They get up early each morning, have breakfast together, and then go to work on their various chores. My friend's dad may go out to plow while his mother prepares the evening meal. Shortly after lunch, every afternoon, his dad comes in from the field and they meet in the bedroom. After forty-five minutes or so, they both emerge and go back to work. They have done this almost every day for over fifty years.

"Every day?" I asked once.

"Yes, unless one of them is under the weather," was the reply.

Maybe taking time off the plow is the secret to a good sex life.

RATE THE INTIMACY IN YOUR MARRIAGE

It's not the men in my life that counts; it's the life in my men.

MAE WEST

What are the two of you doing in your marriage to build intimacy? Are you both working at it, or is one of you trying harder? Answer the following questions:

1. Who is more likely to push for an evening alone instead of meeting other friends?

   You Your Spouse

2. In an argument over which movie to see, which one of you is more likely to give in first?

   You Your Spouse

3. Who's more likely to deliver sympathy and meals in bed in times of illness?

   You Your Spouse

4. Which one of you is more likely to use nicknames or terms of endearment, like "honey" or "sweetie"?

   You Your Spouse

5. Which one of you opens up about your feelings more readily?

   You Your Spouse

6. Who listens more intently when the other one is talking?

   You Your Spouse

7. Which one of you cuddles more, even when sex is not in the picture?

   You Your Spouse

8. Who dresses more often to please the other, both in the bedroom and out?

   You Your Spouse

9. Which one of you is usually more eager to introduce the other to a new friend, special restaurant, or new hobby?

   You Your Spouse

10. Who is more likely to insist that disagreements get discussed rather than just letting the matter drop?

   You Your Spouse

Scoring: You get a point for each time you are the answer to the question. The closer your two scores, the more you two are collaborating on intimacy. If one of you has a much higher score, it is time for the other to focus more on building the intimacy. The rewards are well worth the effort.

IMPROVE THE INTIMACY IN YOUR RELATIONSHIP

If I were asked for a one-line answer to the question, "What makes a woman good in bed?" I would say, "A man who is good in bed."

BOB GUCCIONE

Like any goal, a better sex life requires some effort and investment. Consider the following tools to enhance your sex life.

TOOL #1 Have fun with sex. Marriage provides a safe, secure structure in which to enjoy the gift of sex. Laugh and play as you get to know each other better. Let go of some of the inhibitions that result from the fears of unprotected sex and the negative messages we often learn growing up. Experiment and explore the activities that you both enjoy.

TOOL#2 Talk about it. Discuss with each other what you like and what you don't like. Share your "turn-ons" and what kinds of things you can both do to enhance the enjoyment. The more you talk about sex and intimacy, the less difficult it will become. Create and protect rituals that increase communication in the bedroom, such as lying in bed to talk every Sunday morning.

TOOL#3 Make time for intimacy. It is impossible to have a good sex life if you never make the time to make it happen. Turn off the TV an hour early and meet in the bedroom for talk and lovemaking. Schedule time alone for just the two of you. Go for a walk in the evening to talk about the day's events. Plan getaway weekends to a bed and breakfast or special hotel where you know no one will distract you from each other.

TOOL #4 Avoid boredom. Remember how fascinated you were with each other when you first met? Then, you both paid attention to each other's words and actions. Bored couples aren't paying attention to the details. People keep changing. Make sure you learn something new about each other on a regular basis. Focus on each other, not the rapid wheels of everyday living.

TOOL #5 Try a little effort. Put effort into your own appearance by dressing nicely for your partner, shaving, fixing your hair, and wearing make-up. Consider a "new look" from time to time, with a different hairdo, outfit, or something special for the bedroom.

TOOL #6 Don't forget the extras. Research has shown that other senses such as sight and smell have a dramatic effect on sexual urges. Consider appealing to the voyeur in most of us by wearing revealing clothes around the house. Light a scented candle to set the mood and the scene. Use lotions or cologne to increase the attraction for each other.

TOOL #7 Tell each other about your love. No matter how repetitive it may seem, it is always nice to hear how your partner loves you. Tell each other frequently about your love for each other, especially when intimate. Talk about your physical and emotional attraction to your mate and how special it is to have him or her in your life. Whisper naughty secrets in their ear.

12 It's Your Turn to Get Up with the Kids

STRATEGY 12:
CREATE A SHARED PHILOSPHY OF CHILD REARING

Getting pregnant was not in the plan. At least not right away. Charlie and I were married only a few months when I started to feel tired all the time. Not just a *little* tired, I mean hit-by-a-train tired. So tired, I would fall asleep while eating dinner or taking a bath. You didn't have to be Einstein to know that something was different.

"I think I'm pregnant," I announced to Charlie one evening.

"You can't be," he replied with fierce determination in his voice.

"And just why *can't* I be?" I asked.

"Uh, because, we're so careful. It can't be that easy," he said, squirming in his chair.

A visit to the doctor the following week confirmed what I already knew. Sometimes it *is* easy. Now, I am very grateful that we never had to struggle with the roller coaster of infertility, but we weren't exactly ready for this.

Charlie was just starting his career in data processing, and I was still in graduate school. We had not even unpacked the wedding presents. They were stacked in the spare bedroom with the extra suitcases and cat toys. Our cramped two-bedroom apartment was located between a Big Boy restaurant and a Jiffy Lube. We had a grand total of forty-five dollars in the bank. Scared of the whole idea? You bet.

It's not that we didn't want kids, we did. We just thought we would wait awhile, be prepared, be ready.

I didn't understand at the time that there is NO way to prepare completely for children. Until you have them, you are simply clueless as to the day-to-day demands of raising a child. You think that it will be different for you. After all, you read the books, you studied child development, and *you* have extraordinary patience. You certainly won't make all the stupid mistakes that your parents did. *Yeah, right.*

I find that most of my clients are also clueless. Children come along, and even those people who thought they had everything ready are amazed to find that these tiny seven-pound creatures create a nuclear meltdown and transform perfectly reasonable people into bumbling maniacs.

It is not uncommon at all to turn into a zombie the first year or two after having kids. Now I *have* met couples that brag about how their four-week-old sleeps thirteen hours a night, never cries, and takes long naps. Let me make it clear at this point that these types of people are not my friends, and I rarely talk with them again after they share such information. For most of us, this simply is not our experience.

My children rarely slept, even as newborns. When

Ken was three weeks old, I actually showed him the paragraph in the baby book that outlined the eighteen to twenty hours per day sleeping habits of newborns. (He simply ignored me—which turned out to be a pretty good preview of his teen years.)

Charlie and I *tried* to work together, negotiating the feedings, walking the floor, and rocking for hours to get the baby to sleep. One night, I woke up and was horrified to discover that our beloved child had actually slipped off the couch and onto the floor after I had lapsed into a sleep-deprived coma. Fortunately, no harm was done. He was happily playing with a piece of carpet lint.

There were times when household tension ran deep. After an especially bad siege of 3:00 A.M. awakenings, I was completely frazzled. Half awake, I heard Ken begin to stir in his crib. Poking Charlie in the ribs with my elbow, I insisted, "It's your turn to get up."

He leaped out of bed, startled and confused, and went careening into the TV stand near the door of the bedroom. The lamp perched on top launched like a missile through the air into the kitchen. It landed with a large explosion on the door of the utility closet, which promptly flew open, spewing mops, brooms, and cleaning supplies across the floor. Standing there in his striped Jockeys, Charlie surveyed the spewed Pledge, Comet, and Tidy Bowl, a twisted lampshade and a thirteen-foot-wide girth of glass as Ken broke into blood-curdling screams. By this time, I *was* awake.

I changed, fed, and rocked Ken back to sleep as Charlie attempted to clean up the mess. He was still vacuuming when I crawled back into bed. *Sigh.* So much for getting some extra sleep.

It is now clear to me that there is a medically sound reason why prisoners of war are systematically sleep deprived to make them talk. I can assure you that I would have shared nuclear secrets (if I had known any) in short order when the kids were young.

Smart couples recognize and adjust to the extraordinary strains of having young children. And, by the way, it helps a great deal to have a sense of humor.

Often a troubled couple will seek my services when their marriage is struggling and express the opinion that a child will strengthen their marriage. This is very foolish thinking. Perhaps, some of the most foolish thinking there is. I quickly tell them, "It will only add to your problems. Children are an enormous stress to a marriage."

Myth: Children will strengthen the marriage.

When I was a kid my parents moved a lot, but I always found them.

RODNEY DANGERFIELD

The reduction of leisure time and the lack of opportunity to talk to one another is a major reason for lower satisfaction among couples with children.[1] Numerous studies on marital happiness indicate that couples with children are less happy than childless couples.[2]

There simply aren't enough hours in the day once you have children. Just when you get everything running smoothly, the baby gets an ear infection, the neighbor kid comes over with chicken pox, or the kids use the new chemistry set to blow out the windows in the basement.

The activities once enjoyed as a couple change to family-centered outings, and everything is much more complicated. Your life shifts from a romantic bed and breakfast to Chuck E. Cheese's. From cappuccino on the deck to spit-up on your shoulder. Even a simple weekend away involves multiple suitcases, diaper bags, a portable high chair, boxes of toys, food and formula, and games to introduce when the kids start complaining, which is usually about five miles out of the driveway.

The whole routine does not get easier with more children. Granted, you are more experienced and do not feel panicky when they scream for eight hours, put the cat in the toilet, or remove the back of the TV with a screwdriver. But the second, third, or fourth child creates more demands, which further compresses the time available for each other.

Studies have shown that it is actually the second child that makes the biggest difference in married life. An ongoing study by anthropologist Rebecca Upton indicates that the arrival of the second child causes dramatic changes in married life, with the wife often leaving the workforce or changing to part-time work. The couple may also assume the more traditional roles, with one of the spouses assuming the bulk of the childcare and housework. The second child *now* means that the children are equal in number to the parents, and both parents must attend to the children to give everyone enough attention.

"A lot of men reported that they had been feeling a little bit left out in the bond between the mother and first child," according to Upton. "That changed when the second child was born."[3] Yes, the mother was only too eager to have Dad's help.

Of course, more than two children creates a situation in which the offspring outnumber the parents—a predicament I personally do not think is wise and may be dangerous. I remember growing up with my three siblings and the many times we simply put my mother in her room when we wanted to do something. We not only outnumbered her, we were bigger and stronger.

But the main problem is time. There are only so many hours in the day. The division of time, energy, and resources becomes difficult and couples lose the opportunity to be together.

Children will not automatically strengthen a marriage. The same issues that were there before children will be there afterwards . . . and there will be lots of new things to argue about.

Nothing is more amusing to me than the couples who come to treatment insisting that their lives will be the same *after* children as *before.*

"We still plan to go for Harley weekends across the country," declared one motorcycle aficionado.

"I am going to work full-time and continue in school," announced an expectant executive.

"We fully intend to continue taking overseas tours after the baby arrives," explained a young couple.

Myth: Nothing will change when the baby comes.

It goes without saying that you should never have more children than you have car windows.

ERMA BOMBECK

This type of magical thinking is of the uninitiated. I remember a friend calling after Ken was born, "How about stopping by for some scrapbooking and then we can have lunch at the club?" *Are you kidding, the baby barfed in the bed and I have six loads of laundry to do while he takes his thirty-minute power nap.*

Couples only set themselves up for frustration if they try to lead the DINK (double income, no kids) life with children. You cannot do everything you did before kids. It just doesn't work.

I remember well the evening we went to a nice restaurant for a quiet meal when Ken was a toddler. ("Quiet" and "toddler" do not go together, by the way.) Immersed in conversation, we did not notice that Ken had managed to take the cap off the ketchup and was dumping it over the top of the booth onto a fur coat belonging to the lady at the next table. We quickly paid the bill and left, carrying much of the dinner home in a doggie bag. After that, we only ate at "family-style" restaurants, which is a euphemism for "ketchup everywhere."

As children get older, some things get easier. Sleep, for example. Teenagers sleep a great deal, often awaking at 3:00 P.M. and wondering why breakfast isn't on the table. Parenting is better when you get more than thirty minutes of sleep at a time.

However, other aspects of daily living do not get all that much easier. Couples of older children are constantly running from one activity to the next, finding that they drown in school notices, parents' meetings, and fundraising activities (i.e., selling six dried nuts wrapped in cellophane to your closest friends).

It becomes very difficult to keep track of all this, especially with multiple children. I am embarrassed to report that I actually misread the notice from my son's high school and forgot to send him the first day of school. (He was only too happy to comply with staying home, by the way.)

Parenting means baking cookies at 3:00 A.M. because someone forgot to tell you it was their turn to bring the treat, sewing 963 sequins onto the costume for the school play, sitting at swim meets where the ambient temperature hovers around 105 degrees for six hours to see your child swim exactly 1 minute and 53 seconds, and reading *Curious George* books until you want to strangle that little monkey.

Children will not make your life any easier. They will not suddenly strengthen a marriage. And your house will not look clean for at least twenty years.

But if you stay realistic, work together, strategize a parenting philosophy, it can be one of the most rewarding things you will ever do.

Another area that we must address at this time is the question of money. Children are very, very expensive. Too often, couples look at the cost of "having a baby" as just that . . . what it costs to raise a baby. They don't look at what it costs to raise a child, and these are two very different figures.

According to a recent report by the USDA's Center for Nutrition Policy and Promotion, the average family will spend $233,530 to raise a child. It further reports that the overall cost of raising a child, after adjusting for inflation, has increased 13 percent from 1960 to 2000.[4]

Myth: Children are not expensive.

Never lend your car to anyone to whom you have given birth.

ERMA BOMBECK

This increase in cost does not include additional expenses for education and college. It does not take into account orthodontics, driver's education, additional insurance, school trips, and sports activities. It certainly does not allow for "getaway" family weekends, mountain ski trips, or a Florida vacation. All these extras cost a lot of money.

While I cannot dictate how many children is right for you, I do want to suggest that you give this issue careful consideration. More is not necessarily better.

You will be a significantly better parent if you are not always burned out and exhausted. You will be more fun if money worries do not keep you awake at night. You will enjoy your children more and laugh as a family more if you have the time and money for some family getaways and family vacations.

Talk carefully about how many children you can really afford. Discuss with each other your vision and dreams of family life. It is better to raise a couple of children well than to have a family so large that you cannot meet their needs. Children desperately need your time, attention, and laughter.

I don't quite know where it all started, this idea that each generation should have a better lot in life than the one before, but I hear it all the time. Folks will recount

> Myth: I want things better for my kids than what I had.
>
> **We inevitably doom our children to failure and frustration when we try to set their goals for them.**
>
> DR. JESS LAIR

their own childhoods with a wisp of nostalgia and appreciation, citing the many lessons they learned from hard work, sacrifice, and a focus on time instead of money. Yet in the next breath, they will declare their resolve not to have their own children face such character-building challenges and tribulations. They insist on giving their children the "finest" and "latest"—no matter the cost to them personally or whether these items truly enhance the development of their children.

The constant barrage of advertising through TV, movies, and other media encourages an insatiable appetite for goods and services. Children are very susceptible to these media messages and the influence of their friends. They may beg, urge, argue, cajole, persuade, entice, sweet-talk, and wheedle well-meaning parents into buying them every new toy, item, or electronic device. They are convinced that *more* will make their dreams come true. (Many parents suffer from the same illness. It's called "affluenza.")

Yet, the finest gift you can give your children is an attitude of gratitude for what they have rather than always looking for more. Teach them the pitfalls of the "if-only" game: "if only I had a game-boy, if only we had a large-screen TV, if only I had a new bike, I would really be happy." The "if-only" framework trains your children to chase happiness rather than building it from within, through the development of talents, integrity, and values.

One of the best gifts you can give your children is firm "No's"—especially to material things. Saying "No" has become more difficult as affluence has increased. Years ago, parents could say "No" because they simply did not have the resources to say "Yes." Children intuitively know the financial status of the family and often will not ask if they know the money isn't there.

It is more difficult to say "No" when dollars are readily available. But a responsible parent does just that. They do not try to win favor with the children by giving them everything their hearts desire. They teach their children the value of hard work, a frugal lifestyle, and an attitude of gratitude.

Rather than asking yourself whether you can afford that new TV, car, boat, snowmobile, or electronic gizmo, ask whether it enhances family life. Rather than collapsing into a blob over the constant badgering for more, evaluate whether the next purchase builds the character of your children. And rather than working long hours to give everyone what they want, use your time to be together as a family. This is what children really need.

Myth: There is one right way to parent.

Children have never been very good at listening to their elders, but they have never failed to imitate them.

JAMES BALDWIN

Couples frequently come to treatment because they are arguing about how to raise their children. They may have differing views on discipline, expectations, or authority. Usually one parent is more strict, (a tyrant), while the other is viewed as too lenient (a pushover). They come to the session with bottled anger and passionate energy, talking quickly in an effort to convince me of the fallacy of their partner's parenting skills. Consider the following couple.

CASE STUDY: Chad and Susie

Married five years, this couple has two children, John, age four, and Kayla, age one. Chad works long hours as an architect for a local real estate development company. A full-time homemaker, Susie sells Pampered Chef items at home parties for extra money. They have come to treatment due to their four-year-old's behavior problems and their frequent arguments over parenting.

Susie feels that Chad is much too easy on the children and does not support her disciplinary methods when he comes home. She states that she feels undermined by his actions, which makes John act out more when Chad is not around.

"It's almost like our son just waits for Chad to come home to rescue him," she reports. "He is always the good guy and gives into whatever John wants."

"Susie, I work all day. The last thing I want when I get home is to have to yell at John or give him a time-out for something that happened during the day. It seems like you always call on me to be the bad guy . . . I just want to enjoy the children," Chad responds. "Anyway, I think you are too hard on him."

"Well, I think you are much too easy on him. That's why he is running wild all day and does not listen to me," says Susie.

They both look expectantly at me to make the call, and I let them know, "You are both right. Usually parents disagree on issues related to parenting, with one assuming the role of the disciplinarian. This, actually, is why children need two parents: to balance each other out."

"But how do we solve it?" asks Susie. "Exactly how do we achieve that balance?"

"Two steps: by establishing a shared philosophy of child rearing and then never disagreeing in front of the kids," I explain. "Always present a united front, which makes it clear that you are working together, a close-knit team. Not only will this eliminate a lot of acting out by your children, it will also help them feel safe and secure."

"But what kind of shared philosophy?" Chad asks. "A lot of the time I just guess at what is the best approach, or I find myself doing something just like my parents."

"That is what many of us do," I respond. "We find ourselves responding like our parents. Or we react impulsively or out of anger. We all do our worst parenting when it is a quick response, a "knee-jerk" reaction. We are much more effective when we carefully strategize, work as a team, and present a united front. For that, you need a shared philosophy of child rearing."

"The philosophy I recommend is one of logical consequences. Make the children responsible for their own actions and choices."

I explained to both Susie and Chad that logical consequences take some of the guesswork out of being a parent. Children are given choices, and they take responsibility for the outcome. It provides parents with a framework to help the children see how "the world really works." Parents provide the choices in a non-emotional yet firm approach.

■ ■ ■ ■ ■

Chad and Susie attended a parenting class in their community that taught them the framework for logical consequences. They learned how to discuss, strategize, and negotiate their approach for the children. While occasionally disagreeing, they were able to present a united front.

Myth: I should be a "good" parent.

If children grew up according to early indications, we should have nothing but geniuses.

JOHANN WOLFGANG VON GOETHE

As their arguing decreased, so did the "misbehavior" of their son.

There is no worse handicap for a child than being raised by a "good" parent. "Good" parents are so immersed in their child's life that they believe they must do everything, leaving no stone unturned as they "snoopervise" their child's activities and lives.

"Good" parents may actually become servants to their children, taking responsibility for much of their behavior.

They make sure they get up for school, do their homework, and change their clothes. They are constantly nagging them to "hurry up," "slow down," "finish your vegetables," and "call your grandmother."

While well intentioned, their behavior undermines their children's efforts to be independent and take responsibility. It robs them of self-confidence and encourages dependence. Overly concerned with what others think, they take on responsibilities that really belong to the children to make sure the kids "turn out right." And this takes an enormous amount of energy.

There is a lot of pressure to be a "good" parent in today's world—from school counselors who insist that parents monitor every homework assignment to over-involved grandparents who are critical of parents' efforts.

I remember clearly receiving a telephone call from a neighbor when my son was in elementary school. She was very upset about Ken's behavior on the bus toward her son.

"What exactly did he do?" I inquired, somewhat panicked that he had tried to throw the poor kid out the window, judging by the intensity of her agitation.

"He called Joe stupid," she replied.

"Stupid?" I asked, breathing a sigh of relief.

"Yes, stupid. Are you going to bring him over here to apologize?"

"Well, how did your son handle it?" I inquired.

"He got up and moved to another seat," she stated emphatically.

"Well, it strikes me that he handled it just fine—a logical consequence for unfriendly behavior," I replied.

While I don't think she was particularly happy with me, I was clear that this was an occasion where Ken simply had to take responsibility for his own behavior. When you call people stupid, they are not likely to want to be your friend. I did not want to give the message that I was going to be involved in each and every minute detail of my son's life.

It is much more effective to allow your children to make as many of their own decisions as possible (unless dangerous, of course) and experience the consequences. For example, early in their school careers, we bought both of our children alarm clocks and taught them how to set them for school. We made it clear that getting up for school was *their* responsibility, not ours. We were getting up for our own jobs. If they overslept, they had to explain it to their teacher, not me. I can't recall a time when either kid missed school because he or she overslept (though the snooze button was often used for more than thirty minutes).

The concept of being a *responsible* parent instead of a *good* parent helps to clarify many of the day-to-day decisions that parents face and couples fight about. When confronted with a new dilemma regarding one of the kids, we always ask the question, "Is this something they could do for themselves?" If the answer is "Yes," then we encourage them to take responsibility. If they truly need our help, then this is exactly what we give, some help. We do not make their responsibilities ours.

ARE YOU A "GOOD PARENT?"

Americans, indeed, often seem to be so overwhelmed by their children that they'll do anything for them except stay married to the co-producer.

KATHARINE WHITEHORN

Do you fall into the trap of being the "good" parent? Take this quick quiz to evaluate your own behavior.

1. I feel that my children are a reflection of me.

   Always Sometimes Never

2. I give in to my child's demands if he creates a fuss.

   Always Sometimes Never

3. I feel guilty when I say "No" to my child.

   Always Sometimes Never

4. I feel sorry for my child.

   Always Sometimes Never

5. I demand obedience from my children and feel it is important to win.

   Always Sometimes Never

6. I am very concerned about what others think about my child and my parenting skills.

   Always Sometimes Never

7. I find it hard not to be overprotective of my child.

   Always Sometimes Never

8. I try to give my child everything that I did not get as a kid.

   Always Sometimes Never

9. I feel that my kids "owe" me because of everything I do for them.

   Always Sometimes Never

10. I like to give my children all the latest toys and games.

   Always Sometimes Never

Scoring: How many "never" responses did you have?

8–10: Excellent. You are letting your child take responsibility and creating a respective home environment.

5–8: Good. Talk together about ways in which you can enhance learning opportunities for your child.

0–5: You are "working" too hard. You are taking responsibility for things that your child needs to address. You may find a local parenting group very helpful for additional strategies and support.

CREATE A SHARED PHILOSOPHY FOR RAISING CHILDREN

When you put faith, hope and love together, you can raise positive kids in a negative world.

ZIG ZIGLAR

Remember, "good" parents rob children of self-confidence and independence. Avoid protecting your children from the consequences of their decisions and behavior, as that is how they learn. Use the following tools to keep your marriage strong while raising responsible children.

TOOL #1 Keep the marriage a priority. Yes, you may even feel a little guilty about leaving the kids to go do something together. But it is extremely important. The most critical gift you can give your children is your love for each other. Children do best in stable households with happy marriages. Make sure that you spend time alone together at least one evening a week. Go out at least once a month.

TOOL #2 Discuss child-rearing strategies away from the children. The very best parents take time together, away from the children, to brainstorm approaches, consequences, and other issues related to the upbringing of the kids. And though differing opinions may be the starting point, by the time they are presented to the children, the front is united, clear, and firm.

TOOL #3 Refuse to be a doormat. You do your children no favors when you respond to their every wish, anticipate their every desire, and make them the entire focus of the universe. They will be in for a rude awakening in the real world. Help your children to be responsible for their own lives and also to experience responsibility for the well-being of the family. If all else fails, put up a sign that reads, "THE MAID DIED."

TOOL #4 Teach your children how the world really works. This is the goal of raising children—that they are able to function well in the world when grown. In the real world, no one hands you a car or money; you have to earn it. In the real world, you have to get along with other people and display a positive attitude in order to get ahead. When in doubt with a decision regarding the kids, ask yourself the question, "What happens in the real world?"

TOOL #5 Set realistic expectations. Nothing causes more stress than parents who routinely put themselves in situations in which they have unrealistic expectations of their children. Three-year-olds will not sit still for an hour in church, five-year-olds do not do well in a fancy restaurant, and teenagers are extremely self-centered. You set yourself up for a great deal of frustration if you do not have a basic understanding of child growth and development. Take a course, read a book or two, and attend some parenting classes so that you know your children aren't the only ones with dreadful habits.

TOOL #6 Limits are best served cold. Children need limits and they need boundaries. But the best time to express them is not when you are angry and upset, but in a cold, calm manner after strategizing as a couple. Make sure you both agree, and then serve them cold. Be matter-of-fact, unemotional, and firm. And remember, you can be very firm without being harsh.

TOOL #7 Sprinkle plenty of encouragement. Children grow with encouragement. Constant mention of effort and improvement propels children to do more and work harder. Avoid comparisons with others and focus on the strengths that your children display. Remember, an ounce of encouragement when needed is worth more than a pound of praise when the job is accomplished.

13 Is That All There Is?

STRATEGY 13: REINVENT YOURSELF AND YOUR MARRIAGE

Sometimes I see clients who present as the perfect couple. They pause upon entering the office, as if asking, "What am I doing here?" and sit on the edge of the couch in a hesitant pose. Smiling at each other demurely, they maintain: "We don't have any problems, no problems at all. Why, we don't even know why we made this appointment. Silly us! We get along perfectly. Everything is perfect." *Yes, perfectly boring.*

This is the type of couple whose marriage has appeared to roll so smoothly through life that it feels like a deep rut has been dug, allowing little sunshine. There are no ups and downs and no real conflict or debate. The partners are bored with each other, tired of their lives, and disinterested in the world. Even a new home entertainment system with Dolby surround sound does not bring a spark to this couple's existence.

Couples like this do not fight anymore; they do not want to squander the energy. It seems easier to agree and not make any waves. They long ago gave up the pursuit of individual interests; it seemed to involve too much work. Life is boring and they are too.

These couples have resigned themselves to a tedious, fairly predictable and monotonous life with no excitement and even less passion. One morning they wake up and ask, *Is that all there is?*

That's when my phone rings.

The visit to counseling is usually initiated by the least happy partner. Depressed and feeling trapped, the precipitating partner realizes that something is amiss but cannot seem to put his or her finger on exactly what. As he or she describes his or her unhappiness and despair, the spouse stares in amazement.

"I didn't even know anything was wrong," one wife told me after hearing her husband's lament. *No, you both stopped talking to each other long ago.*

The situation is even more pressing when the visit is driven by one of the partners questioning whether they want to remain in the marriage. This individual knows his or her life is boring, but does not know what to do about it. He or she knows the marriage has no pizzazz but is not sure how to add the spice.

He or she may have toyed with the idea of finding something—or someone—new and exciting as a solution. He or she may have already tried an infidelity or flirtation. I suggest that the guy or girl who gets on the bus in Milwaukee is the same one who gets off in Los Angeles. The problems travel with you.

I tell a couple that it is necessary for each partner to reinvent themselves periodically to keep the marriage fresh and alive. And there are times that this takes work, re-commitment, and energy.

I share with clients the famous story of Gary Player, the golfer. One morning while practicing, he hit a chip shot about fifty yards off the green that rolled directly toward the pin and dropped in the hole. His caddy came running and said, "Wow, that's amazing! What great luck!"

"Luck?" Player responded. "What are you talking about? I've practiced that shot every day for the last twenty years."

Great marriages work the same way. They are less about luck and more about hard work. Sometimes the work you have to do is on yourself, your attitude, and the amount of energy you bring to the marriage.

Myth: Any long-term marriage gets boring.

Family jokes, though rightly cursed by strangers, are the bond that keeps most families alive.

STELLA BENSON

Marriage does not need to be boring, and constant conflict is not necessary in order to keep it interesting. Living without the roller coaster of crisis is a good thing. Other ways exist to keep life exciting, without becoming a case history on the *Jerry Springer Show*, sitting next to folks who are contemplating a sex-change operation.

No, you really do not need constant craziness in your life.

One of the advantages of stability is that it allows you to reach a point where you are no longer running around foolishly trying to put out brush fires. Energy is there for focusing on more appealing things—like a champagne brunch on Sunday, a golf weekend with friends, or, let's say, a trip to London. Stability makes it a whole lot easier to bring new and positive excitement to a marriage.

The long-term marriages that are the happiest are those in which both partners are invested in personal growth and the growth of the relationship. According to the husband and wife team of Floyd and Harriett Thatcher, "If a marriage is to last, to be exciting and adventurous, to be satisfying and fulfilling, the couples somehow will have to discover growth patterns that are mutually rewarding."[1] To be more succinct, it is important to continue to notice the world together.

Myth: Marriages can go on autopilot.

Keep yourself clean and bright. You are the windows through which you must view the world.

SOURCE UNKNOWN

The main problem with boring marriages is the mistaken belief that it is okay to go on autopilot. This happens, by the way, more frequently in so-called "good marriages" (i.e., marriages without a lot of discord). The lack of disagreement is usually part of the problem. Research has demonstrated that couples that habitually keep quiet about issues to avoid an argument "are less happy over the long-term than 'conflict-engaging' couples."[2]

A certain amount of conflict brings energy into a relationship and spurs discussion, understanding, and resolution. I enjoy the couples who come into my office arguing up a storm because I usually find that they are deeply invested and willing to put a lot of themselves into making their marriages better.

In contrast, autopilot marriages are filled with routine and schedules. Little stress equates to too little investment, as most daily activities are predictable and practical.

CASE STUDY: Jim and Sally

Married for more than twenty-four years, this couple first came to see me after Jim announced that he wanted to quit his job. He has worked for a large advertising firm for over twenty-five years and climbed the corporate ladder to a comfortable salary and generous benefits package. Sally works at a local department store in the accounting department. They have three grown sons; two are married and one is finishing college in another city. Jim and Sally have lived in the same neighborhood for years and long ago paid the mortgage in full. Living frugally, they have a nest egg for retirement and no other debts. Both are in good health, exercise regularly, and take two weeks off every summer to vacation at a lake.

Handsome and reserved, Jim states: "I don't want to work at that job any more. I have been there for years and would like to see what else is out there."

He continues to clarify how the corporate culture has changed over the past decade with more emphasis on quarterly earnings than people.

"I just don't feel I belong there anymore. It's not very fulfilling."

"But what about our retirement?" asks Sally. "We have counted on this for years and worked toward this goal. What happens if you leave now?"

Looking sad and discouraged, Jim does not answer.

In a subsequent one-to-one session with Jim, he talks at length about how discouraged he is with his life. He is tired of his job, his routine, and his marriage. He feels there is little to look forward to and his days are void of any high points.

"Even the vacations are boring," he laments. "We go to the same place at the same time every year. There are so many other things to see."

"Like what?" I ask him.

"Like sunsets in the Rockies, stingrays in the Caribbean, archeological treasures in Israel, and museums in Paris," he replies, his eyes welling with tears. "We have always been so practical; I sometimes feel that we have missed what life is all about."

"Have you shared your feelings with Sally?"

"Yes, I have, but she's happy with things the way they are. She says she wouldn't do anything differently. Sometimes I find myself wondering if I wouldn't be better off getting out of the marriage and finding someone else."

Over the next several sessions, it becomes clear that part of what is driving Jim's feelings is that he has indeed met another woman. Describing an infatuation with a coworker at the office, he reports that he feels alive with her energy, that an aura of excitement surfaces when she is around. He believes that she is also taken with him, as she flirts with him on a regular basis in a very forward manner. He admits guiltily that he likes the attention and feels attracted to her.

"I never dated anyone other than Sally," he confides. "All of a sudden, I have this woman practically throwing herself at me. I feel flattered. I was always the nerd in school, the practical one at work. I've never done anything crazy in my life, and all of a sudden I feel like doing something outrageous with her. I don't because I am deeply committed to my marriage and I know I would lose everything. But it is tearing me apart. A part of me wants to do something wild and passionate."

"Have you ever thought about doing something wild and passionate with your wife?"

"Huh?" Jim looks up, surprised. "What do you mean?"

"Why don't the two of you plan something really exciting, like a rafting excursion down the Colorado River, or a trip to London or Paris, or a balloon ride?"

"Sally wouldn't be interested."

"What would happen if you told her that you were going to do them anyway?"

"I don't know," said Jim looking thoughtful.

In future sessions, Jim was able to recognize that the person who needed to change his life was himself. He could not blame Sally totally for the lack of excitement nor expect someone new to just magically fix it. Part of the answer rested with him.

As Jim began to plan more activities and take the lead with booking some adventures, Sally started to become interested in participating. Though they both recognized that they were cautious people by nature, they pushed themselves to try new things. Sally, in particular, found it difficult in the beginning to take calculated risks in new areas. After a raft trip down the Colorado River, she expressed surprise that she could "do it."

"I always thought of myself as the quiet one, the bookworm, the unadventurous type," she reports. "Now I am doing things that I never thought possible."

■ ■ ■ ■ ■

This couple was able to revitalize their marriage by reinventing themselves. They pushed themselves in new directions and expanded their horizons as a couple. Over time, they found that much of the passion returned to their marriage as they shared adventures.

Marriages do not do well on autopilot or on the back burner. They need to be directed and driven where you want them to go. And, sometimes a new highway needs to be constructed to liven up the scenery.

Myth: Boring is bad.

The foolish man seeks happiness in the distance; the wise grows it under his feet.

JULIUS ROBERT OPPENHEIMER

Am I suggesting that boredom is always a bad thing? Actually, many times in my own life I have welcomed a sense of boredom. Routine and predictability have certain advantages, and these rewards become quickly evident when a true emergency, crisis, or tragedy occurs.

Charlie and I came to appreciate monotony a great deal after the spring of 1990.

It was the day before Easter, and Charlie had run out to get last-minute candy for the Easter baskets. Finishing breakfast, both of our children were running and laughing through the living room. Suddenly, Ken burst into the den where I was on the phone.

"Steph is acting really funny," he said.

"Yes, I know. I hear you laughing," I responded.

"No," he insisted, "there is something wrong."

I hung up the phone and walked quickly into the bedroom where Stephanie was lying on the floor, unconscious, with a small amount of foam in the corners of her mouth.

Unable to waken her, I asked Ken to call 911 and I quickly assessed her condition. Though breathing with a steady pulse, she appeared ashen.

The ambulance arrived and took her to Children's Hospital. Shortly after entering the emergency room, she began to have a seizure. Within minutes she stopped breathing. As the staff feverishly worked on her, Charlie arrived. We stood together, looking through the emergency room windows, not believing what was happening.

The doctor pulled us aside and told us he had no explanation for Stephanie's condition, but was very concerned, as her condition had changed so quickly. After routine questions regarding overall health status, history, and access to poisons, Stephanie was transported for a CAT scan. We were left to pray. In a state of shock, I could not believe how rapidly our lives had been turned upside down. An hour ago, we were eagerly looking forward to Easter and now our world was crumbling around us.

With no remarkable results from the CAT scan, Stephanie was transported to ICU and placed on a ventilator. She lay in a coma, and the hospital called in expert after expert. After each expert ran tests, we were told there was still no diagnosis. While I hoped and prayed for answers, I was also relieved as one serious explanation was ruled out one after the other. In spite of the uncertainties, I knew that no diagnosis was good news.

We took turns at her bedside, making sure that someone was with her at all times. After six days, little improvement was evident. The doctors informed us that they believed she had viral encephalitis and that little could be done to help her, except provide supportive care. They also cautioned us that children with encephalitis often do not make a full recovery. We should brace ourselves for a child with severe disabilities if she did get better. We were very discouraged but hoped for a miracle.

Later that evening, Stephanie began to move her feet and hands. By the following morning, she was breathing on her own and the nurses detached the respirator. As I was washing her face, she suddenly put her arm around my neck and said my name. I thought I was dreaming and just stood there and stared.

From that day on, Stephanie showed steady improvement. With great courage, she approached her recovery with energy and humor. She never complained or asked, "Why me?" She simply would ask, "What's next?

We met with a series of rehabilitation specialists who outlined a program to help Stephanie regain her strength and her skills. After a day at physical therapy, where many of the kids were coughing and sneezing, we decided it would be better to rehabilitate her at home. Both Charlie and I took a leave from work and my mother came to help. We helped Stephanie relearn to walk, feed herself, ride her bike, and read again. We focused on small improvements and watched her slow, steady progress.

To the doctors' surprise, Stephanie totally recovered. She is now a freshman in college and interested in medicine. A National Honor Society student, she was also on the varsity swim team for her school.

Now, I do not know how you look at things in life, but I think her recovery was a miracle. Einstein says there are two ways to look at the world, "Either everything is a miracle or nothing is a miracle." I prefer to believe in miracles. And that miracle changed our attitudes and our lives.

We never looked at boredom or our problems quite the same again. The next year, our brand-new van was stolen. I walked out the front door and it was gone. Not believing my eyes, I walked around the block thinking maybe I had parked it elsewhere. Talk about denial! It was gone.

When the police arrived, the officer was quite surprised how we calmly enjoyed our coffee while telling him of our mishap.

Myth: We have no time for church.

When you examine the lives of the most influential people who have ever walked among us, you discover one thread that winds through them all. They have been aligned first with their spiritual nature and only then with their physical selves.

ALBERT EINSTEIN

"Most folks are pretty upset when a brand-new vehicle is stolen!" he exclaimed. "You two don't seem concerned at all."

"Officer, it *is* just a vehicle. This is not a big problem," Charlie replied. "The whole event is rather boring."

I routinely suggest to couples that they go to church together. Any church. Any time. Any religion. Just make a commitment and go. I tell them of the magic in leading a spiritual life and how it will help bond the two of them closer together. Sometimes they tell me they simply do not have the time.

Charlie and I long ago discovered that we seemed to have less conflict, less rudeness, and more gratitude when we went to church. It is very difficult to listen to wonderful words, beautiful hymns, and prayers of guidance and then go home and treat each other like garbage. A spiritual framework helps your life function differently.

Like many, I have found that once you make the decision in your life to follow God, many other choices become easier. A spiritual life is one of love, compassion, and understanding. It involves a surrender—understanding that there are forces in the universe much larger than us. As we stop trying to control everything, events fall into a more natural order, sometimes as they are meant to be.

A spiritual framework means fewer struggles, less worry, and more freedom to love. As we "let go and let God," we create an attitude of faith and trust that establishes our relationship with God, with each other, and with ourselves. The surrender to a life of faith is a conscious decision—a letting go that allows love to grow and us to learn.

Most of my clients are looking for this kind of love and peace in their lives. While I have seen many people who have found it, I have yet to see it accomplished without a focus on spiritual growth. People who have found serenity always have faith, hope, and spirituality wrapped around it.

I talk with my clients about the power of prayer: talking with God, not just when we want something, but sometimes just to say "thanks." I let clients know that everything I have ever prayed for has come my way—maybe not the way I thought it would happen, but the way God thought best.

I have learned over the years to pray for what I need rather than what I want, to seek significance rather than success, to search for God's way rather than my own, and to look at what I can give rather than what I can take.

As I have allowed God to steer my vessel in life, I have found the course easier and the direction simple. I worry less and trust more. I use things and love people rather than using people and loving things. It has cleared my eyes, heart, and soul for what is really important.

I gently urge my clients to explore the spiritual side of their lives, talking with God and learning the Scriptures. Besides, I sometimes say to them, "It doesn't hurt to have the big guns on your side."

IS YOUR MARRIAGE IN A RUT?

A rut is simply a grave with no ends.

AUTHOR

Evaluate the excitement and "newness" of your relationship.

1. I look forward to coming home each day.

   Always   Sometimes   Never

2. We have things to talk about and "catch up" on when we see each other.

   Always   Sometimes   Never

3. We try new activities on a regular basis.

   Always   Sometimes   Never

4. We have special traditions for holidays, birthdays, and anniversaries.

   Always   Sometimes   Never

5. We surprise each other with something new for no reason at all.

   Always   Sometimes   Never

6. I say kind things to my spouse every day.

   Always   Sometimes   Never

7. We attend church on a regular basis.

   Always   Sometimes   Never

8. I practice an attitude of gratitude on a daily basis.

   Always   Sometimes   Never

Scoring: How many "always" responses did you have?
7–8: Excellent. You are a reinventing yourself and your marriage.
5–7: Good. Keep working. You will find your relationship more exciting by investing more effort.
Fewer than 5: Get busy. Use the following tools to build traditions and rituals that strengthen your marriage.

BUILD RITUALS AND TRADITIONS IN YOUR MARRIAGE

Now and then it's good to pause in our pursuit of happiness and just be happy.

GUILLAUME APOLLINAIRE

TOOL #1 When you enjoy a new activity together, establish it as an "annual event." Each year, relive the experience by scheduling the trip, dinner, or other activity that was so enjoyable. These traditions will help the two of you bond as you recount previous experiences and adventures.

TOOL #2 Find at least one new, exciting thing to do together each year. It could be a new hobby, a restaurant, or a special trip. At least once a year, "vision" together some of your dreams for the future. Some couples find it helpful to establish a theme for the year (i.e., "The Year of Travel," "The Year of Accomplish-ment," "The Year of New Friendships"). Review the interest list from Chapter 6. Discuss as a team some new things you could try together.

TOOL #3 Create special ways to celebrate birthdays, anniversaries, and other occasions. We have a tradition that you can do most anything you want on your birthday, and other members in the household have to attend to your every need or wish. You can demand a certain channel on the TV, ask for breakfast in bed, or request a particular dish for dinner. It is great fun for all involved and can be hilarious if it gets a bit out of hand. Create traditions for holidays that work just for you.

TOOL #4 Practice daily affirmations. Review at the end of the day three wonderful qualities for you and for your spouse. Repeat the positive thoughts for yourself out loud. Share your thoughts and comments with your spouse.

TOOL #5 Attend the church of your choice. Get involved, form friendships, and join in the activities. Study the Scriptures and historical documents together. You will find the answers to many of your questions and struggles. As you open your hearts to God's love, it will release the love you have for each other.

TOOL #6 Let gratitude be your attitude. Spend a few moments each night reviewing all the wonderful gifts that you enjoy together. Consider writing down a few thoughts on a calendar or in a journal. Talking and writing about what you are grateful for amplifies these feelings and will help keep your life in focus. Happy people make it a habit to reflect on their blessings and savor the small pleasures that life has to offer.

14 The Second Time Around Will Be Easier

STRATEGY 14: BUILD A FRIENDSHIP FOR THE FUTURE

After the first edition of *Why Did I Marry You Anyway?* was published, a number of readers asked why I did not include information about second, third, and fourth marriages. After all, 50 percent of first marriages end in divorce, with the median duration of first marriages approximately 7.8 years, according the most recent U.S. Census report.[1] The median age at first divorce is 30.5 years for males and 29 for females, so there is plenty of time to try again (and again). This material was not included in the first edition simply because it was off my radar screen. Though I come from a divorced family and had a step-family, I have only been married to Charlie.

Yet, I do know firsthand some of the difficulties of second, third, and fourth marriages from living with a stepdad and working with clients for over twenty-five years. Most of my divorced clients want to try again and dream of the perfect relationship that eluded them the first time around. They yearn for the kind of union they see with friends and families. And most are convinced that they can make it happen if they just find the right person.

Divorcées do get remarried, and fairly quickly at that. The median number of years people wait to remarry after their first divorce is 3.3 years for males and 3.1 years for females. Fifty-four percent of divorced women remarry within five years.[2] The percentage of weddings that are remarriages for at least one partner is 43 percent. The statistics, however, for second marriages are more dismal than the first time down the aisle. Remarriages have a 60 percent failure rate with a median duration of 7.3 years for males and 6.8 years for females.[3]

Myth: It will be easier the second, third, or fourth time.

Instead of getting married again, I'm going to find a woman I don't like and give her a house.

LEWIS GRIZZARD

At first glance, this may not make sense. One would think that folks tying the knot for a second time learned from previous mistakes and recognize the problems they had. They have more experience and, hopefully, more maturity. One would also believe that they would be more careful in their choices. But often this is not true.

Many of the clients I see make the same mistakes over and over again. They go into their second marriage with all the problems they had in their first. They often don't take time to reflect on what went wrong or what they need to change. Rather they focus on all the wrongs of their ex-spouse with very little insight into their own role in the dissolution of the marriage.

Sometimes the problem is in the choosing. Some folks pick the same type of partner over and over again. This is especially true when alcoholism and chemical dependency are part of the mix. I have had many clients who divorce one alcoholic only to marry another. Then they express confusion over the problems in the new marriage and wonder where they went wrong. I have never seen a happy marriage where alcohol or drugs are involved.

It may be that the partners aren't really ready for a mature marriage. They want to party, live the single life, but with a partner. As I explained in Chapter 5, that simply does not work. The bar life and party scene does not build a solid home life. Does this mean you can never go out or have fun? Of course not. Marriage is a lot of fun, but you do things together. You don't sit on a bar stool flirting with someone else.

The top three things that couples fight about, kids, money, and sex, remain constant in second marriages. Only now it is more complicated. Now there are my kids–your kids, (covered in the next chapter), my money–your money, and little time for sex. If couples haven't taken the time to learn how to argue and communicate effectively, the marriage is doomed.

Myth: This spouse will be perfect.

I hate to be a failure. I hate and regret the failure of my marriages. I would gladly give all my millions for just one lasting marital success.

J. PAUL GETTY

Often the problem is in the expectations of marriage. The partners may believe that romance will conquer all; they don't have to work at it. Or that marriage will solve all the problems, including loneliness. After all, the courtship was so much fun. Of course it was. When we date someone, it involves going out, spending time together, and sharing activities. It does not involve mortgages, laundry, bills, and family problems. If you take the work and responsibilities out of your lifestyle, it always looks good.

But reality sets in shortly before or after the wedding. Many a second time newlywed discovers that they not only have all the problems they had before, they now have new ones.

Case Study: Eric and Tiffany

This couple came to the clinic after eighteen months of marriage. Eric is a successful entrepreneur and recently sold his software company for several million dollars. Married previously for three years, he is angry and bitter that his ex-wife got money from the sale and half of his assets.

Tiffany works as a social worker for a local hospital. She puts in long hours and often comes home physically and mentally drained. Her ex-husband has not accepted the divorce, let alone her remarriage to someone else. He frequently calls and tries to manipulate Tiffany into contact with him. Tiffany feels sorry for him and guilty that she has moved forward with her life even though she knows she could not have stayed with him.

Both Eric and Tiffany report that they frequently argue about their previous relationships. Eric is very guarded with his money as he fears "another wife will take it all." Tiffany doesn't understand why Eric gets upset when she speaks with her ex-husband, "after all, it is over."

I carefully explained to both of them that their previous relationships did not appear "over." Rather, they were spilling into the present marriage.

"Let's start by talking about money a bit," I suggested, "since this is the number one issue that couples fight about. Have you discussed how you are going to handle your money?"

"Well, we both just handle our own checking accounts," Eric reported. "We split the bills down the middle."

"That's one way that is common with second marriages," I replied. "What about assets that you both brought into the marriage?"

"Well, we worked that out too with our attorneys," Eric said. "We have a prenuptial that we are both comfortable with."

"It sounds like you have had some great discussions and problem-solving around the money issue," I said. "Now how much longer are you going to hang on to your resentment over what your ex-wife got?"

"But it wasn't fair," Eric explained. "She did nothing to build my company and she still got half the assets."

"Whether you agree with it or not, it is the way things work in a marital property state, and, even more importantly, it is over," I replied. "It is time to move on. That resentment is interfering with your current marriage and poisoning your heart. This will take a conscious decision from you to let it go."

"I'm trying," said Eric softly. "But it is so hard."

"Yes, I know," I replied. "This will be some of the most difficult work you do, but it is critical for your current marriage."

"I think it is time for me to let go of my ex too," said Tiffany. "He calls a lot and tells me his problems. I find it hard to get off the phone because I feel sorry for him."

"You would actually be doing him a favor by cutting it off," I said. "It is time for him to solve his own problems and not to lean on you. Perhaps you could suggest to him that he receive some counseling. I would be happy to give you some names of therapists."

"I don't think he would ever do that," said Tiffany. "He thinks counselors are all quacks."

"Currently, he is manipulating you into being his counselor," I replied. "You really can't assist him since you are not objective, and it is interfering with your current marriage."

"But how do I tell him I don't want to speak to him anymore?" Tiffany asked.

"Just like that. You tell him and then get off the phone," I said. "And stay firm. He will move on. Both of you need to focus on your new relationship and let go of the past. There is nothing you can do about either of these two situations and they are only clouding the happiness you can find now."

■ ■ ■ ■ ■

Both Tiffany and Eric had to let go of the past if they were going to build a future together. For some couples, "letting go" involves talking a great deal about the previous relationship so they are sure that their new spouse understands their history. One couple I worked with called it "The 'Can You Top This' Game?" They told stories of the problems and failings in their prior relationship and then spent some time discussing and analyzing what they would do differently. It helped them get to know each other with an open and honest discussion.

For widows and widowers, letting go can be even more complicated. Whether the previous marriage was happy or fraught with problems, there are memories, emotions, and anxiety as one opens up to the possibility of another marriage. It is important that there has been time to grieve and heal from the pain of losing a spouse. You do not want to simply latch onto a new relationship to try to fill a void.

Myth: My last spouse was perfect.

The difficulty with marriage is that we fall in love with a personality, but must live with a character.

PETER DE VRIES

You may even feel guilty or unfaithful to your deceased spouse for getting involved with someone else. These feelings are normal but need to be set aside. If you are ready to date and find yourself fortunate enough to be in a positive relationship, you deserve another opportunity at finding happiness and a soul mate.

Love may feel different this time around than when you both were younger. Yet maturity has taught you of the many different kinds of love that can grow between two people. The love grows as the friendship deepens and you begin to build a new life together.

It is very important to talk about the many issues that face a couple where one or both have previously lost a spouse. The past must be embraced, not run from. It is a part of the history, and some of the feelings will move forward with the two of you. There may always be some grief over the lost spouse(s). This provides an opportunity to honor the past while moving forward.

A word of caution about possessions and blending two households into one. People accumulate personal items that reflect their history and their emotions. These can include most anything but often involve pictures, knickknacks, dishes, etc. I have seen relationships absolutely devastated by a spouse carelessly disposing of something, not realizing the emotional impact on their new spouse or family.

One of my clients had lost her mother suddenly to pancreatic cancer and was deeply depressed and distraught. She was still reeling from her mother's death when her father remarried a woman quite a bit younger. Though my client had long been married and on her own, her loss was further exacerbated by the sale of the family home where she grew up. While I am sure the new wife was trying to be helpful, she threw away the family Christmas ornaments that had been accumulated and collected for years. For my client this loss was almost as devastating as the loss of her mother. Many of the ornaments had been made by her mother and had special memories attached. She viewed them as family heirlooms and grieved the loss of this connection to her mother.

It is important with a marriage to a widow or widower to avoid comparisons or expectations that the new relationship will be like the last one. There is a tendency to idealize the past and remember the good times, but it is a mistake to expect the new husband or wife to live up to these expectations. After all, we are all different with diverse strengths and weaknesses.

I had one couple who sought counseling because the

man, who was a widower, wanted his new wife to treat him just like his deceased partner. "She never nags me," he complained. "My former wife would nag me about eating right, watching my weight, and exercising. Look at how heavy I am. I don't think she cares."

"He's a big boy," the wife responded. "I think he's old enough to take responsibility for his own actions. Of course I care, but I'm not going to babysit him."

Myth: If I do what I always did, I will get different results.

I never hate a man enough to give him his diamonds back.

ZSA ZSA GABOR

This man seemed to have the opinion that his new spouse should act, behave and think just like his deceased wife. This simply does not work. I found myself smiling in the session, because odds are he complained during his first marriage about all the nagging.

One of the reasons that remarriages fail at such an alarming rate is that often the partners simply operate like they did in their first relationship. They think they can do what they always did, but get different results.

Case Study: Pete and Tricia

Married only a few months, Pete and Tricia came to the clinic because of constant bickering and arguing. Both were bitterly disappointed that the marriage wasn't going better and wasted no time in blaming each other.

"She's just like my first wife," complained Pete. "She's always nagging me to pick up around the house. It drives me crazy."

"Well, he's a slob," reported Tricia. "I had no idea before I married him. When we dated, his place was always tidy and clean. Now he expects me to do all the housework."

"I'm tired of hearing about it," said Pete. "My first wife was the same way. Why can't I find someone who just accepts me like I am?"

"I didn't marry you to become your maid," said Tricia. "I thought this would be more of a partnership."

"What kind of agreement do you have about housework and chores?" I asked.

"We haven't really talked about it," said Tricia. "We just kind of moved in together and went back to working full time."

"So you both work full time?" I asked.

"Yes," responded Pete. "And I come home really tired. I work in a factory . . . I don't sit at a desk all day."

"I'm not clear what you are saying Pete," I said. "Are you implying that Tricia is less tired because of the nature of her job?"

"Well, I'm not saying that . . ." Pete paused. "It's just that I work so hard and come home exhausted."

"I know you do," said Tricia. "But I'm tired too. I can't do all the work at home and work full time at the office."

"This is one of many situations where you have to talk things through and decide what is fair," I explained. "I sometimes refer to it as 'negotiating the deal.' You do both work full time, so expecting Tricia to do all the housework isn't fair. And Pete, you do come home very tired, so it may not be reasonable to expect you to do a lot after a long day. But, do you two think it may be possible to work out a schedule on Saturday where you both pick up and clean? That is what my husband and I do and it actually goes very quickly. We divide up the chores and work together until it is done."

"We could make a list," said Tricia. "Our house really isn't that big. I don't think it would take very long."

"I'd be willing to try," added Pete.

■ ■ ■ ■ ■

Pete and Tricia are a good example of a couple who did not really discuss some of the most basic issues in living together harmoniously. It seems obvious, but all too often couples just expect "things will work out" without any discussion or compromise. They avoid the discussions because they don't want to make waves, only to find that anger and resentment build over time.

There is perhaps no greater battleground in second marriages than money. Agreeing on financial goals and priorities before the wedding is critical, yet too often money is not discussed before the marriage. In fact, many remarries actively avoid talking about money. There are many reasons for this. Some think that a conversation about finances puts too much emphasis on money in the relationship instead of romance and love. Others reason that money caused problems in their previous marriage, and talking about it with the new spouse will guarantee that history will repeat itself.

Myth: Money should not be an issue.

> This would be a much better world if more married couples were as deeply in love as they are in debt.
>
> EARL WILSON

Statistics show, however, that avoiding discussions about money can sabotage long-term happiness. If financial issues are not addressed early on, they will become the front line for problems. Some of the common money issues that occur in second marriages include:

- Undisclosed past financial problems of one of the spouses. This can be previous bankruptcies, high credit card bills, IRS audits or penalties, etc. In most states the new spouses inherit these problems and become equally responsible after saying "I do."
- Failure of one spouse to save for retirement. This becomes a significant problem especially when the marriage is later in life as there are fewer years to save and build a nest egg.
- Inconsistency in child support payments from an absent parent. Unable to budget and anticipate income, it can put an unfair burden on both partners and lead to anger and resentment.

- Income disparity between partners. Money often is the war zone for power and control. Too often, the spouse who is making the most money feels that this gives them the upper hand in decision making.
- Financial commitments to a previous spouse. Second marriages often involve baggage from a previous marriage including alimony, maintenance, and child support.
- Costs of raising children from a previous marriage. The new spouse may resent the money going back to the ex-spouse and the children. This is especially true if money is tight and it is viewed that this money would be better spent at home.
- College expenses for children. The legal financial obligation for children ends at age eighteen but most divorcing couples make some kind of agreement as to how they will pay for college. An enormous expense, it gets even more complicated if one of the parents does not agree on a costly choice for schooling. There are also a lot of additional expenses besides tuition and books.
- Changes in child custody arrangements. New spouses need to understand that legal agreements regarding children can change over time. It is not uncommon to "go back to court," to modify custody or financial arrangements.
- Inequity in the payment of household expenses. Who pays what is an important discussion to take place. Regardless of who makes the most money, any marital property state operates that the partnership is 50/50.
- Financial commitments to parents, siblings and other family members. Again, there may be additional baggage that a spouse brings to the table simply because they are older and more affluent than the first time

around. Elderly parents and dependent family members can put a strain on family finances.

While it may be difficult to talk about money, this discussion is essential to prevent future misunderstandings. Prepare for the discussion by gathering your important documents and records and answering the following basic questions:

- What are your assets?
- What is your current income?
- What are your current and potential liabilities?
- What insurance coverage do you have?
- How much do you have saved for retirement?
- How would you like to handle checking accounts and expenses after marriage?
- Have you had previous financial problems?
- Do you have financial obligations to others?

The answers to these questions give you both a starting point. It will also help to flush out issues that need to be discussed further. We all have different attitudes, fears, and goals about money that shape how we handle our resources. It is important that you both explore your money management style. Are you a spender or a saver? Are you impulsive or a planner with money? Research has shown that savers and planners are the people most likely to find financial security.

In a second marriage, there needs to be a decision as to whether money will be combined or kept separate. How will household expenses such as mortgage and utilities be handled? What about any previous debt? Make sure that you set up a workable system to handle day-to-day issues so that each decision does not become an argument.

As partners are usually older at the time of a second or third marriage, planning for long-term security is even more important than the first time around. Saving for a new home or a comfortable retirement should start as soon as possible. Some of the long-term issues for discussion include:

- Your most important financial goals
- Housing
- Estate planning
- Medical and life insurance

It may be helpful to hire a financial adviser to help you formalize your plans. There are a number of professional organizations that you can contact for a referral, such as the American Institute of Certified Public Accountants, Financial Planning Association, or the Society of Financial Service Professionals. It is also helpful to ask for recommendations from friends and family.

Interview candidates and ask specific questions regarding their experience, philosophy, and fees. Make sure you feel comfortable with the adviser that you choose and develop your financial plan together. Even the most complex money issues can be worked out and solid plans for the future solidified. Many couples tell me that working together for agreed upon future goals was one of the most satisfying parts of their marriage.

WHAT MYTHS DO YOU NEED TO OVERCOME TO HAVE A SUCCESSFUL MARRIAGE?

A happy home is one in which each spouse grants the possibility that the other may be right, though neither believes it.

DON FRASER

1. I believe marriage is based on love.

   Always   Sometimes   Never

2. I think if I find the "right person," we will live happily ever after.

Always Sometimes Never

3. I know exactly what I am looking for in a spouse.

Always Sometimes Never

4. There must be sparks, or it is not love.

Always Sometimes Never

5. I don't believe that you should have to work at marriage, it should just work out.

Always Sometimes Never

6. If only my partner would change a few things, our relationship would be perfect.

Always Sometimes Never

7. I can see what my partner does wrong but do not see anything I could change.

Always Sometimes Never

8. I frequently bring up my or my partner's previous marriage, especially when angry.

Always Sometimes Never

9. I wish my spouse was more like my previous partner.

Always Sometimes Never

10. I think that money discussions are too difficult so I avoid them.

Always Sometimes Never

Scoring: How many "always" responses did you have?

8–10: Time to go back to the drawing board and read again about the myths that hinder a happy marriage. You may find it helpful to seek some counseling to build your skills for a mature marriage.

4–7: Making progress, but some additional effort will help you make this marriage successful. Consider taking a communication course or marriage encounter together.

0–3: Congratulations! You are overcoming the myths that sabotage marriages. Continue your efforts together to build a solid future.

MAKE THE SECOND TIME AROUND SUCCESSFUL

Many marriages would be better if the husband and the wife clearly understood that they are on the same side.

Zig Ziglar

TOOL #1 If you are re-marrying your former spouse, don't get back together just for the sake of the kids. Make sure that you that you are really committed to make it work.

TOOL #2 Understand your own marital history. What went wrong? What was your role in the problems? Unfinished business and feelings will resurface the second time around if you don't recognize the past.

TOOL #3 Take a communications or marriage encounter course together. This can help you to learn the skills that are needed to effectively solve problems in your marriage.

TOOL #4 Learn how to argue fairly and effectively. Retake the "How Do You Argue?" quiz in Chapter 9.

TOOL #5 Know what defense mechanisms you use and work at tearing down the walls. Have both partners take the inventory on page 183 and post the results on the refrigerator.

TOOL #6 Skip the comparisons. Comparisons always lead to someone coming up short. Focus on your spouse's strengths and understand the weaknesses.

TOOL #7 Don't dwell on your (or your spouse's) mistakes. Focus together on building the future.

TOOL #8 Work on building a solid friendship of shared activities, laughter, and talking. Build on your common interests to build a life together.

TOOL #9 If marrying a widow or widower, be sensitive to the past and empathetic with your spouse and family. There will always be anniversary dates and memories that trigger grief and sadness.

TOOL #10 Know your money personality. Take the free profile at www.asec.org and click on Savings Tools.

15 Your Kids, My Kids, and Our Kids

STRATEGY 15: BUILD THE BLENDED FAMILY WITH REALISTIC EXPECTATIONS

Getting remarried is difficult enough, but remarriage with children can be overwhelming. There are *my kids, your kids,* and sometimes *our kids.* There are ex-spouses, visitation, and custody to deal with. There are histories, parenting philosophies, and often kids who don't like the whole arrangement. Arguing about children is common in first marriages, and it is even more of a problem in second marriages.

Unfortunately, our culture provides few guidelines to navigate through the transition to blended family. Most of our rituals and assumptions about marriage relate to the intact first marriage, though this version of family is now in the minority. Every day, 1,300 stepfamilies are formed with 500,000 adults becoming new stepparents every year. Some 6.4 million children, representing a tenth of the nation's children, live with one stepparent and one birth parent.[1]

Many therapists are not equipped to deal with the complexities of a blended family. Most graduate schools of psychiatry, psychology, and social work provide no specific training in dealing with the dynamics of stepfamilies. Many of the methods and information appropriate to the nuclear family can be destructive if applied to the highly specific dynamics of the stepfamily system.

Stepfamilies are, by definition, born of loss. They combine members of original families who are now divided. This can be because of divorce or death, but each represents the loss of a dream. This dream includes a history and a future that will now not take place. Children of all ages feel this loss. Research by Judith S. Wallerstein and others demonstrates that the influence of divorce on children lasts a lifetime and is a cumulative experience.

"Its impact increases over time and rises to a crescendo in adulthood. At each developmental stage divorce is experienced anew in different ways. In adulthood it affects personality, the ability to trust, expectations about relationships, and ability to cope with change," according to Wallerstein.[2]

It is not uncommon for children to expect, hope, and dream for their biological parents to get back together. They come to my practice expressing a misplaced optimism that things will still work out. I remember clearly when my own father passed away, thinking, "now they will never get back together," even though my parents had been divorced for more than thirty-five years. Children yearn for the stability they once experienced and want it back. They find it hard to accept that the positive, intimate relationship between their biological parents no longer exists and won't be returning.

With a stepfamily, new problems quickly emerge

even as family members are adjusting to the new "normal." Due to custody arrangements, children often move between two homes. They no longer have one home with both parents; rather they face different rules, expectations, and dynamics between two households.

Myth: Our family will be like the Brady Bunch.

Marriages are all happy—it's having breakfast together that causes all the trouble.

IRISH PROVERB

Too often, couples marry with an idealized version of what their new blended family will look like. Like the myths that surround marriage, many new spouses believe that their families will simply come together and live happily ever after. It amazes me how many folks with kids get remarried with very little discussion about how they will handle issues and problems. Some of the common unrealistic expectations of a blended family include:

- Belief in the Brady Bunch or instant family myth. Expecting everyone to love each other immediately with no conflict.
- Belief that the step-children will love you. Not only may they not love you, they may dislike and resent you.
- Belief that the stepchildren will respect and/or obey you. So different than your biological children, you have to earn the respect of your new stepchildren. It will not be given automatically.
- Belief that a step-family will be like a first marriage family. It is so much more complicated and involves feelings and baggage from the first union.
- Belief that the biological parent, your spouse, will support you in all matters related to the kids. Quite the contrary, your spouse may align with the children

on certain issues, undermining your authority.

- Belief that the stepchildren will be fair to you and give you a chance. The new stepchildren may not feel that the whole arrangement is fair, so why should they give you a chance? Especially if changes have uprooted the kid's lives; i.e., new house, new school, they may be resentful of you coming on the scene.
- Belief that the stepchildren can think/operate like adults. Even the most mature and articulate children are still children and have the emotions of a child. They may struggle with feelings that they don't understand and lack the maturity to express them appropriately.
- Belief that the biological parent, your spouse, will want to function as a team. Often parents simply repeat some of their difficulties in the second marriage.

Many experts believe it takes four to seven years for blended families to come together. Elizabeth Einstein, MA, of Stepfamily Solutions, notes that blended families go through five stages toward reaching a resolution with the new blended structure:[3]

Stage One: Fantasy. This is the first introduction of family members into a blended living situation. Einstein describes the "trio of uns" which includes unresolved grief, unrealistic expectations, and uninformed adults.

Stage Two: Confusion. During this stage the new couple begins to realize that their fantasies of instant love and bonding are not going to happen. There are multiple bumpy relationships that cause divisiveness and tension in the household. The couple is often confused and finds it hard not to take rejection of the new stepparent personally.

Stage Three: Crazy Time. Turmoil reaches a new crescendo at this time with the pain of unresolved issues and loss evident. There may be confusion over loyalties to the non-custodial parent and fears about a two household system.

Stage Four: Stability. Lessons and growth become evident as family members begin to integrate into a new lifestyle. Crises occur less frequently and aren't viewed as seriously. While there are setbacks, they are seen as less significant. The blended family begins to form its own history, traditions, and rituals.

Stage Five: Commitment. This is a time of reflection and introspection for all family members. What is working? What have I learned? Often arrangements for custody and family relationships have been realigned and the family settles into a routine. Ideally, the adults also do forgiveness work and form a positive friendship with the ex-spouse to continue parenting.

Myth: Children are resilient.

Even a minor event in the life of a child is an event of that child's world and thus a world event.

GASTON BACHELARD

All too often I hear parents, therapists and professionals say that children are resilient. They insist the kids will adjust; it's just a phase, and after all, their friends are more important. In my experience working with families for more than twenty-five years, this is simply not true. Children have very soft hearts and do not have the emotional maturity to deal effectively with the major changes that divorce or death and remarriage present. After all, many adults reel from the turmoil. Why would it be different for children?

Children react to the changes in profound and dramatic ways. Their world is shaken apart and they often feel very much alone. In spite of the fact that approximately half of all Americans are currently involved in some form of step relationship, it is rarely addressed in school or the community.[4] Children find that they do not have anyone to talk with about the transitions at home. Too often their own parents are not available due to their own problems.

Parents and family are the primary focus of a young person's life. Spending time with family was the top answer to the open-ended question, "What makes you happy?" in a recent poll conducted by the Associated Press and MTV. More than one hundred questions were asked of 1,280 people ages thirteen to twenty-four on the nature of happiness. Nearly three-quarters of young people said their relationship with their parents makes them happy. When asked to name their heroes, nearly half of the respondents named one or both parents.[5] Clearly, what happens at home makes significant waves in a child's life.

There is often conflict of loyalties in blended families. This conflict occurs in cycles and reflects the child's confused emotions. Often just as the child is beginning to have warm feelings for the stepparent, he/she will suddenly pull away and negatively act out. Children sometimes feel that if they love a stepparent, it means they are choosing *against* their biological parent. Children have to be reassured that they can love more than one person and there does not need to be someone who comes "first."

Here are some key points to remember to help children adjust to a blended family setting.

- Provide reassurance that it was not them or their behavior that led to the divorce or death, thus bringing them into a blended family. Make sure you allow questions and their expressions of grief and loss.
- Children may not understand why their biological

parents do not "get back together." This is especially true if they are lucky enough to have their parents forge a friendship and work together in parenting. Their disappointment is natural and should be talked about.

- Children, especially young ones, may worry about seeing their non-residential parent. They fear that reduced contact will lead to no contact and further loss. Make sure that there is a clear parenting plan put in place including frequent time with the parent the child doesn't live with.
- As much as the new couple would like to have a family life again, remember that the children have suffered a loss. Stepchildren may resent or rebel when asked to participate in this new venture, which they did not choose. As one child in my practice said, "Why do I have to have problems just because my parents can't solve theirs?"

  Make sure you allow time and patience while the children adjust to the new arrangement.

> Myth: Stepparenting is just parenting.
>
> **You can learn many things from children. How much patience you have, for instance.**
>
> FRANKLIN P. JONES

One of the most common mistakes that I see stepparents make is trying to act "like a stepparent." That is, they mistakenly believe that they can parent the stepchildren like they did their own biological children. Or if they don't have other children, like they believe it "should be done." In my experience, the only time that works is when the children are very young and/or the other biological parent is not in the picture.

As children get older, they are not interested in obtaining "another parent" just because mom or dad has a new spouse. Many view the new person on the scene as simply their parent's spouse, not their parent. This is especially true if the child is close to their biological parents.

It works much better for the stepparent to assume a role more like a mentor or coach to the stepchildren. Provide gentle guidance and focus on building a friendship. Entering the family as disciplinarian, competitor, or replacement parent greatly hinders the opportunity for a smooth transition.

Case Study: Mark and Jeanne

This couple, both in their mid-forties, came to treatment after one year of marriage. Both were married previously, but only Mark had a daughter, Shannon, from the previous union. His ex-wife had moved across the country when Shannon was five years old, so Mark had raised her primarily alone until his remarriage to Jeanne. They came to treatment at this time due to constant arguing and tension at home. They also reported that Shannon, now age thirteen, was doing poorly at school and "hanging with the wrong crowd."

"Things have really gotten unbearable," Mark said. "There are days I hate to come home because I know that Jeanne and Shannon will be arguing."

"Yes, and when you do come home, it just gets worse," said Jeanne. "Sometimes I feel like an outsider in my own house."

"What do you mean, 'an outsider'?" I asked.

"Mark and Shannon seem to have their own secrets. I often feel that he sides with her about things," responded Jeanne.

"That's not true," said Mark. "It's just that it was just the two of us for a long time."

"What you both are describing is actually pretty common in blended families, especially when the history is essentially one of a single-parent family," I said.

"Though your ex-wife saw Shannon occasionally," I said

turning to Mark, "you have raised her alone for the last seven years."

Both Mark and Jeanne nodded as I continued. "Single-parent households like you describe tend to develop their own unique culture. There is a special bond, a silent code, between single parents and their children that is closed to outsiders. The longer the parents and children are together, the more entrenched they are likely to become. Some even develop their own methods of communicating."

"That's exactly what it is like," said Jeanne. "Sometimes I feel resentful or even jealous about Mark and Shannon's relationship."

"Again, that is normal," I said. "I think it is very common to underestimate the bond that a single parent has with their child. And this can give rise to very negative feelings and even occasional dislike for the child."

"But, what can we do?" asked Mark. "I really want this to work. I think Jeanne would be good for Shannon if Shannon would just give her a chance."

"Well, let's brainstorm a bit. How often do you do things with just Shannon?" I asked.

"Since we got married, I've really pushed to do things as a family, making sure that Jeanne is always included," said Mark.

"Is it possible that this may be part of the problem? Shannon was used to having you all to herself. Maybe it would work better to have some scheduled time with just you," I said. "Children love one-on-one time. It makes them feel special."

"She has mentioned that she misses fishing with me," said Mark. "We used to go all the time."

"I think it is important when people are moving forward in a new direction that they take with them the parts of the past that were positive. It sounds like fishing together could be one of them," I said. "Now Jeanne, what do you do alone with Shannon?"

"Other than argue, not much," responded Jeanne.

"What does Shannon like to do that the two of you could do together?" I asked.

"Well, she loves to shop and so do I," said Jeanne.

"A shopping trip with just the two of you might help you begin to forge a friendship. And yes, her bond with her father will always be stronger, but you could become a significant mentor for her, especially during her teen years," I said.

"I would be willing to give it a try," said Jeanne.

■ ■ ■ ■ ■

Both Mark and Jeanne had to realign their expectations of how their blended family would come together. While Shannon desperately could use the guidance and compassion of a mother figure, Jeanne needed to focus on building friendship and respect first. That required patience, understanding, and compassion, which are sometimes very difficult with a teenager.

Myth: Our exes will not be a problem.

Marriage is the only war in which you sleep with the enemy.

FRANCOIS DE LA ROCHEFOUCAULD

A biological parent will be a part of your new married life whether they are alive or deceased. Deceased parents create a spectrum of emotions from grief to guilt as a child starts to move on with their life. There may be visits to the cemetery and difficult anniversary dates. For the new spouse there may be expectations of living up to an idealized parent and possibly an idealized former spouse.

A former spouse who is still in the picture presents a whole different set of challenges. There is an old saying that you can't really divorce someone if you have children together. You will always have that connection and at least some contact. There are holidays, family events, and involvement with school. It is not unusual for biological parents with their new spouses in tow to all attend the school conference.

This can be very uncomfortable for the new spouse, as you now have someone in your life that you may never have seen or met. You may also find that you don't particularly like them when you do meet them. Stepmothers and stepfathers are forced to have contact with, either directly or indirectly, a person they would not have contact with under normal circumstances. It may be even more complicated with feelings, resentments, and disagreements about parenting that make the relationship very tense.

But smart couples make an effort to make it work. The old saying is "you have to love your children more than you hate each other." The growing trend for blended families is for biological parents to have holidays together to avoid the splitting that occurred a generation ago.

Many of today's remarrieds are themselves the products of broken marriages. They remember the tension, going house to house, and exhaustion of multiple family gatherings. More and more families are having the holidays together; exchanging gifts and enjoying the children. Sometimes to everyone's surprise the ex and the new spouse forge a friendship that is good for all involved.

Here are some tips for couples to build positive relationships for a blended family:

- Respect the parenting skills of the former spouse. Make sure that you do not undermine them or criticize them in front of the children.
- Don't put children in the middle. Deal directly with parenting adults in other households. Children quickly pick up on disagreements and may try to manipulate one parent against the other.
- Follow the child's lead as to how they wish to address the new stepparent.

- Maintain family rituals and traditions even as you develop some new ones.

One area of frequent conflict with former spouses centers on rules and structure when the child is at their house. Many parents mistakenly believe that they have to agree on everything and both houses should be exactly the same. They may argue about how chores, money, gifts, or friends should be handled. They may unintentionally put the child in the middle with comments about the other parent. This can lead to power struggles between the households and tension when the parents see each other.

Myth: We all need to parent the same.

Unhappiness in a child accumulates because he sees no end to the dark tunnel. The thirteen weeks of a term might just as well be thirteen years.

GRAHAM GREENE

While it certainly is nice if the parents agree on these issues, it may be unrealistic. After all, you did not agree on all the parenting issues before the divorce. Why should you now?

Children quickly learn that things are different at the two houses. If parents keep a matter-of-fact attitude and are consistent with the structure at their home, children usually do not have a problem with this. The most important thing is to be unfailing in following the structure that is established at your house. Kids feel more secure when they know what to expect and the rules are clear. This is especially important with teenagers.

Some common areas to address for structure include:

- *Money.* Will the child receive an allowance? Are they expected to get a job or earn some of their own spending money?
- *Chores.* What is the child expected to do around the house as a family member? Is there a structure in

place such as a chore chart, coupons, or a similar motivational tool to make sure that the chores are completed?

- *Curfew.* What are the rules for older children who go out with friends? What time do they need to be home on school nights? Weekends?
- *Mealtimes.* Does the family eat together? Are children expected to be home for meals?
- *Car.* What are the rules for using the family car? Is this privilege tied to any other responsibilities like grades or chores?

Life gets even more confusing when there are children from prior marriages and now "our" children. One spouse may feel his or her children are treated unequally in the family. Or the children from a previous marriage may feel that a new arrival is getting all the attention. Whatever the circumstances, the focus of family members becomes comparison and keeping score.

> Myth: We will treat all the children the same.
>
> **Before I got married, I had six theories about bringing up children. Now I have six children and no theories.**
>
> John Wilmot

These constant comparisons are poison in a family. When comparisons are made, someone always ends up short. Members start to focus on what is "fair" as if there were some magic formula for fairness. In reality, smart parents know that what is fair for children can vary with time and circumstance. Many parenting issues can be resolved through communication and discussion.

Case Study: Joe and Debbie

This couple came to treatment after several days of arguing. Reportedly the precipitating event was a baseball game that was attended by Joe and his son, Billy, from his first marriage.

"He didn't even ask my daughter, Maggie, to go along," complained Debbie.

"It honestly never occurred to me to do that," said Joe. "Billy and I always go to opening day, so I just bought the tickets for us."

"But you never invite her along when the two of you go places," said Debbie. "She feels like you don't even like having her around."

"That's not true," said Joe. "I love her a lot, but I really don't know how to do 'frou frou' kinds of things, like playing with dolls. I've only raised a boy. I feel at a loss sometimes."

"Well she feels that you favor Billy," said Debbie.

"How do you respond to her when she expresses those feelings?" I asked.

"I just say that I will talk with him," said Debbie.

"Perhaps it would be helpful to also explain that Joe and Billy do have a special relationship and building relationships take time," I said. "I think it is important for Maggie to know that Joe and Billy will always have a special bond, but that doesn't mean that she can't also have a special relationship with Joe. Now, I understand that opening day is a special ritual for you and your son, but what about another ballgame where you could take both kids?" I asked.

"Sure," said Joe. "I think it would be a lot of fun."

"While dealing with a girl may be new territory for you, it is important that you create your own bond with Maggie through shared activities," I said. "What other things could you two do together to build your relationship?"

"I don't know," said Joe.

"She would love to go on the boat with you the next time you go sailing," said Debbie.

"Well, I asked her once and she said 'no,' so I haven't asked her again," said Joe.

"That is one of the guidelines for blended families," I said. "You have to keep trying to build the friendships and the relationships. It really is the parent's responsibility to initiate and reach out. Most children do not have those skills."

"Would it be possible for you to make some suggestions to Joe when you see some potential opportunities for him and Maggie to connect?" I asked Debbie.

"Yes, I can do that," said Debbie. "I know Maggie can be moody at times and difficult to reach."

"That's part of the problem I have," said Joe. "I don't know how to read her very well."

"This is where both of you have to work together to understand each other's child," I said. "No one knows them like you do. It is important that you coach each other in how to connect individually and through family time."

■ ■ ■ ■ ■

Joe and Debbie came for several more sessions and gradually built positive relationships with the children. They recognized that building their blended family involved a lot of time, energy, and patience but in the end would be very rewarding.

It is clear that a blended family is a lot of work. But the positives can outweigh the negatives. There is the potential for both partners to find marital happiness. Having a long-term partner in life makes things so much more fun. Building a blended family can be a process of forgiveness, understanding, lessons, and healing.

It gives parents an opportunity to provide a healthy marriage model for children rather than being left with only the model of the divorce. The blended family gives the children a positive representation that they can use as they move to adulthood and form relationships. Children thrive in stability and routine.

Stepparents have a unique opportunity to have special relationships and friendships with children who are not their own. Often they find that the mentoring process brings great rewards and lifetime closeness when the children are grown.

I strongly encourage couples and families to consider some counseling to help get a positive start. It will shorten the learning curve and give the new couple tools to solve whatever problems come their way.

WHAT MYTHS DO YOU NEED TO OVERCOME TO HAVE A BLENDED MARRIAGE?

Children need love, especially when they don't deserve it.

HAROLD HULBERT

1. How often do you think/wish that everything will just "come together"?

   Always Sometimes Never

2. Do you believe that the kids should "just adjust"?

   Always Sometimes Never

3. Do you believe that children are resilient?

   Always Sometimes Never

4. Do you think step parenting is just like parenting your own kids?

   Always Sometimes Never

5. Are you having difficulty dealing with your spouse's ex?

   Always Sometimes Never

6. Do you feel that all children in the family should be treated the same?

   Always Sometimes Never

7. Do you believe that the rules and structure must be the same between parents' homes?

   Always Sometimes Never

8. Do you feel that all the children in the household should be treated the same?

   Always Sometimes Never

Scoring: How many "always" responses did you have?

7–8: Reexamine your beliefs and expectations about a blended family. You and your spouse will have to work hard to make the adjustments to make it work. Go for some marital and family counseling to receive additional tools.

4–6: Making progress; talk with your spouse about the areas you both need to work on.

1–3: Good; continue using the tools in this chapter to help your new family come together.

BUILD YOUR BLENDED FAMILY WITH LOVE AND FRIENDSHIP

There are few successful adults who were not first successful children.

ALEXANDER CHASE

TOOL #1 Nourish the couple bond by having alone time. Use this opportunity to talk and have fun. Resist spending all the time talking about "step" issues.

TOOL #2 Predictability and structure create intimacy in families. Talk about the structure and routines that you want established for the family.

TOOL #3 Decide household rules together as a couple. Communicate rules to the children together so that it is clear that both partners were involved.

TOOL #4 Expect and accept different parent-child, stepparent-stepchild feelings. Every relationship is different and needs to be treated as unique.

TOOL #5 Support one another with the children. Discuss disagreements about parenting styles behind closed doors.

TOOL #6 Accept the custody agreement. Remember children love their parents. When you complain about the arrangement or the ex-spouse, you are only putting your child in the minefield between the two of you. They have enough problems of their own to work out.

TOOL #7 Be considerate of your spouse's time with his/her biological children. They have history and traditions that will always be special to just the two of them.

TOOL #8 Spend alone time with your stepchild and let them decide on the activity. Look for opportunities to connect with common interests.

TOOL #9 Model the concept that ways of doing things can be different without being "right" or "wrong."

TOOL #10 Remember to keep your sense of humor. A little laughter can help relieve family tension and promote a sense of wellbeing.

POSTSCRIPT: WHY DID I MARRY YOU ANYWAY?

The Answer.

We are at the last session. I have pretty much shared with you all I know about marriage—at least so far. Sometimes clients come to the last session not wanting to leave. They worry that their progress has only been a Band-Aid, and that at any moment they might slide down the slippery slope of marital discord and succumb to sad statistics and lonely nights. Let me assure you, this will not occur. While new challenges will always come your way, your promise to each other will keep you together.

I describe the calm joy that so often occurs in a long-term marriage. I share the comfortable familiarity Charlie and I experience with Sunday morning coffee on the deck, routine conversations, shared memories, and walks by the lake. I guarantee them that the "Art of Everyday" becomes easier each year, until a contented lifestyle emerges. That contented lifestyle represents home—home for the body, the mind, and the soul.

I tell couples that the work they do on their relationship is worth it, that it is very gratifying to look at the events in your life and know that you did your very best. There is great peace in this position. At the end of the day, at the end of your life, to look in the mirror and feel proud of what you have done and what you have become is priceless.

I almost forgot to tell you that once I jumped out of a perfectly good airplane. It happened more than twenty years ago, but the memory is still vivid. Back in those days, student sky divers jumped the old Army 1-1, which was a round canopy that brought a diver down very hard. It was not like today, where inexperienced jumpers can complete a "tandem" jump, after little instruction, by harnessing to an experienced jumpmaster who takes care of all the important details, like pulling the ripcord.

Twenty years ago, the student sky diver actually had to learn a bit more about the sport by going to ground school. The course emphasized four basic things. Upon leaving the aircraft, it was imperative that the student arch his or her body with arms and legs spread wide. This was to prevent rolling out of the aircraft, which could result in a tangling of ropes or the parachute. It was also stressed that the student must pull the ripcord—a very critical safety issue! After deployment, the diver was to look up to make sure that the chute actually opened. Again, quite important. And last but not least, it was important that the proper landing position be assumed as the diver neared the ground, with legs together in an executed roll to minimize what can be a very hard drop.

I spent the better part of a Saturday at the airport ground school. Working very hard, I practiced the four key items judiciously. *Arch, pull, look up, and roll. Arch, pull, look up, and roll.* I knew the response upon leaving the airplane had to be automatic and instinctive. With repetition and practice, each significant element was burned into my brain. I trained with my class until late in the day.

Finally, the jumpmaster believed the students were ready. We strapped the heavy gear onto our backs, buckling our helmets snugly as we loaded onto the jump plane. No one spoke a word as we gained altitude to 8,000 feet for the jump run. Suddenly I heard the engine slow and the jumpmaster say, "Okay, Bartlein. You're first. Step outside."

I took some deep breaths and pulled myself out onto the strut of the airplane wing, holding on to the handles by the doorway. All I could think was: there is no way I am letting go.

But suddenly . . . I did.

For a split second, it seemed like I was suspended in the air next to the aircraft. Then I felt the rush of wind push against my body as I started to fall. I watched the jump plane bank to the left and quickly fly away.

As the adrenaline surged through my bloodstream, I became acutely aware of the amazing scenery and beauty in the sky. I could see for miles in every direction. The treetops looked like tiny brushstrokes on the horizon. Bright orange streaks flamed from the high cirrus clouds as the sun began its descent. I could see a hint of purple where the sky blended toward the earth.

I never arched. I never pulled the ripcord. Fortunately, I was on a static line that automatically pulled the chute as I fell. I never looked up to check whether the chute actually opened. And when it came time to land, I hit the dirt like a ton of bricks. My helmet flew off, and I plummeted into the dirt.

As I staggered slightly dazed to my feet, all of the other sky divers came running toward me. They were excitedly yelling: "How did you like it?" "Did you have fun?" "Was it what you expected?" "Was it everything you dreamed it would be?"

Beaming from ear to ear, I nodded, "Yes."

See, I think that is the way life is too. You sky dive through this world, sometimes forgetting what you are supposed to do, omitting the details, and just enjoying the moment. And when you dive into the next world—whatever you believe that to be—I think all the people you know who are already there come running up to see you. And they ask: "How did you like it?" "Did you have fun?" "Was it what you expected?" "Was it everything you dreamed it would be?"

The key to a great life is to be able to say, "Yes!"

ADDITIONAL RESOURCES

Chapters 1, 2

Public policy related to marriage:

The Institute for American Values
David Blankenhorn, President
1841 Broadway, Suite 211
New York, NY 10023-7603
Phone: (212) 246-3942
Email: IAV@worldnet.att.net
Web site: www.americanvalues.org

The Howard Center for Family, Religion and Society
Allan C. Carlson, President
934 North Main Street
Rockford, IL 61103
Phone: (815) 964-5819
Email: howdctr@bossnt.com

The Urban Institute
C. Eugene Steuerle, Senior Fellow
2106 M Street, NW
Washington, D.C. 20037
Phone: (202) 833-7200
Email: paffairs@ui.urban.org
Web site: www.urban.org

Information on divorce law reforms:

Americans for Divorce Reform
John Crouch, Executive Director
2111 Wilson Boulevard, Suite 550
Arlington, VA 22201-3057
Email: divorcereform@usa.net
Web site: www.divorcereform.org

Chapter 5

For more information on drinking and alcoholism, please contact:

Al-Anon Family Group Headquarters, Inc.
1600 Corporate Landing Parkway
Virginia Beach, VA 23454-5617
Phone: (757) 563-1600; Fax: (757) 563-1655
Email: WSO@al-anon.org
Web site: www.al-anon.alateen.org

Makes referrals to local Al-Anon groups, which are support groups for spouses and other significant adults in an alcoholic person's life. Also makes referrals to Alateen groups, which offer support to children of alcoholics. Free information, materials, and locations of Al-Anon or Alateen meetings worldwide can be obtained by calling the toll-free number (888) 425-2666 from the United States or Canada, Monday through Friday, 8 a.m.–6 p.m. (Eastern time).

Alcoholics Anonymous (AA) World Services, Inc.
475 Riverside Drive, 11th Floor
New York, NY 10115
Phone: (212) 870-3400; Fax: (212) 870-3003
Email: visit AA's Web site
Web site: www.alcoholics-anonymous.org

Makes referrals to local AA groups and provides informational material on the AA program. Many cities and towns also have a local AA office listed in the telephone book. All communication should be directed to AA's mailing address at P.O. Box 459, Grand Central Station, New York, New York, 10163.

National Council on Alcoholism and Drug Dependence, Inc.
20 Exchange Place, Suite 2902
New York, NY 10005
Phone: (212) 269-7797; Fax: (212) 269-7510
Email: national@ncadd.org
HOPE LINE: (800) NCA-CALL (24-hour affiliate referral)
Web site: www.ncadd.org

Offers educational materials and information on alcoholism.

Provides numbers of local NCADD Affiliates via the above toll-free, 24-hour HOPE LINE.

National Institute on Alcohol Abuse and Alcoholism (NIAAA)
Scientific Communications Branch
6000 Executive Boulevard, Willco Building, Suite 409
Bethesda, MD 20892-7003
Phone: (301) 443-3860; Fax: (301) 480-1726
E-mail: niaaaweb-r@exchange.hih.gov
Web site: www.niaaa.nih.gov

Makes available free informational materials on all aspects of alcoholism including the effects of drinking during pregnancy, alcohol use and abuse, and help for cutting down on drinking.

Use the following tool to evaluate your own drinking behavior.

THE MICHIGAN ALCOHOL SCREENING TEST (MAST)

The MAST is a simple, self-scoring test that helps assess if you have a drinking problem. Please circle the answers to the following YES or NO questions:

1. Do you feel that you are a normal drinker? ("normal"—drink as much or less than most other people)

   Yes No

2. Have you ever awakened the morning after some drinking the night before and found that you could not remember a part of the evening?

   Yes No

3. Does any near relative or close friend ever worry or complain about your drinking?

   Yes No

4. Can you stop drinking without difficulty after one or two drinks?

   Yes No

5. Do you ever feel guilty about your drinking?

   Yes No

6. Have you ever attended a meeting of Alcoholics Anonymous (AA)?

Yes No

7. Have you ever gotten into physical fights when drinking?

Yes No

8. Has drinking ever created problems between you and a near relative or close friend?

Yes No

9. Has any family member or close friend gone to anyone for help about your drinking?

Yes No

10. Have you ever lost friends because of your drinking?

Yes No

11. Have you ever gotten into trouble at work because of drinking?

Yes No

12. Have you ever lost a job because of drinking?

Yes No

13. Have you ever neglected your obligations, your family, or your work for two or more days in a row because you were drinking?

Yes No

14. Do you drink before noon fairly often?

Yes No

15. Have you ever been told you have liver trouble such as cirrhosis?

Yes No

16. After heavy drinking, have you ever had delirium tremens (D.T.'s), severe shaking, visual or auditory (hearing) hallucinations?

Yes No

17. Have you ever gone to anyone for help about your drinking?

Yes No

18. Have you ever been hospitalized because of drinking?

Yes No

19. Has your drinking ever resulted in your being hospitalized in a psychiatric ward?

Yes No

20. Have you ever gone to any doctor, social worker, clergyman or mental health clinic for help with any emotional problem in which drinking was part of the problem?

Yes No

21. Have you been arrested more than once for driving under the influence of alcohol?

Yes No

22. Have you ever been arrested, even for a few hours because of other behavior while drinking? (If Yes, how many times? ________)

Yes No

Scoring for the MAST:
Please score one point if you answered the following:

1. *No*
2. *Yes*
3. *Yes*
4. *No*
5. *Yes*
6. *Yes*

7 through 22: Yes

Add up the scores and compare to the following score card:
0–2: No apparent problem
3–5: Early or middle problem drinker
6 or more: Problem drinker

Chapter 10

Calculate your retirement needs by using the planning calculator available at the Choose to Save Web site (www.choose-tosave.org).
To discover your money personality type, check the Retirement Personality Profiler at the Savings Council's Web site (www.asec.org).

Chapter 14

National Endowment for Financial Education, 5299 DTC Blvd., Suite 1300, Greenwood Village, CO 80111. www.nefe.org

Chapter 15

The Stepfamily Association of America. 1–800–735–0329. www.stepfam.org

National Stepfamily Resource Center. http://www.stepfamilies.com

Kaufman, Taube. *The Combined Family, A Guide to Creating Successful Step-Relationships.* Insight Books, Inc., 1993.

Wisdom, Susan and Green, Jennifer. *Stepcoupling: Creating and Sustaining a Strong Marriage in Today's Blended Family.* Three Rivers Press, February 2002.

NOTES

Introduction

1. Dennis Orthner, David Blankenhorn, Steven Bayme, and Jean Bethke Elshtain, eds., "The Family in Transition." In *Rebuilding the Nest: A New Commitment to the American Family* (Milwaukee: Family Service of America, 1990), 98.
2. Judith Wallerstein, Julia Lewis, and Sandra Blakeslee, *The Unexpected Legacy of Divorce* (New York: Hyperion, 2000), 295.
3. Arlene Saluter, Marital Status and Living Arrangements: March 1994, U.S. Bureau of the Census, March 1996; series P20-484, vi.
4. Paul R. Amato and Stacy J. Rodgers, "Do Attitudes Toward Divorce Affect Marital Quality?" *Journal of Family Issues* 20 (1999): 69–86.
5. Karen S. Peterson, "Unhappily wed? Put off getting that divorce," *USA Today,* July 11, 2002, reporting on research by Linda Waite, University of Chicago.
6. Linda J. Waite and Maggie Gallagher, *The Case for Marriage: Why Married People Are Happier, Healthier and Better Off Financially* (New York: Doubleday, 2001).
7. Sara McLanahan and Gary Sandefur, *Growing Up with a Single Parent: What Hurts, What Helps* (Boston: Harvard University Press, 2001), 95–115, 39–63.

Chapter 1: Why Did I Marry You Anyway?

1. Permission requested through the William Morris Agency.

2. Paul D. McLean, "Man and His Animal Brain," *Modern Medicine,* February 3, 1964.
3. Judith Wallerstein, Julia Lewis, and Sandra Blakeslee, *The Unexpected Legacy of Divorce* (New York: Hyperion, 2000), 59.
4. Used with permission of Bill Cosby through the William Morris Agency.
5. Paul W. Coleman, *The 30 Secrets of Happily Married Couples* (Hanover, MA: John Adams, Inc., 1992), 84.

Chapter 2: I Can Never Count on You

1. Joseph Nowinski, *A Lifelong Love Affair: Keeping Sexual Desire Alive in Your Relationship* (New York: W.W. North, 1989), 48.

Chapter 3: You're Absolutely Perfect . . . Now Change

1. N. S. Jacobsen, V. Follette, and D. McDonald, "Reactivity to Positive and Negative Behavior in Distressed and Non-distressed Married Couples," *Journal of Consulting and Clinical Psychology* 50 (1982): 706–714.
2. Debra Umberson, "Family Status and Health Behaviors: Social Control as a Dimension of Social Integration," *Journal of Health and Social Behavior* 28 (1987): 306-319.
3. Linda J. Waite and Maggie Gallagher, *The Case for Marriage: Why Married People Are Happier, Healthier and Better Off Financially* (Doubleday: New York, 2000), 51.
4. E. E. Filson and S. J. Thoma, "Behavioral Antecedents of Relationship Stability and Adjustment: A five-year longitudinal study," *Journal of Marriage and the Family* 50 (1988): 785–795.

Chapter 4: You Are Just Like Your Mother/Father

1. Joan Druckman, David Fournier, Beatrice Robinson, and David H. Olson, "Effectiveness of Five Types of Pre-Marital Programs," *Education for Marriage,* Grand Rapids, Michigan, 1979.
2. Judith Wallerstein, Julia Lewis, and Sandra Blakeslee, *The Unexpected Legacy of Divorce* (New York: Hyperion, 2000), 54.
3. Glenn Norval and Kathryn B. Kramer, "The Marriages and Divorces of the Children of Divorce," *Journal of Marriage and the Family* 49 (1987): 811–825.

Chapter 5: You're Going Out Again?

1. Oakley Stern Ray, *Drugs, Society and Human Behavior* (St. Louis: C.

V. Mosby, 1978). Referenced in Debra Umberson, "Family Status and Health Behaviors: Social Control as a Dimension of Social Integration," *Journal of Health and Social Behavior* 28 (1987): 316.

2. National Institute on Alcohol Abuse and Alcoholism, NIH Publication, No. 96-4153.
3. Alcohol Epidemiological Data System. Yi, H., Stinson, F. S., Williams, G. D., and Bertolucci, D. *Surveillance Report #46: Trends in Alcohol-Related Fatal Traffic Crashes, United States, 1977–96.* Rockville, MD: National Institute on Alcohol Abuse and Alcoholism, Division of Biometry and Epidemiology, December 1998.
4. *The Louie Anderson Show,* Louzell Productions, Inc., 1988.
5. Lawrence Jeff Johnson and research team, "Key Indicators of the Labor Market 2001–2002" study available through the United Nations International Labor Organization.
6. Worldwatch Institute estimate of consumption since 1950.
7. Melissa Compton-Edwards, "Living to Work," survey by Institute of Personnel and Development (IPD), copyright 1999.
8. C. Leslie Charles, *Why Is Everyone So Cranky? The Ten Trends That Are Making Us Angry and How We Can Find Peace of Mind Instead,* (New York: Hyperion, 1999), 229–231.

Chapter 6: We Never Do What I Want to Do

1. Quoting Dr. Roy Rhodes, a Dallas, Texas, psychologist, in "Cheating" by Jeanne Sara Dorin, *Dallas Morning News,* May 28, 1978.
2. John C. Howell, "Under Attack: The Christian Home," *Home Life,* November 1982, 6.
3. L. and Keith B. White, "The Effect of Shift Work on the Quality and Stability of Marital Relationships," *Journal of Marriage and the Family* 52 (1990): 453–462.
4. Mitch Albom, *Tuesdays with Morrie: An Old Man, A Young Man, and Life's Greatest Lesson* (New York: Doubleday, 1997), 149.

Chapter 7: I'm Going to the Hardware Store, Honey

1. Dianne Hales, "The Female Brain," *Ladies' Home Journal,* May 1998, 173.
2. Michala De Leonardo, "The Female World of Cards and Holidays: Women, Families and the Work of Kinship," *Signs* 12 (1987): 440–453.
3. S. Merriam and M. Clark, *Lifelines: Patterns of Work, Love, and Learning in Adulthood* (San Francisco: Jossey-Bass, 1991).

Chapter 8: If You Really Loved Me, You Would Know What I Like!

1. Permission requested through ICM Artists.
2. John Faul and David Augsburger, *Beyond Assertiveness* (Waco, TX: Word Books, 1980), 23.

Chapter 9: Why Can't You Fill the Ice-Cube Tray?

1. Patrice Noler and Mary Anne Fitzpatrick, "Marital Communication in the Eighties," *Journal of Marriage and the Family* 52 (1990): 832–843.
2. Erich Segal, *Love Story* (New York: Bantam Books, 1970), 80–81.

Chapter 10: We Still Have Checks, So How Can We Be Out of Money?

1. Richard L. Strauss, *Marriage Is for Love* (Wheaton, IL: Tyndale House Publishers, 1973), 101.
2. Bernice Kanner, *Are You Normal About Money? Do You Behave Like Everyone Else?* (Princeton, NJ: Bloomberg Press, 2002), 2.
3. Ibid., 2–3.
4. Ipsos-NPD, reported in *Readers Digest,* August 2001.
5. Richard M. Ryan and Edward L. Deci, "On Happiness and Human Potentials: A Review of Research on Eudaimonic Well-Being," *Annual Review of Psychology* 52 (February 2001)
6. Aristotle, "Politics," quoted in Goldian VandenBroeck, Ed., *Less Is More: The Art of Voluntary Poverty* (Rochester, VT: Inner Traditions, 1996), 978.
7. Lewis H. Lapham, *Money and Class in America: Notes and Observations on Our Civil Religion* (New York: Weidenfeld & Nicolson, 1988).
8. Brooke Kroeger, "Feeling Poor on $600,000 a Year," *New York Times,* April 26, 1987; stockbroker quoted in Lapham, *Money and Class in America.*
9. Kanner, 83–84.
10. J. Lauer and R. Lauer, "Marriages Made to Last," *Psychology Today,* June 1985, 26.
11. American Savings Education Council Web site. Permission requested.

Chapter 11: We Never Have Sex Anymore!

1. John Gagnon, Ph.D., as reported in "Am I Normal?" *Good Housekeeping,* March 2001, 72–73.
2. Linda J. Waite and Maggie Gallagher, *The Case for Marriage: Why Married People Are Happier, Healthier and Better Off Financially* (New York: Doubleday, 2001), 87.
3. Gina Ogden, Ph.D., as reported in "Am I Normal?" *Good Housekeeping,* March 2001, 74.
4. John Gottman, Ph.D., research findings, as reported in *Family Therapy Networker,* May/June 1994.

Chapter 12: It's Your Turn to Get Up With the Kids

1. L. White, A. Booth, and J. Edwards, "Children and Marital Happiness: Why the Negative Correlation?" *Journal of Family Issues* 7 (1986): 131–147.
2. N. Glenn and S. McLanahan, "Children and Marital Happiness: A Further Specification of Relationships," *Journal of Marriage and the Family* 44 (1982): 63–72.
3. Sandra G. Boodman, "Second Child's Impact on Parents Weighed," as reported in *The Washington Post,* December 3, 2000.
4. Mark Lino, *Expenditures on Children By Families,* 2001 Annual Report, U.S. Department of Agriculture, Center for Nutrition Policy and Promotion. Miscellaneous Publication No. 1528-2001.

Chapter 13: Is That All There Is?

1. Floyd and Harriett Thatcher, *Long Term Marriage. A Search for the Ingredients of a Lifetime Partnership* (Waco, TX: Word Books, 1980).
2. John Gottman, "How Marriage Changes," in Gerald R. Patterson, Ed., *Depression and Aggression in Family Interactions* (Hillsdale, NJ: Laurence Erlbaum Associates, 1990).

Chapter 14: The Second Time Around Will Be Easier

1. U.S. Census Bureau, 2002.
2. Ibid.
3. National Center for Health Statistics.

Chapter 15: Your Kids, My Kids, and Our Kids

1. U.S. Census Bureau, 2002.

2. Wallerstein, Judith, Lewis, Julia and Blakeslee, Sandra. *The Unexpected Legacy of Divorce, A 25-Year Landmark Study,* p. 298.
3. Einstein, Elizabeth, MA. "Blended Families," *In Touch-APS Healthcare,* Volume 1-Issue 2.
4. U.S. Census Bureau, 2002.
5. Noveck, Jocelyn, and Tompson, Trevor. "Young People Name Family as Key Happiness Factor," *Associated Press,* August 2007.

ABOUT THE AUTHOR

Barbara Bartlein, RN, MSW, CSP, is The People Pro®. A clinical psychotherapist, she has provided couples counseling for over twenty-five years and frequently presents at professional conferences and workshops. She is adjunct facility for the University of Wisconsin-Milwaukee Continuing Education.

Barbara is a Certified Speaking Professional, CSP, a designation by the National Speaker's Association held by fewer than eight percent of all members worldwide. She offers keynotes, seminars, and consulting across the United States and Canada. She is past president of the National Speaker's Association, Wisconsin Chapter, and has been featured on FOX, CNN, and CBS.

Barbara is the author of the column, "The People Pro®," which appears widely in professional journals including *The Business Journal* and *Corporate Logo Magazine.* Several of Barb's articles are featured in the *Chicken Soup for the Soul* series.

For information about Barbara's presentations and consulting services, please contact her at barb@ThePeoplePro.com

To receive Barb's free e-mail newsletter, "The People Pro®," please visit: www.whydidimarryyouanyway.com.